WHAT LIES
BENEATH:
CALIFORNIA

WHAT LIES BENEATH

CALIFORNIA

PIONEER CEMETERIES
AND GRAVEYARDS

GAIL L. JENNER

TWODOT®

GUILFORD, CONNECTICUT
HELENA, MONTANA

A · TWODOT® · BOOK

An imprint and registered trademark of Globe Pequot, the trade division of
The Rowman & Littlefield Publishing Group, Inc.
4501 Forbes Blvd., Ste. 200
Lanham, MD 20706
www.rowman.com

Distributed by NATIONAL BOOK NETWORK

British Library Cataloguing in Publication Information available

Library of Congress Cataloging-in-Publication Data available

ISBN 978-1-4930-4895-3 (paper : alk. paper)
ISBN 978-1-4930-4896-0 (electronic)

♾™ The paper used in this publication meets the minimum requirements of American
National Standard for Information Sciences—Permanence of Paper for Printed Library
Materials, ANSI/NISO Z39.48-1992.

*To my two sisters, Patricia Mae Peterson and
Teresa M. Davis.*

CONTENTS

INTRODUCTION

Everyone loves a mystery and as you enter through the battered gates of old, overgrown cemeteries or graveyards, there is a decided air of mystery that hovers over them. Perhaps that is why we are drawn to them—much like looking over into the dark abyss where you cannot see what is beyond sight—and why our imaginations are ignited.

The importance of such places cannot be underestimated, particularly in terms of history. Not only do the variety of headstones or crypts or monuments pique curiosity about the lives once lived, there is something more. Is it the tangible but fragile link we have to death itself? Whether we believe or don't believe in what follows this life, the desire to find a connection to the possibility of an afterlife draws us to these places of "eternal rest."

As an avid lover of genealogy and anything historical, cemeteries have always interested me. Who were these people and what did they suffer? What did they overcome? Those lives cut off at birth or ten or forty-eight or ninety-four—whether by illness, age, or accident—cause me to stand and ponder the circumstances surrounding their living and

Grave of Maybelle Alice, daughter of C. E. and C. E. Stovall, June 20, 1901, Williams Cemetery, Colusa County, feels eerie.

dying. To see a family plot where one, two, or three children or infants have been laid to rest is tragic. You see the small headstones, topped with a lamb or angel, with the simple but devastating words: "At rest" or "Sleep, Our Baby." To lose one child would be heartbreaking, but to witness the heartbreak of multiple losses feels grotesquely unfair and terrible.

Take, for instance, **Mark Schofield** (1835–1890) of New York. After marrying **Eliza Ann Schofield** (1840–1877), the couple traveled cross-country to California and settled in Sierra County, where Mark took a job as a superintendent for a mining company. They were off to a wonderful beginning and then their first child, a daughter—Amelia Adaline—was born on Christmas Day, 1868. However, in May 1871, Amelia passed away and they laid her to rest in the **Whiskey Diggings Cemetery**, in Sierra County. A second child, Alice, was born in January 1872, and she died in June of 1873; she was only seventeen months old. A third daughter, Ida, was born in May 1876.

What more could happen? Eliza Ann passed away a year later, on May 2, 1877. She was 37 years old and one month later, in June 1877, little Ida passed away. Mark Schofield had lost three daughters and his wife in the spread of nine years. All four of them were interred in Whiskey Diggings Cemetery.

As if this were not grievous enough, on November 23, 1890—thirteen years later—Mark Schofield, superintendent of the North America Mine, near Gibsonville, Sierra County, entered the mine with several other employees to retimber a portion of it. Suddenly the men began scrambling about as they tried to back out of the mine. It only took a few minutes before they realized they were being overwhelmed by a toxic gas, known as "white damp." Six men collapsed on the car track before they could escape and others rushed in to rescue as many as they could, but Schofield, who had been the first in, could not be resuscitated. It was too late. Even the horse that had been pulling the mining cart died from the gas. Mark Schofield was laid to rest beside his wife and three daughters in the Whiskey Diggings Cemetery in Sierra County in November 1890. At fifty-five years, his life and legacy had been brought to an end.

And then there is the **Hiram Page Cemetery** in Yreka, Siskiyou County. Hiram and his sons are interred in a private, off-the-road, singular graveyard, with one large marble headstone that sits outside a white picket fence. The plot measures about eight by eight inches, and it's a spot that people suddenly see as they're driving by. It is not a

Hiram Page and two of his sons were killed when their wagon rolled over.

destination, but sits at an angle—almost resting against a tree—alongside a residential road not far from a senior living project. Apparently, in 1863, the site was close to the Page family farm. Were they headed home, or headed to town?

Hiram Page (1822–1863), **Hiram Balpher Page** (1849–1863), and **Salathiel Page** (1851–1863) were all killed when their wagon turned over. Rather than trying to haul them away, rescuers buried them near their home. One more name was added to the tombstone one year later, that of six-year-old **Julian Page** (1857–1864). No doubt, it would have been a relief for the boys' mother, **Ellie Dodge Page,** and sister **Minnie Page** (1857–1944) to have them buried close at hand. If families find proximity to their dead a comfort, though it may be "small comfort" to some, the poem "One Final Gift" by D. J. Kramer reflects an apt emotion for Ellie and Minnie. Here are the final lines:

> Don't leave my resting place unmarked
> As though you never cared.
> Deny me not one final gift
> For all who come to see . . .
> A single lasting proof that says
> I loved . . . and you loved me.

A third story from 1878 rests in the **Angle Cemetery** in Willits, Mendocino County. Located on a small knoll in the middle of a pasture and nestled under a copse of trees are the graves of **Rench Angle** (1828–1889) and nine of his fifteen children—six of whom died between May 30 and June 13 from diphtheria. Originally from Pennsylvania, Rench Angle was the first owner of the now-famous Ridgewood Ranch of Seabiscuit fame. He was, at one time, one of the wealthiest men in Mendocino County. After his death, his widow, **Mahulda Catherine Orender Angle** (1840–1925), married Sylvester Drew, and after he died, she married John H. Christy. When she passed at eighty-three, she was buried in an unmarked grave in the **Ukiah Cemetery**, in Ukiah, Mendocino County, beside her father, **Joel Orender** (1813–1891). The question lingers: How does one handle that much grief?

The stories of these and others from California's earliest days need to be remembered and not just by those whose lives were connected in time and space. No, for me, the desire to recapture and preserve a dying history is what propelled this project. My research and journey to over 100 cemeteries up and down California was not conducted to share the names or deeds of well-known individuals who already fill history books or local lore, but to uncover lesser-known or even unknown individuals, whose lives and challenges, deeds and foibles should not be lost to time.

It was obvious from the outset that there would be no way to collect or locate all—or even a small percentage—of the named and unnamed graves and cemeteries in California! In each of California's fifty-eight counties, there are hundreds (and hundreds) of cemeteries or burial sites—let alone abandoned graveyards, some tucked away behind storefronts or under paved streets. "Burying grounds" are found in neighborhoods, pastures, and fields, in downtowns, backyards, or deep in the woods. I have barely scratched the surface of uncovering the lives still buried beneath the soil, pavement, and rocks or under the waters of this state.

Finally, in organizing this volume, my first hope was to keep the names of cemeteries connected to individual towns and counties, but as I began to collate family groups—who were many times buried in separate cemeteries—I realized that would be difficult, and thus the book has been organized by "regions" (with some cross/references), and most of these regions include several counties. That being said, it was impossible to include cemeteries from every county. Traveling the state made it clear that I would have to exclude some counties and many, many towns, regardless of how many historic and fascinating cemeteries would be overlooked. It also became clear that every county deserves its own collection of cemetery books! Until then I have gathered as many intriguing stories as I could in the limited time I had—some involve disappointment and despair, intrigue and murder, a rise to fortune or a fall to shame, love, hate or unrequited love, ambition, and hope.

CHAPTER 1

SAN DIEGO AND THE IMPERIAL REGION

The span of California's frontier history can be divided into five major periods: the Native American period or "pre-contact"; European exploration, from 1542 to 1769; the Spanish colonial and/or mission period, from 1769 to 1821; the Mexican period, from 1821 to 1848; and, finally, the 1849 Gold Rush, Settlement, and Statehood.

After landing in San Diego Bay in 1542, the explorer Juan Cabrillo claimed the region for Spain. In 1769, *Padre* (Father) Junipero Serra and Gaspar de Portola, the Spanish military commander, established **El Presidio Real de San Diego**, the first permanent European settlement on the Pacific coast. Set upon a hill (above Old Town), the Spanish fort's cemetery no longer exists as a cemetery. The Presidio, now known as **Presidio Park,** was the first of the Spanish presidios and missions in California to be built. The line of missions eventually stretched north 700 miles, from San Diego to Sonoma. In all, twenty-one missions were built from 1769 to 1833.

This is the broken headstone of Dannier Herold, aged six months old. Born in 1890, he passed away in 1891 and was laid to rest in Dutch Flat Cemetery, Placer County. Note that the small, narrow grave has sunk below the edges of the surrounding sod.

After Mexico won its independence from Spain in 1821, *Alta* California became Mexico's northern frontier. This period saw the demise of the "mission system" and much of the land was doled out by the Mexican governors as land grants to those who fought for or swore allegiance to Mexico, including Americans who came to be identified as *Californios*.

Seventeen years later, after the Americans defeated the Mexicans in February 1848, the Treaty of Guadalupe Hidalgo ended the war and defined the new boundaries of Mexican and American territories. The United States acquired Alta California, including the lands stretching from San Diego up to present-day Oregon in the north.

Presidio Hill Cemetery is the oldest cemetery site in San Diego. Located above Old Town San Diego, it looks out over the town; it was a well-chosen location for the Spanish with its extended views of the surrounding area. Today, Presidio Hill Cemetery is Presidio Park. Those originally interred here included Spanish soldiers, Mexican settlers and soldiers, missionaries, American soldiers, and Californios. Old broken down clay walls give a hint as to the cemetery's sloping location, and about halfway down the hill stands a statue of Father Junipero Serra. Just a few yards from him stands an immense cross, constructed of layers of red tile. From there the hill fans out to a broad expanse of green grass. One can only envision what a cemetery there might have looked like.

The last recorded burial in the Presidio Hill Cemetery was for Old Town San Diego's first *alcalde,* or mayor, **Captain Henry Delano Fitch** (1799–1849), in 1849. Take note, this Yankee sea captain

Presidio Hill's cemetery no longer exists, but a statue of Junipero Serra and an immense stone cross stand as reminders of the site.

would alter the history of Alta California *and* impact an entire nation. A tall, blue-eyed, handsome young man, while working for Henry Edward Virmond of Mexico, Fitch sailed into San Diego Bay, in spite of the ban against merchant ships. When he landed, he immediately caused "quite a stir among the eligible senoritas."

The Captain and His Bride

It was the fifteen-year-old daughter of Joaquin and María Ignacia Carrillo who caught Captain Henry Fitch's attention when she boarded his ship with her cousin Pio Pico to shop for fabric. The young **María Antonia Natalia Elijah Josefa Carrillo** (1810–1893)—better known as Josefa—was also intrigued and invited the attractive American to her parents' home. Attending the gathering was California's governor, **José María de Echeandia** (unknown–1871), a tall but imperious man, who must have grown jealous. As the story is told, he had been attempting to woo the young woman himself. Henry and Josefa fell in love and, while her parents reluctantly approved the match, the marriage had to be approved by Mexico City and the church. Henry agreed to be baptized into the Catholic Church in 1829 and adopted the Spanish name Enrique Domingo Fitch. The governor was able to assert his influence, however, and the marriage's approval was denied. An attempt at a secret marriage was also foiled by the governor, so, after much to-do, the couple eloped aboard Henry's ship and sailed to Valparaiso, Chile. In Valparaiso, they were married.

This tempestuous love story does not end here: a year later, the couple returned to San Diego with their infant son. María's vexed mother locked herself away and her father only embraced her after she crept along the floor begging for his forgiveness. The vicar general interrogated Henry who refused to denounce the union. Instead, he and Josefa left and sailed north to Monterey. There they were arrested, Henry for the heinous crime of abduction. Three months later, they were taken to **Mission San Gabriel** to face trial. In the end, the marriage was declared legal under the law, but not within the church. As penance, "the couple was ordered to attend high Mass for three feast days while holding lighted candles, and to recite part of the rosary for 30 consecutive days." Henry was also required to give a fifty-pound bell to the plaza church in Los Angeles.

Henry and Josefa settled in San Diego with their young son where they eventually had ten more children. Henry became influential and not only ran the only store in Old Town but also served as police commissioner, justice of the peace, and was the first to survey the area. In 1846, he became the town's first alcalde. In addition, he was given a land grant of 48,000 acres in northern California on which to build his estate, but Captain Fitch would not live to see Rancho Sotoyome as he died of pneumonia in 1849 and became the last person to be buried in the Presidio Hill Cemetery. Remarkably, in the 1960s–1970s, excavation uncovered what turned out to be Fitch's remains under the former chapel's tiled floor.

Josefa moved to the rancho and lived out her life there. Unfortunately, she suffered from financial woes for many years and died in 1893 at the age of eighty-two. Her body was not returned to San Diego; instead, she was buried in Healdsburg's **Oak Mound Cemetery**. This couple's legacy continued to live on, however, in the life of one of their many descendants, Franklin Delano Roosevelt, the thirty-second president of the United States.

The **Mission San Diego de Alcalá Cemetery** was located east of the mission. More than 4,300 individuals were buried there between 1769 and 1832—most of them unnamed Indian converts—and that number does not include U.S. soldiers. In 1873, however, it was reported that the old cemetery "contains but one lonely monument of marble" marking the grave of **Sergeant Richard Kerren** (1814–1856) of the U.S. Army who had been thrown from his horse and killed. In 1887, Kerren's monument, along with his remains, were reinterred at Point Loma, now **Ft. Rosecrans National Cemetery.**

Indian Converts

While a number of mission Indians who had been baptized into the Catholic Church were buried in the Presidio Hill Cemetery, few of their names were recorded and none was provided headstones. One exception was **"Benito" Malac**, originally from the Rancheria Apusquele. He was baptized with his wife **Taltal** and their children,

Most of those buried in any of California's mission cemeteries were unidentified Indian converts.

Sinusin and **Malac (Jr.)**, at **Mission San Diego de Alcalá** in September 1775. When Benito (Sr.) died, his family carried his body up Presidio Hill to the cemetery to be buried on February 1, 1779. Benito's daughter Sinusin married José Antonio Ruiz y Leyba a few months later. The couple had six children, but four of them passed away at young ages. Two of the stricken children were buried at the Presidio Hill Cemetery with Benito (Sr.). When Sinusin passed away at age forty-one or forty-two, she was buried at the **San Juan Capistrano Mission Cemetery**. This cemetery is on mission grounds and, though there are at least 2,000 people buried there, there are only eighty-four individuals whose identities were recorded, and Sinusin, also known as "Clara" Bustamante, was one of those.

Mason Carter (1834–1909) was also interred at Fort Rosecrans National Cemetery. His father, John Carter, was a well-respected physician. Mason married **Lucie Maria Downing Wellington** (1850–1938) in 1870. As an Indian Wars Congressional Medal of Honor recipient, he received his medal for "gallantry in action against the Nez Perce at Bear Paw Mountain, Montana on September 30, 1877, in leading a charge under a galling fire." He retired as a major and then taught military science in Tennessee before moving to California. Carter was the first Medal of Honor recipient to be interred at Fort Rosecrans National Cemetery. He died in San Diego at age seventy-five, in 1909.

It's been said that Ft. Rosecrans National Cemetery sits on the most valuable piece of land in San Diego County. Some would add that it is one of the most beautiful cemeteries, as well. Comprised of seventy-seven plus rolling acres at Point Loma, it overlooks the bay and the Pacific Ocean. It dates back to 1882 when soldiers who had been buried in mass graves after the Battle of San Pasqual were reinterred here. In 1934, Ft. Rosecrans became a national cemetery. Others buried in San Diego's Presidio Hill Cemetery included several Mexican soldiers. One, **José Carlos Rosas** (1769–1805), came north with the 1781 Rivera Expedition as one of its first pioneers, called *pobladores*, to help settle Alta California. He married **María Dolores** (1768–1809) on July 4, 1784 at **Mission San Gabriel.** When he died in 1805, he was laid to rest in the Presidio Hill Cemetery, while Maria Dolores was laid to rest in the **San Gabriel Mission Cemetery.**

Jose Manuel Perez Nieto (1748–1804), an Afro-Latino soldier, traveled in the 1781 journey and is credited with escorting the pobladores as part of Rivera's Expedition to settle Los Angeles. He received the largest individual land grant, called Rancho de Los Nietos, ever given while Spain ruled Alta California. He married **Maria Teresa Morillo** (1756–1816) in 1778. Sadly, they lost one of their three children, **Antonia Maria de los Santos Perez Nieto** (1788–1796), at age seven. She was buried in the San Gabriel Mission Cemetery, as were Jose and Maria and their two sons years later.

As with the Presidio, Father Junipero Serra established Mission San Diego de Alcalá in 1769. While burials of great significance were dug within the church, whether under the floor, inside the walls, or near the altar, those of less significance were placed outside the church in the cemetery. The cemetery—the oldest known *mission* cemetery in California—was located in the courtyard where the unmarked remains of Indian converts lay under the plaza garden. Inside the church, the following *padres*, or mission priests, rest under the floor, just to the right of the altar and in front of the *retablo* or *reredos* (the structure against the wall behind the altar where stand statues of Saint Joseph, the Crucified Christ, and the Virgin Mary and Child). The marble tiles are set into the shape of a cross, each tile inlaid with the name of an early priest. Under the center tile lays **Father Luis Jayme (Jaime)** (1740–1775), the second pastor of the church and California's first Christian martyr. He was only thirty-five years old when he was killed in a raid on November 5, 1775, when 800 Indians attacked and burned the mission to the ground.

In addition to Father Luis Jayme, the other mission padres interred under the floor include **Father Juan Figueroa** (unknown–1784), who arrived in California in 1772 and passed away in 1784; **Father Juan Mariner** (unknown–1800), who arrived in 1785 and died in 1800; **Father Jose Pinto**, who arrived in 1810 and died in 1812 after being poisoned by a Native American cook; and **Father Fernando Martin**, who arrived in 1812 and died in October 1838. Also martyred in the November 1775 attack was **José Manuel Arroyo**, a blacksmith, whose remains were interred in the sanctuary of the chapel.

Another early cemetery in San Diego was **El Campo Santo Catholic Cemetery**, or Holy Field, which was created for the emerging community of San Diego's Old Town in 1849, eighty years after the Presidio and its cemetery were first built. It's located at 2414 San Diego Avenue, San Diego, right in the heart of today's Old Town district. While this cemetery was home to many more gravesites in the early days, most of which were later relocated, there are still about 450 graves here. The oldest known original headstone, which has been restored, belongs to twenty-one-year-old **Rosa Serrano de Cassidy** (1848–1869), daughter of Jose Antonio Serrano. She was the first wife of a San Diego administrator, Andrew Cassidy, who emigrated from Ireland.

Approaching the small, protected graveyard, visitors have to stop and glance up. The cemetery sits between shops along the main drive, enclosed by an adobe wall and, above that, a white fence. There is a gate and a couple of steps up to the site, but as you enter, it opens up to scattered headstones, some wooden and very primitive, painted white, some carved stone tombstones. A few have iron fencing around them.

The ground is dry, but the effect is not that the area is dirty; it simply has the look of being old and intriguing. In addition, as you step down to the sidewalk and look out on the street, and up and down the sidewalk, you suddenly see them—graves—each marked by a small brass medallion. They are so unremarkable that most tourists walk by, unaware of their existence. On each medallion is written: "Grave Site."

Who knows to whom these abandoned, forgotten graves belong?

One who is identified at El Campo Santo is **Antonio Garra** (unknown–1852), chief of the Cupeño tribe. On January 16, 1851, it was reported that "an Indian chief, named Antonio Garra, attempted to unite all the Southern Indians with the Californians to drive out the Americans," and "he and his few braves attacked the Warner Ranch, to the east, and killed nine whites." Thomas Whaley, early settler of San Diego, wrote this about the attack:

El Campo Santo is located in the heart of Old Town, San Diego, and situated between places of business and enclosed by an adobe wall.

The first attack the Indians made was upon the rancho of J. J. Warner, member of our State Legislature, burning his house, stealing everything belonging to him and murdering a man in his employ. Four men have been murdered upon the Gila and four more Americans from this place at the Springs of the Agua Caliente who had gone there for their health. . . . I am well armed with a brace of Six Shooters and have a horse ready to saddle at any moment.

When Garra was finally captured, he confessed he'd induced members of various tribes to unite against the Americans. He was declared guilty of murder and theft and sentenced to death by a firing squad of twelve men. One report noted, "When Garra was asked to state any last words, he simply said, 'Gentlemen, I ask your pardon for all my offenses, and expect yours in return.'" Then, "as he [Garra] was shot, he fell backwards into his gravesite within the cemetery (El Campo Santo) and was subsequently buried." Antonio Garra's headstone reads, "Sacred to the memory of Antonio Garra Sr. A leader among his people Cupeño-Kavalim Clan. Died January 10, 1852. Rest in Peace. Erected 1992 H.S.F."

One soldier interred at El Campo Santo Cemetery was **Juan María Osuna** (1785–1851). Married to **Maria Juliana Josepha Lopez** (1791–1871) in 1806, Juan fought in the Mexican Revolution of 1831, and he and his family were the first to build on the lowland beyond the Presidio of San Diego. In 1833, Juan María Osuna and five other citizens urged Alta California's governor to replace the sixty-year military rule with a town (*pueblo*) government for San Diego. As a result, Juan María Osuna was elected the first alcalde of the San Diego pueblo, defeating Pio Pico by thirteen votes. Pio Pico

The author taking a photo of Antonio Garra's grave, which is a favorite at El Campo Santo Cemetery in Old Town, San Diego.

would later become the last governor of Alta California under Mexican rule. Osuna's land grant lay north of San Diego, along the coast. Today his Rancho San Dieguito is known as Rancho Santa Fe, and his adobe overlooking the river valley has been restored. It is now part of The Inn at Rancho Santa Fe. Juan María Osuna died in 1851 and was buried in El Santo Campo. His epitaph reads: "Juan María Osuna

Died 1851 First Alcalde of San Diego." His wife died in 1871 and was buried alongside him.

A third, but infamous individual interred at the El Campo Santo Cemetery was **Jim Robinson** (unknown–1852). Known as "Yankee Jim," many stories have since been told about the thief. Having spent time in the gold fields of northern California, where the six feet four inch stranger had supposedly murdered and stolen gold from other miners, he was eventually arrested in 1852, along with two accomplices, after stealing a boat belonging to two San Diego men, Stewart and Wall.

Yankee Jim's Hanging

As recalled in the October 1873 *Los Angeles Herald*, Volume 1, Number 5, the jury announced Yankee Jim's punishment—death by hanging:

The gallows consisted of two beams planted in the ground with a heavy beam across the top. It was located in Old Town, on the spot where Whaley's brick house now stands. On the 11th day of September, Yankee Jim was taken from his little adobe jail room, where he had been closely guarded, and placed in a wagon. Two Catholic priests accompanied him and did their best to convince him that his time was near. They hoped to impress him with the importance of being prepared for his future state.

To the wagon was attached a span of mules with old Gustave Fisher as driver. On reaching the gallows the priests alighted and the wagon was driven under the fatal noose. The rope was adjusted around Yankee Jim's neck and he delivered a farewell speech to the large crowd gathering to witness his execution. He told them he had been a good man and given piles of gold to help poor men.

Undersheriff Crosthwaite, who was to superintend the execution, stood on the ground near the wagon and listened patiently to Yankee Jim's story until it was a quarter to three o'clock. He finally ordered Fisher to drive on, and the old man applied his whip to the mules. Yankee Jim kept his feet in the wagon as long as possible, but was finally pulled off as the mules plodded on. He swung back and forth like a pendulum, until he strangled to death.

And thus ended the career of the dreaded desperado, Yankee Jim. Subsequently his accomplices in the crime were tried by the same jury but were sentenced to the State Prison for only a year. They never returned to San Diego.

While Yankee Jim was buried in El Santo Campo Cemetery, his legend—and, some say, his ghost—has lived on, especially since on the very site where he was hung entrepreneur **Thomas Whaley** (1823–1890) later built his stately home. According to the *San Diego Union*, "Soon after the couple and their children moved in, heavy footsteps were heard moving about the house. Whaley described them as sounding as though they were made by the boots of a large man, and he came to the conclusion that the unexplained footfalls were made by Yankee Jim Robinson."

The Thomas Whaley House

Today the Whaley House is considered one of the most haunted houses in America. Visitors swear that not only Yankee Jim's ghost has been seen and heard walking the floors, but the ghosts of Whaley's infant son **Thomas Whaley, Jr.** (1856–1858) and daughter **Violet Whaley** (1862–1885) have also been spotted. According to the family history, Thomas Whaley left New York City and his family's hardware and woodworking business to sail to San Francisco in 1849. He was so successful that he was able to build a lovely home and establish a store. A fire in 1851, however, destroyed his business, so Whaley moved his enterprise to Old Town San Diego. Within a short time, he again grew successful and was able to return to New York to marry **Anna Eloise DeLaunay** (1832–1913) in 1853. Returning to San Diego with his wife, Thomas began construction on a new home in 1856, on the site of Yankee Jim's hanging. By 1858, Thomas and Anna had three children (ultimately they had six), including **Francis Hinton** (1854–1914); **Thomas,** who died at eighteen months from scarlet fever; and **Anna Amelia** (1858–1905). Unfortunately, in 1858, another fire destroyed Thomas's place of business. Despairing, he moved his family back to San Francisco.

Over the next few years, Thomas's financial success fluctuated. Daughters Anna Amelia and Violet were both married, but Violet's marriage was a disastrous one. Having been deceived, the marriage ended in divorce, after which the young woman fell into a deep depression. In July 1885, she attempted suicide by jumping into the cistern in the yard. Her father rescued her just in time. But on August 18, 1885, Violet was able to complete the task; she shot herself through the heart. Thomas Whaley passed away five years later, in 1890. His wife lived several more years. But in the end, Thomas, his wife, and nine members of the Whaley family were all buried in San Diego's **Mount Hope Cemetery**. A tall, impressive marble monument stands to honor Thomas Whaley and all he had hoped to achieve and all he had achieved as one of San Diego's early citizens.

Two years after the last burial took place at the El Campo Santo Cemetery, a streetcar line was built right through the center of it. Outraged at the indignity, citizen Walter P. Temple purchased the cemetery in 1917 and began its restoration. In 1933, the San

Diego Historical Society took on the restoration. Using information provided by an old photograph, members reset markers and rebuilt individual fences encircling particular graves. They also constructed an adobe wall to protect the entire gravesite. Scattered around the hard dirt rectangular site are aging olive trees and cacti. Only one original headstone still marks the grave of **Edward L. Greene,** and a large white cross stands at the center of the Old Town Catholic cemetery.

San Diego's **Mount Hope Cemetery** is the final resting place for over 70,000 people. Located at 3751 Market Street, the cemetery encompasses more than 100 acres. The original Mount Hope Cemetery opened in 1869, east of the "New Town" of San Diego. Initially the cemetery was established for members of the International Order of Foresters, the Masons, the Grand Army of the Republic, the Fraternal Order of Eagles, and the County of San Diego's Indigent Burial Program. In 1973, a veterans' section was added.

There is a long list of notables interred at the Mount Hope Cemetery, including **Alonzo Erastus Horton** (1813–1909). Born of Puritan stock, he was an enterprising man—a cooper, a sailor, and even an amateur wrestler. He came to California in 1851, thinking to mine gold or invest in cattle. Instead he began to trade in and sell gold dust. One interesting anecdote was that he "went into the mountains where there were fine fields of ice" and was able to ship and sell 312 tons of "frozen snow" at a great profit. Even as he made money, Horton also invested in San Diego and was often called "The Father of San Diego" for the vision and promise he saw in the future.

At Alonzo Horton's funeral the *San Diego Union* reported, "The men were bareheaded, the women touched with emotion, the children subdued. All sounds of the busy Saturday afternoon rush were stopped—the 'tramp, tramp' of his marching brethren was the only music heard and it was a fitting requiem." And Laurie Bissell wrote, "Eight thousand people had come to bid this man, who founded modern San Diego, farewell. . . . The casket passed through a double line of Masons and Elks to the hearse."

One of the most intriguing individuals buried at Mount Hope was **Tom Chong-kwan**, also known as **Ah Quin** (1848–1914), and often dubbed the "Unofficial Mayor of San Diego's Chinatown." Born in China in 1848, he converted to Christianity and attended missionary school where he learned to write in both Chinese and English. After working in Alaska and California as a laborer and a cook, he settled in San Diego where he was hired to work as a railroad labor contractor, especially because he could translate for Chinese workers. Quin also kept a diary, and his journals are filled with San Diego history as well as history of the Chinese in California. Ah Quin married **Leong Sue Quin** (1861–1927) in 1881 and fathered twelve children. His son George was the first Chinese male born in San Diego. Sadly, in 1914, Ah Quin was struck and killed by a motorcycle. He was buried at Mount Hope Cemetery.

Another famous individual interred at Mount Hope is **Nate Harrison** (1833–1920), a former slave who traveled to California with his master during the gold rush and at some point gained his freedom. He built a cabin and lived out his life on

The obelisk monument built to honor Alonzo Horton is a testament to his enterprising and creative spirit.

Palomar Mountain. So much has been written about Nate that he has become almost larger than life. In trying to separate myth from fact, members of the Nate Harrison Historical Archaeology Project accumulated fifty-five different secondary sources that offered biographical information about Harrison, including how he gained his freedom: "Early accounts claim that Harrison escaped from his owner; interim narratives assert that Harrison obtained his freedom as soon as his owner died; later stories state that Harrison's owner granted him liberty; and the final histories relate that Harrison purchased his freedom from his owner."

Which story is true?

Though not much is known about him, Nate Harrison lived for years on Palomar Mountain where he assisted many on the road between Doane Valley and Pauma.

Courtesy Esperer Collection/Tom Allain/ Tom K. Cubes

Nate Harrison's Legacy

What *is* known about Nate Harrison is that he homesteaded on Palomar Mountain where he built a cabin and provided passersby assistance as they traveled the wagon road between Doane Valley and Pauma. It's reported he helped motorists in the early days of the automobile, too, offering water from his spring, while preparing meals and selling fruits from his garden. In failing health, he left his homestead in 1919 and died the next year at the age of ninety-seven. In 1955, a plaque was placed at the site of Nate's cabin and spring, which was the *first* U.S. Historical Monument dedicated to an African American. A sleek, upright gray granite headstone was also placed at his grave at Mount Hope Cemetery. It reads, "Born a slave, died a pioneer." A final honor came from San Diego County when Palomar Mountain Road was renamed Nathan Harrison Grade Road.

Sam Brannan (1819–1889), California's first millionaire is also buried at Mount Hope Cemetery. Born in Maine in 1819, he moved with his family to Ohio where he apprenticed as a printer. He joined the Church of Jesus Christ of Latter-Day Saints, then moved to New York where he began publishing *The Prophet*. Brannan married **Ann Eliza Cowan** in 1844, and in 1846, he and Ann sailed to California with a group of Mormons on board the *Brooklyn*.

When Sam Brannan reached San Francisco in July 1846, he immediately set up his printing press and began producing the *California Star*. He next moved to Sacramento and opened a general store where he sold thousands of dollars of supplies to incoming miners and settlers; his wealth grew, as his was the only store between the Gold Country and San Francisco. By the early 1860s, Sam Brannan became known as the richest man in California, and he helped build some of San Francisco's most important buildings. He also purchased 3,000 acres in Napa with the idea of building a resort to be called Calistoga. However, Brannan also supported the controversial, even notorious, San Francisco Vigilance Committee, which tackled problems like theft, arson, murder, and criminal gangs, often ruthlessly. In 1868, Ann Eliza Brannan divorced Brannan, and one wonders if his ambition overshadowed his character. Ultimately, Brannan's numerous schemes proved reckless and futile, and he lost money.

In the end, Brannan lived out his life in San Diego, where he died, penniless, on May 5, 1889. His nephew paid for his burial and the "rent" on his "vault," for a total of $47.00. The "headstone" was nothing more than a wooden stake marking his plot, and for almost forty years, nothing more was done to identify Sam Brannan's grave. Finally, a monument was built, which reads: "Sam Brannan 1819–1889 California Pioneer of '46 Dreamer, Leader, Empire Builder."

Today both Sam Brannan and Samuel Brannan Jr. (1845–1931) are interred in the Mount Hope Cemetery.

Young **Alta M. Hulett** (1854–1877), a pioneer lawyer, was also buried at Mount Hope Cemetery in 1877. An ambitious young woman, she was one of the Hulett's six children, of whom four died in childhood. Alta, eager to learn, learned telegraphy at age ten, enabling her to work as telegraph operator. After that, she taught school while studying law. This was a time when women were not seen as capable of becoming attorneys, so although she passed the Illinois law examination in 1872, she was refused entrance to the bar. Outraged, she moved to Chicago, where she became successful in effecting change. Alta became Illinois's first female attorney in 1873.

Alta Hulett moved to California for health reasons and established her law practice. Sadly, however, she died in March 1877 at the unlikely age of twenty-two and was buried at Mount Hope. Eighty years after her death, women lawyers of San Diego County placed a new headstone on her grave, and in 2004, the first "Alta M. Hulett Award" was established in Illinois.

Another intriguing young woman buried at Mount Hope Cemetery was **"Kate" Kathleen Farmer Morgan** (1865–1892). On December 30, 1885, the nineteen-year-old Kate married Thomas E. Morgan, aged twenty-five. Hopeful, in love, things changed when the couple's first and only child **Thomas E. Morgan** was born ten months later, on October 31, 1886. The infant died two days later. The mystery surrounding Kate Morgan's untimely death occurred in 1892 when she checked into room 3312 (now room 302) at the luxurious Hotel Del Coronado in Coronado, San Diego County. She signed in as "Lottie A. Bernard," from Detroit. Five days later "Lottie" was found, a bullet wound to the head. The coroner declared it self-inflicted, that Kate, aka "Lottie," had committed suicide. She was laid to rest at Mount Hope Cemetery. Following the event, however, strange movements were reported, not only in Kate's Del Coronado hotel room but also throughout the resort and grounds. To this day, people report seeing a troubled young woman gliding in and out. Others report they have even felt her presence. The staff has had to continually foil questions as to her intentions and presence.

"She's harmless," is the general consensus of those who work at the hotel.

Three notables laid to rest at Mount Hope were **John Stone Stone** (1869–1943), inventor and mathematician and arguably the first to invent the radio-tuning apparatus two years before Marconi; **Gustaf Kletus Akerlundh** (1883–1961), member of Captain Roald Amundsen's 1903 expedition to the magnetic north pole; and **Elisha Spurr Babcock** (1848–1922), who built the exquisite and famous Hotel Del Coronado.

In 1861, Marcus Schiller and Adath Joshurun established a **Jewish Cemetery** in San Diego. **Louis Rose** (1921–2008), who was actually the first Jew to settle in San Diego in 1850, donated five acres for the creation of the cemetery. Both Marcus Schiller and **Joseph Mannasse** (1831–1897) donated lumber for the fencing, and the local Jewish population planted pepper trees. As the area's population grew, however, the location became inconvenient and inadequate, and Congregation Beth Israel sought a place within the much larger Mount Hope Cemetery that would suffice. The request was granted, and San Diego's **Home of Peace Cemetery** was dedicated in 1892. Those buried in other plots, including Louis Rose and Joseph Mannasse, were reinterred at Home of Peace in 1937.

Marcus Schiller (1819–1904) was born in Prussia and immigrated to the United States in the 1840s. He first settled in New York, then traveled to San Francisco, and finally moved to San Diego in 1856. He married **Rebecca Barnett** (1843–1921) in 1861 and together they had nine children. He became successful in real estate

Located on 1502 Second Avenue, San Diego's Temple Beth Israel was constructed in 1889, making it one of the earliest synagogues in California. LIBRARY OF CONGRESS

and became a political figure, even serving as president of Congregation Beth Israel until his death. He helped fund the first telegraph line to San Diego and also helped in acquiring land for what became Balboa Park. When he passed away in 1904, he was interred at Home of Peace. Many have likened Schiller to a San Diego "Jewish Horatio Alger," and according to Samuel Fox, historian, "Mr. Schiller was a leading spirit in all welfare and charitable work in San Diego."

Jewish Burial Customs

As with many cultures, Jewish burial traditions are especially important to orthodox believers. For example, burials generally take place within twenty-four hours. Another tradition: the Jewish faith prohibits cremation. It also prohibits embalming. These prohibitions go back to the Lord's words: "Dust to dust," emphasizing the natural process of decomposition. The casket needs to be biodegradable and should not include nails. The body is not open to viewing, and no flowers are placed on the grave. Likewise, music and flowers are not permitted at the funeral. It is acceptable to place stones on the grave (or headstone after it is set). The placement of stones likely originated in ancient times when Jews were nomadic and lived in the desert. Stones are dry and found in arid places; they also don't deteriorate. For some, they represent the strength and perseverance that marks Jewish history. Or, as a personal gesture, stones pay tribute to the dead and communicate to the family that the deceased still lives in the minds of those who have come to pay respect. Some contend that rocks or stones help keep evil spirits out and help prevent the soul from being taken over by demons. At the funeral, whether at the burial site or in another location, only the rabbi walks in front of the casket. Mourners follow the casket. In addition, there are typically seven pauses; as the casket moves forward and is halted, the living are given time to consider their own lives. According to one source, during the procession, *"the very beautiful and moving Psalm 91 is recited. . . . It is said to have been recited at the building of the Tabernacle in the desert. . . [and] is an expression of confidence that God will watch over His people."*

Finally, those who carry the casket must be Jewish, and it is a violation of Jewish law to allow the deceased to be handled or covered by anonymous gravediggers. The coffin must be lowered to the bottom of the open grave, and the grave must be filled at this point. Only one person handles the shovel at a time and it should not be handed off but slipped into the soil so that the next person reaches for it without touching anyone. Tradition asserts that in this way, one person's grief is not handed off to another.

San Diego's **Calvary Pioneer Memorial Park** has been known by various names, as the Catholic Cemetery, Mission Hills Cemetery, Old Catholic Cemetery, or as Pioneer Park. Originally it was simply called the **Calvary Cemetery**. Located at 1501 Washington Place, San Diego, Calvary Pioneer Memorial Park was established in 1870 with separate burial areas for Protestants and Catholics.

Elmer Ignatius Otis (1830–1897) was laid to rest at Calvary Pioneer Memorial. An U.S. army officer, he fought in both the Civil War and the Indian Wars. He graduated from West Point in 1853, after which he was assigned to the First Cavalry in Texas. During the Civil War, he served as part of the Army of Tennessee. In 1861, he married **Agnes Reid Boone** (1840–1916), the daughter of Indian agent Albert Gallatin Boone and the great-granddaughter of Daniel Boone. They had ten children.

The Last Major Indian War

Elmer Ignatius Otis is noted for having participated in the Modoc War of 1872–1873, which took place along northern California's borderlands. Refusing to relocate to the Klamath Indian Reservation (a generations-old enemy), *Kintpuash*, also known as Captain Jack, and a group of Modocs retreated to a stronghold in the rugged lava beds near Tule Lake. At least 150 held off 1,000 U.S. troops for almost six months. Otis, however, was determined to help negotiate some kind of peace, but when peace negotiations erupted in bloody violence, it looked doubtful. Eventually, Kintpuash surrendered after a betrayal, but there would be no peaceful resolution. Three of the Modoc leaders, in addition to Kintpuash, were found guilty of war crimes, including the murder of General Edward Canby. They were hanged on October 3, 1873. Afterward, their fingers and other body parts were shipped around the country as if they were some kind of show-and-tell trophy. The "last major Indian War" was a tragedy for all.

Kintpuash and his band of Modocs held out against 1,000 U.S. troops in the 1872–1873 Modoc War. After their capture, Kintpuash and three of his warriors were hung.
COURTESY FORT JONES MUSEUM

In 1892, after his retirement, Elmer Ignatius Otis moved to San Diego. When he passed away in 1897, he was interred at Calvary Pioneer Memorial Cemetery.

María Amparo Ruiz (1832–1895), born in Loreto, Baja California, was also laid to rest in the Calvary Pioneer Memorial Cemetery. As a member of an influential family, María Amparo was well educated in the classics and spoke several languages. As a young woman, she also witnessed U.S. forces invading her hometown of La Paz during the Mexican War of 1846–1848. But it was then she also met the man who would become her husband, **Captain Henry S. Burton** (1819–1869), commander of the New York Volunteers.

María Amparo Ruiz, Writer and Wife

The marriage of María Amparo Ruiz and Captain Henry S. Burton in 1849 is a romantic tale. María was a member of the conquered country, while Captain Burton was an officer of the oppressing nation. He was a Protestant, and she a devout Catholic where any marriage had to be approved by the governor and the church. Rushing ahead, however, the couple found a Protestant minister in Monterey to perform the ceremony, only days after María's seventeenth birthday.

In 1852, Burton became the commander of the San Diego Army Post. When he was reassigned to Fort Monroe, in Virginia, 3,000 miles from home, María and their children accompanied him. For the next few years, María witnessed the Civil War from her position as wife of a Union Army general. She also became friends with First Lady Mary Todd Lincoln and was granted a one-on-one meeting with President Lincoln. These experiences are what prepared her for her next career, as an author of real importance, because María Ampara Ruiz de Burton became the *first* writer of Mexican-descent to write in English, and she's also considered the *first* authentic Mexican American writer.

Henry Burton died in 1869 after battling an illness brought on by malaria that he had contracted years earlier. This left María a widow at age thirty-seven. She returned to California and their rancho, but all had fallen into disrepair and portions of land sold to clear her husband's debts. Although devastated by what she'd lost, María Ampara's literary abilities eventually brought her "redemption." She authored two important novels and a play, and through them, "addressed crucial issues of ethnicity, power, gender, class and race." Modern readers and critics have noted that "her life and writings demonstrate(d) the historical contradictions of the Mexican American identity." María passed away in 1895, and she was interred at Calvary's Pioneer Memorial Cemetery.

The last funeral to take place at Calvary Pioneer Memorial took place in 1960, and by 1968, the cemetery was closed. At that time, at least 1,800 people had been buried there. In 1969, Calvary Pioneer Memorial Cemetery was declared an historic site. Aboveground vaults were opened and bodies interred below ground, plus a bronze memorial was placed in the center of the park to commemorate those who had not been found but still lay under the surface. In 1970, the former Calvary Cemetery was dedicated as a public park, and most of the headstones that had been removed were taken to Mount Hope Cemetery where they were somehow abandoned. In 1988, they were rediscovered and several were set in cement. A memorial was built, recognizing those whose names and lives had been nearly forgotten.

Another important historic location in San Diego County is San Pasqual, located east of Escondido along State Highway 78. San Pasqual Valley was named after the *Kumeyaay* village of San Pasqual and is part of the Santa Ysabel Creek watershed. The area was also the site of one of the bloodiest battles during the Mexican American War of 1846. **The Battle of San Pasqual**, which broke out on December 6, 1846, pitted the forces of the American general Stephen W. Kearny against Mexico's General Andres Pico and his detachment.

The Bloodiest of All Battles in California

The Battle of San Pasqual took place near the Indian village of the same name. Apart from the ongoing battles fought against the various tribes of California Indians, this battle has been dubbed the "bloodiest of all battles fought on California soil." In hindsight, it has also been regarded as an unfortunate and unnecessary encounter.

In December 1846, as General Kearny's exhausted army marched toward San Diego—after leaving New Mexico and crossing the Sonoran Desert—a communication arrived stating a formidable force of Californios was waiting for them in the narrow San Pasqual Valley. At the same time, Kearny—from earlier communications via Kit Carson—believed that the Californios had been contained or eliminated by Commodore Robert Stockton and John C. Fremont and his California Battalion. How formidable, then, could such a force really be?

Coupled with an unusually severe winter for the region, Kearny's men were ill-prepared for the battle, but Kearny decided his men could still mount a surprise attack and succeed. Come morning, however, the men's equipment, ammunition, and guns were wet from rain, and as soon as they set out, they were also overtaken by fog. In the first waves of battle, the Californios killed seventeen of Kearny's troops. By the time Kearny was able to assemble his artillery, the wet gunpowder proved almost useless. In addition to the death toll, more than a dozen troopers were seriously wounded and one was either missing or captured. The men hurriedly buried their dead in one mass grave. Kearny's army then retreated to a rocky hillside where it remained until December 11. Meanwhile, Kit Carson and Lieutenant Beale, who had traveled with Kearny, slipped out to seek reinforcements from San Diego, twenty-eight miles away. Unfortunately, the remaining men, hoping to be resupplied, were forced to kill and eat their mules to stave off starvation.

The area tagged as the Battleground of San Pasqual sits on the north side of San Pasqual Valley Road (Highway 78) in Escondido, San Diego County. Almost adjacent to the highway, it slopes upwards where a crude rock wall encircles it. Today, a large bronze plaque set against an enormous boulder stands in the center of the area listing the names of the soldiers and officers lost in battle.

Some of those who died were also taken to the quaint **San Pasqual Pioneer Cemetery** down the road. The cemetery sits atop a knoll above the bridge across Santa Ysabel Creek. Once known as "Cemetery Hill," it contains more than 200 graves. The sloping entrance to the cemetery is rocky, not paved, and a rather dilapidated gate hangs limply from its hinges. But as you move up the incline, you suddenly take note of the plateau-like area ahead of you, where white headstones, some shaped in half circles, stand in tidy rows under the trees. A few whitewashed wooden markers list names and dates in bold black print. The scene is quite peaceful and pleasant.

Also located on the same side of the San Pasqual Valley Road (Highway 78)—actually between the battlefield and the Pioneer Cemetery—is the **San Pasqual Indian Cemetery**. Sitting off the road a few yards, and next to an old school (now the Museum of Archaeology), the fenced enclosure includes a number of wooden, well-worn crosses, none bearing names or dates. The fencing has deteriorated, and knee-high weeds and stinging nettles have overtaken the enclosure. In the center stands a tall cross, looking as forlorn as the scattered wooden crosses surrounding it. To reach the center of the square patch requires a little bit of grit as the nettles inflame bared ankles.

Felicita La Chappa (unknown–1911), aka *Hal-ah-wee*, is interred here. She was the daughter of **Pontho**, the last hereditary chief of the San Pasqual Indians. Felicita lived to be over 100 years old and witnessed not only the Battle of San Pasqual but also the tragic degradation of her people. She died in 1911 and was buried here, although there is no headstone indicating which might be her burial site. The one marker that does exist is for "Andres A. Alvarado, Nov. 1912–Mar. 1919."

Another small and old cemetery in San Diego County is the **Meadowlark Pioneer Memorial Cemetery** in San Marcos, originally established in 1894 by Salvador Gonzales. Over many decades, there have been attempts to move or destroy it, but each time the

A memorial was installed at Fort Rosecrans in honor of the soldiers who died fighting in the 1846 Battle of San Pasqual.

families of those interred here have intervened. Most recently, when the city thought to move the graves to enlarge a thoroughfare, the road was finally rerouted and the cemetery's location spared. Now the cemetery lies within the median of the Rancho Santa Fe Road at the intersection of Meadowlark Ranch Road, and the graves are marked with squares of stone laid in the shape of a cross. According to the dedication plaque, there are seven people buried within the median, including **Casildo Figueroa** and his seven-year-old grandson, **José Figueroa; Felipe Sanchez**, a rancher from the region; **José Urbano** and **Ramon Moralez**, two LaJolla Indian ranch hands; and **Tomasa Gonzales Tico** and her nine-year-old son, **Alfredo Joaquin Tico**. Ramon Moralez died after being shot by the sixteen-year-old grandson of Colonel Cave Couts. Though tried for murder, the boy was acquitted, a decision that remained controversial for years. Tomasa Gonzales Tico was born in 1867; she was the great great granddaughter of **José Francisco de Ortega** (1734–1798), the "pathfinder" who traveled with Father Junipero Serra a hundred years earlier. At fourteen, Tomasa married **Victorino Peralto**; they had four children, although two died young. After Peralto died in 1887, Tomasa married **Juan Tico**, whose grandfather had marched north from Baja California with the Spanish army. Juan and Tomasa also had four children. At thirty-eight, Tomasa died of tuberculosis (TB).

On the plaque listing the names of those buried in the cemetery, it is written:

In the 1880s, a group of colonists of European Spanish descent from Ventura and Ojai, California, settled here in the Meadowlark region, then known as the Fresno Valley, and homesteaded land. This monument commemorates the memory of those colonists who died here and lie buried in the Meadowlark Pioneer Memorial Cemetery adjacent to this monument. Among the pioneers buried in this cemetery are members of the **Figueroa**, **Gonzales**, and **Tico** families . . . in whose bones and dust rests the heritage of their Spanish ancestors, who explored and settled California.

Greenwood Memorial Park is located on 4300 Imperial Avenue in San Diego. A number of interesting individuals have been laid to rest here: several Civil War **Medal of Honor** soldiers; **Dr. Charlotte LeBreton Johnson Baker** (1855–1937), San Diego's first woman physician; and **Ulysses Simpson "Buck" Grant, Jr.** (1852–1929), son of General Ulysses S. Grant. The younger Grant's memorial is one of the most unusual ones in the entire cemetery; a black, forbidding sculpture of the Angel of Death sits atop the solid stone monument. Its distressed appearance and formidable size raise a number of questions: was "Buck" a haunted or troubled man? Or, like his famous father, had he struggled with issues of addiction or depression?

Moses Augustine Luce (1842–1933), who rests at Greenwood Memorial Cemetery, enlisted in Company E, Fourth Michigan Infantry, U.S. Army, in June of 1861. During May of 1864, as the Confederates engaged the Union at the Battle of the Spotsylvania Court House, Luce courageously moved into the advancing Confederate line to carry a wounded comrade to a place of safety. After Luce mustered out in June 1864, he studied law and began practicing in Illinois. He moved to San Diego and founded the practice of Luce, Forward,

Ulysses S. "Buck" Grant Jr. is interred in Greenwood Memorial Park where the black "Angel of Death" sits atop his rock monument, peering down as if in serious contemplation.

Hamilton, & Scripps. He also served as county judge, postmaster, and vice president of the Santa Fe Railroad. It wasn't until 1895 that Moses Augustine Luce was awarded the **Medal of Honor** for his actions in the Civil War Battle of the Spotsylvania Court House. He retired from law in 1922, at age eighty. He lived until 1933 and was then buried at Greenwood Memorial Park. His son, **Edgar Augustine Luce** (1881–1958), was also buried at Greenwood, as was his daughter, **Grace Adelaide Luce Irwin** (1877–1914)—who married **William Irwin** (1875–1995), noted author of *The Rubaiyat of Omar Khayyam.*

Dr. Charlotte LeBreton Johnson Baker (1855–1937) was born to privilege in Massachusetts in 1855. She attended Vassar followed by medical school at the University of Michigan where she studied obstetrics. She completed her residency at a women's penitentiary, and this is when she decided she wanted to improve the lives of women and children. Charlotte married **Dr. Fred Baker** (1854–1938), also a physician. When they moved to Southern California, they worked at St. Joseph's Hospital where it was reported, "Dr. Charlotte delivered 1,000 babies and never lost a mother." When she died in October 1937, she was buried at Greenwood Memorial Park.

Another resident of Greenwood Memorial Park is **Marvel Crosson** (1900–1929). At thirteen, she and her brother Joe saw their first "flying machine" and were immediately determined to have one of their own. They purchased a dismantled World War I "Jenny," which they rebuilt, and by 1922, the plane was ready to fly.

Marvel Crosson, Pioneer Aviator

Joe Crosson earned his pilot's license first and then taught his sister Marvel. An adept learner, she became an accomplished aviator, described by one newspaper as "so steeped in aviation that she carries you into the clouds." In 1927, Marvel joined her brother in Alaska, where she became the first female pilot in Alaska. She worked as a bush pilot and flew freight for Western Canada Airways, but then returned to San Diego. Doing stunts and flight exhibitions, she set a new world altitude record on May 28, 1929. In August 1929, she entered the First Women's Air Derby, along with women fliers like Amelia Earhart and Bobbie Trout. Though Marvel was the youngest pilot, she was the most experienced. Later, it would be debated as to whether there had been any foul play; female pilots were fighting for recognition and several had complained about sabotage and sand in fuel tanks. Nothing was discovered, however, and on day two of the competition, Marvel crashed near Wellton, Arizona. Even her parachute failed to open as she jumped free.

The mystery surrounding Marvel's death has never been solved. At twenty-nine, she was laid to rest in Greenwood Memorial Park cemetery.

The geographical region of the Imperial Valley actually lies in two counties, Imperial and Riverside. Located in the southeastern portion of Southern California, the valley is bordered in the east by the Colorado River. To the north lies Coachella Valley and to the west lies the Salton Sea and, further west, San Diego County. To the south lies the boundary between California and Baja California.

Fort Yuma, originally named Fort Independence then renamed Camp Yuma, was established in 1848 at the end of the Mexican

American War. It sat near the Colorado River and below the mouth of the Gila River. It was built to protect emigrants and settlers in Yuma (then within the New Mexico Territory, later to become Yuma, Arizona). Today, Fort Yuma is part of the Yuma Indian Reservation. When the fort's cemetery was closed in 1889, the remains of 149 uniformed soldiers were reinterred at the **San Francisco National Cemetery**, but the rest were left behind in the now defunct **Fort Yuma Post Cemetery**.

Mrs. Sarah A. Bowman (1812–1866), originally from Tennessee, was one of those relocated to San Francisco's National Cemetery at the Presidio in 1890; she had been a well-known camp follower, laundress, and cook, attached to Zackary Taylor's army during the Mexican War and at Fort Yuma. Mrs. Bowman was given full military honors at her (second) burial in San Francisco.

One soldier left behind at the fort was **Charles August Reidt** (1828–1870). He had enlisted as a first lieutenant at the start of the Civil War, and before mustering out was brevetted to lieutenant colonel. With retirement, he decided to move west but was attacked and murdered by Mexican bandits before he could reach California. It was Christmas Eve, and he was forty-two years old when he was buried at Fort Yuma.

A second soldier "left behind" was **Francis Stanton** (1838–1859). Born in New York, he was the seventh of eleven children, the son of General Henry Stanton. Captain Henry Whiting Stanton, older brother to Francis, died in a skirmish with Mescaleros in 1855, and Fort Stanton was named in his honor. Unfortunately, twenty-year-old Francis fell ill while on assignment. Left behind to recover at the fort, he died on October 1, 1859. A monument—a large white obelisk—was raised in his honor and still stands against the bare landscape, just across the border from Yuma, Arizona, in Winterhaven, California.

Private Lee Rainbow (1901–1918), the son of Nelson Rainbow and stepson of Ruth (Yuma) Rainbow, was a member of the 158th Infantry Regiment, Fortieth Division during World War I. Nelson had been a scout in the Yuma Indian contingent that served General Miles during the Indian Wars in Arizona. Sadly, Nelson received a telegram telling him his son had been killed in action during the Meuse-Argonne Offensive in France during World War I.

Nelson Rainbow took the telegram to the superintendent of the Yuma Indian school and told him, "I received the telegram telling of the death of my son. . . . It is our custom never to mention the name of our dead relatives, but his name should be remembered and honored forever. . . . I gave my son as one of the Yuma Indians. A meeting will be called to arrange to ask for his body and to erect a memorial to his memory." In lasting tribute, a memorial was built on the Phoenix Indian School grounds in front of Memorial Hall. It honored not only Lee Rainbow but also sixty-three other students who had served in the war. Lee Rainbow, however, was the first student "to lose his life for his country." In November 1922, Nelson Rainbow was presented Private Lee Rainbow's posthumously awarded Cross of Malta—the highest honor given by the Veterans of Foreign Wars. In tribal fashion, Lee Rainbow was cremated and his ashes interred at the **Quechan Indian Cemetery** in Imperial County. He was only seventeen years old.

A second cemetery in El Centro is the **Evergreen Cemetery**. Also known as the **Central Valley District Cemetery**, it is located on 201 E. Gillett Road, in El Centro. One of the most intriguing individuals buried in El Centro's Evergreen Cemetery is **Austin Ira Aten** (1862–1953), known to most as Ira Aten. Born in Illinois, he was the son of an itinerant Methodist minister who moved his family to Texas in 1876. This event proved to be an important episode because at age sixteen Ira witnessed the killing of the notorious outlaw, Sam Bass, by Texas Rangers.

Austin Ira Aten, Texas Ranger

Ira Aten joined the Texas Rangers in 1881 and served first as a Regular Ranger and then as a Special Ranger. From 1886 to 1888, he faced one of his most famous challenges, the "Fence Cutting Wars." These "wars" often led to violence and murder between those who tried to fence off the wide-open plains and those "fence cutters" who cut the wires. In 1893, Ira Aten was hired as sheriff of Castro Valley. Finally, in 1904, he moved his family to the Imperial Valley where he joined the Imperial Valley District Board, which helped direct the construction of Boulder Dam and the American Canal.

Ira and his wife, **Imogen Boyce** (1867–1957), had five children. Their second son, **Albert Boyce Aten** (1894–1918), served during World War I as a lieutenant of Company D, 129th M. G. Battalion Thirty-Fifth Division. The twenty-four-year-old Albert Boyce Aten was the last officer in his division to fall in the Argonne Forest, in France. He died in the hospital but was brought home to be buried in the Evergreen Cemetery. Ira's oldest son, **Marion Hughes Aten** (1892–1961), joined the Royal Flying Corps, also known as the Royal Air Force (RAF), in 1917. Though he did not arrive in

Ira and Imogen's second son, Albert Boyce Aten, was the last officer in his division to die in the Argonne Forest in France in World War I. He was twenty-four.

Europe until the summer of 1918, he did participate in the Russian Civil War from 1918 and 1920 as part of an RAF unit. For "scoring 5 victories in the air against the 'Red' Air Force," he received the British Distinguished Flying Cross. Eventually, he returned to the Imperial Valley and the Aten family farm. He passed away in 1961 and was also buried in the Evergreen Cemetery in El Centro.

Austin Ira Aten died of pneumonia in 1953, at age ninety-one, and was buried in the Evergreen Cemetery in El Centro. In honor of his service, he was inducted into the Texas Rangers' Hall of Fame in Waco, Texas.

Julian, California, with a population of about 1,000, is a frontier-like town located at the intersection of California highways 78 and 79, an hour northeast of San Diego in the Cuyamaca Mountains. At 4,226 feet, it does see occasional snowfall. While an out-of-the-way place these days, it was Southern California's first and only gold rush town.

The first gold "strike" in this rugged terrain occurred circa 1869, when **A. E. "Fred" Coleman** (1829–unknown) discovered flecks of gold in a stream while watering his horse. Coleman, a former slave, worked as a cattle herder and lived in the area with his *Kumeyaay* wife Marian and their eleven children. The stream where Coleman discovered gold is now called Coleman Creek; the mining district was named the Coleman Mining District (and Coleman was elected its recorder). Finally, there is a street in Julian named Coleman Circle in Fred Coleman's honor.

Julian's Gold History

Julian was officially founded by two former Confederate soldiers, **Drury "Drue" (Dobbins) Bailey** (1844–1921) and his cousin **Mike Julian**, who came west to seek their fortunes. Bailey laid out Julian's town site, offering free lots to anyone who would build on them, and he named the town after his cousin Mike who had found a "fine nugget" in a creek near the cabin they had built. Following their discovery, others arrived in waves, each filing claims and establishing mines. The Washington mine was one of the first (having been filed on George Washington's birthday). A few other early mines included the Owens and High Peak, the Eagle, Helvetia, Big Blue, the Stonewall Jackson, and the California. Though San Diego's first and only gold rush did not last long, from 1870 to 1880, Julian was a lively mining town, boasting five stores, two livery stables, two blacksmith shops, two hotels, two cafes, and eight saloons. By 1880, almost $7 million in gold had been extracted from the area's mines.

One of the most notable sites in Julian is the Julian Hotel. Established in 1897 by a former slave, **Albert Robinson** (*c.* 1845–1915), and his wife **Margaret Tull Robinson**, it was called the Robinson Hotel until Albert's death. Margaret and Albert had met in Julian, where Albert, who emigrated west with his former slave owner, worked as a cook. They were married in the 1880s, and in 1887, they opened a restaurant and bakery and razed the old structure to build the hotel.

After falling ill, Albert died in 1915 and, while there has been controversy over his final resting place because of a possible "whites only" policy—in 2005, historian David Lewis was able to identify the grave of Albert Robinson at Julian's **Haven of Rest Cemetery**, also known as the **Julian Pioneer Cemetery.** It is a fairly large granite, manicured headstone, especially when compared to many of the primitive or rougher stones scattered around the hillside. It simply states: "ALBERT ROBINSON 1845–1915 Loving Husband of Margaret."

The entrance to Julian Pioneer Cemetery is located at 2656 Farmer Road, Julian, which is up A Street, only a block or two from historic Main Street. There are actually two entrances, one that allows

The Julian Hotel has been open consistently since the years when Albert and Margaret first opened it in 1897.

cars to drive into the cemetery, and the second a rather battered, wooden stairway, where some of the oldest graves are located. The cemetery actually sits on a hill that overlooks the community. Though not large or showy, it is an intriguing and eclectic collection of headstones, some made of rocks, others little more than etched bricks, even some that are simple "punched" metal signs. There are a few family plots enclosed by cement borders and/or iron fencing. Written on a plaque at the lower entrance is the following statement:

Primitive living conditions, violence, alcohol, disease and fatal accidents, all common in the Julian gold mining district, created an urgent need for a graveyard. Such use began on this then private property with the burial of stillborn babies under a sheltering oak tree. The earliest burials recorded are those of two teenage boys who died in the winter of 1875. Soon other victims were buried, some 'with their boots still on' in unmarked graves, some in family plots and some alone in what became a family cemetery.

According to Julian historian and author David Lewis, the oldest grave may belong to a young boy who was accidentally killed while cutting down a tree with his father, around 1870. A second burial was noted in 1873, but records and identifications were not kept until much later. In 1922, there was a proposal to build a hotel on the cemetery site, so in order to maintain the cemetery a meeting was held to form an association. Since many of the markers were nothing more than bricks or rocks with numbers scrawled or etched into them, Lewis explained how he and other volunteers have determined who is buried where. As he wrote in his book, *Last Known Address*, "For seven years now, I have searched the Julian Cemetery grounds looking for the locations of seventy lost graves. Finding one or two a year has been good progress." He added, "Sometimes the discovery of a gravestone can be incidental to routine maintenance. . . . While removing soil adjacent to a headstone I discovered a concrete wall that encircled the plot. . . . I was about to move on when I suddenly realized what I had found. It was one of the 1923 vintage concrete markers that had fallen on its side. The inscription read, '15-SMITH INFANT.' I had discovered the grave of a baby unknown to today's family members."

The Bailey Family

The Bailey family is well represented in Julian's Pioneer Cemetery. **Drury "Drue" Dobbins Bailey** (1844–1921), who was born in Georgia, enlisted in the Confederate Army in May 1862. He served until 1865 after which he and his brothers and cousins headed west. Early on Drury was considered one of Julian's leading citizens. In 1874, when he and his partners ceased mining operations, he settled permanently in Julian, opening a blacksmith shop, livery stable, and stageline. Reportedly, he donated land for several important buildings, including the high school and grammar school, a jail, a church, and even a public hall. In addition, at his death in 1921, Drury's daughter Ida Bailey Wellington became concerned with preservation of the cemetery. She maintained that interest until her death in 1962.

Both Drury Dobbins Bailey and **Annie Laurie (Redman) Bailey's** (1859–1927) headstones are large—made of granite, set on roughly edged stone bases. Not far from their headstones are several smaller flat stones belonging to other family members, and a scalloped black iron fence encircles the entire family plot. Drue and Annie had twelve children, but two young ones did not survive, including **Jennie Bailey** (1881–1882) and **Julia Bailey** (1889–1891). Their flat markers sit just in front of Drury and Annie's larger headstones.

One of Julian's more interesting residents was **America Newton** (c. 1835–1917). An ex-slave originally from Missouri, she came west in 1872 with a Mr. and Mrs. James A. Cole. Cole mined for a time but decided to leave Julian around 1885. Before he left, however, he assisted America in filing for an eighty-acre homestead, on a site that is now located on Routes 78 and 79. He built her a cabin not far from a spring, and a cart, and he gave her a horse with which to pull it. She received her document of ownership in 1891. In 2005, the Julian

Independent and well known, America Newton was laid to rest in the Julian Cemetery in 1917.

Black History Committee placed new markers on the graves of Albert Robinson, America Newton and Susan Tull, all pioneers of Julian. America's headstone's dedication reads, "Not forgotten."

Not Forgotten

America Newton became a well-known figure in Julian. She allowed travelers to drink freely from her well; she loved visitors and encouraged them to sit and visit; she was illiterate and therefore she occasionally asked individuals to help her by signing her name whenever she had business matters to attend to. While not fat, she was large and her feet were equally large. Whenever she needed new shoes—because she walked everywhere—she asked townsfolk to help her out.

Julian pioneer, Lulu Juch, wrote that America always received a new pair of shoes. America hired out to do laundry for residents and local miners. According to the locals, "No one was so skilled as America in fluting ruffles, baby clothes and shirts. The rods of her fluter and her irons were all heated over a grill in her fireplace." When America sold her property in 1913, she retained a life estate so she could live out her life in her cabin. In the end, she lived fifty-plus years in Julian before dying of pneumonia. In her honor, there is a half-mile stretch along Highways 78 and 79 known as America Grade. America Newton was laid to rest in the Julian Cemetery in 1917.

Lula Yancey Juch, who lived almost 100 years, was one of Julian's historians and descended from historic families.

One interesting side note: of the fifty-five African Americans living in San Diego during the San Diego Census of 1880, thirty-three lived in Julian.

PIONEER CEMETERY
1870

FOR OVER 50 YEARS GRAVE SITES ON THIS HILL WERE INACCESSIBLE TO WAGONS. COFFINS WERE CARRIED FROM THE WAGON TO THE GRAVE UP THIS WALK WHICH BEARS DUE WEST ALONG THE 3RD STANDARD PARALLEL SOUTH. IN 1896 MARY CLOUGH DIED DURING A STORM. IT TOOK SIXTEEN MEN TO DRAG A SLED BEARING HER CASKET FROM THE CHURCH UP THIS WALK THROUGH 3FT. OF SNOW TO HER GRAVE. CARRYING COFFINS UP THIS WALK WAS DISCONTINUED ABOUT 1924 WHEN VEHICLE ACCESS TO THE CEMETERY FROM "A" ST. WAS COMPLETED. THE WALK BECAME A PUBLIC ACCESS EASEMENT, 1991.

JULIAN HISTORICAL SOCIETY

A plaque located at Julian Pioneer Cemetery gives a brief history of its creation.

CHAPTER 2

ORANGE COUNTY REGION

Most present-day residents of Orange County have little connection to the early exploration of their county. Its history, however, is part of Alta California's colorful past: from the original Native American tribes that lived off the land and suffered under the succeeding generations; to the Spanish who claimed the land for the crown and established missions; to the Mexican period, where settlement included awarding land grants to various people groups and individuals willing to adopt Californio rule; and then into the Gold Rush Era, American Settlement, and Statehood.

As with the early history of San Diego County, the first travel into this region dates back to Portola's expedition of 1769. As Portola and his men passed through the low mountain country, they met up with a village of Native Americans. Reportedly, two small Indian girls, very ill, were baptized, making their conversion the first official Catholic baptisms in Alta California.

Portola's mission was to find the port of Monterey. He and his company crossed the valley of San Juan Capistrano and skirted the

Griffith Griffith, originally from Wales, became a giant in the granite industry of California during the gold rush, as evidenced by his large gray granite memorial found in the Old Auburn Cemetery in Placer County.

foothills east of the Santa Ana Valley. They rested at what would become the Irvine Ranch then camped along the Santa Ana River where, again, they encountered a friendly Native American village. From here, they reached "a very green little valley, which has a small pool of water, on whose bank there is a very large village of very friendly heathen." Today, that stop would have been in the town of Fullerton.

Long before the Spanish settled the area that would become Orange County, it was home to the *Acjachemen* people, but as the Spaniards built the **San Juan Capistrano Mission,** the Acjachemen people became known as the *Juaneño* band of Mission Indians. The mission's construction in 1776 brought obvious challenges and devastation to the Acjachemen.

As with other areas of Alta California, the people contracted diseases and thousands died. It's been estimated that by 1830, California's entire indigenous population had declined by 74 percent. The church itself was only used six years as it collapsed during the earthquake of 1812, and forty people were killed. A chapel is the only original building still standing.

After Mexico won its independence from Spain in 1821, San Juan Capistrano's mission and grounds continued to decline. Thousands of acres were handed out by the territorial governor or his representatives to individuals and families loyal to the Mexican government. One such individual was **Bernardo Antonio Yorba y Grijalva** (1801–1858). Born in San Diego, Bernardo was a Californio, born to the Spanish soldier **Jose Antonio Yorba** (1746–1825). Bernardo received more than 35,000 acres in land grants, and in 1834, he received an additional

Mission San Juan Capistrano was constructed in 1776, but the church was destroyed in the earthquake of 1812. The chapel is the only original building standing today.

13,328 acres, known as the Rancho Canon de Santa Ana. Bernardo developed the land by planting orchards and gardens, raising cattle, constructing irrigation systems, even building a gristmill.

Bernardo Yorba was also a womanizer. He married three times, each time to a woman many years younger. In the end, he had twenty children. In his will, dated only two weeks before his death in 1858, Bernardo Antonio Yorba deeded a plot of land, roughly 100 square feet, with an adobe chapel already under construction, to the Catholic Church. The order? To be used as a cemetery for his family—the **Yorba Cemetery**, the oldest private cemetery in Orange County. Only the **Mission San Juan Capistrano Cemetery** predates it.

Unfortunately, the cemetery was not prepared in time for Yorba's own burial, so he was interred in the **Old Calvary Cemetery** in Los Angeles. In 1923, Bernardo and nine other family members were reinterred at the Yorba Cemetery, along with members of other Californio families, including the Castillos, Peraltos, Acostas, Ames, Navarros, Estradas, Romeros, and others.

Another Yorba relation laid to rest in the Yorba Cemetery was **Audel Ramon Carrillo** (1881–1919), the great grandson of Bernardo Antonio Yorba and son of **Jose Ramon Carrillo** (1848–1921) and **Adelina Bernarda Yorba Carrillo** (1853–1933). At twenty-seven, Audel Ramon Carrillo was living with his widowed mother, a brother, and a sister, on the family estate. It was May 1919, and as Audel walked through the front door of the adobe, unexpectedly a shot was fired. Audel fell, shot through the abdomen. According to John M. Foster, who wrote about Audel's death, "A man who had shot two Chino policemen was hiding in the home. He panicked—thinking Audel an officer about to apprehend him—he shot first and asked questions too late." Audel was interred in the Yorba Cemetery in Yorba Linda, Orange County.

Audel's mother, Adelina Bernarda Yorba Carrillo, was later laid to rest, as acknowledged in the *Los Angeles Times* of April 12, 1933:

> [Today] this section lost one of its ties with the days of the Dons. She was 79 years of age, the widow of Jose "Joseph" R. Carrillo, a native of Los Angeles. Death occurred on the family's ranch home in Santa Ana Canyon about eight miles east of Placentia.... Burial will be in the old Yorba Cemetery, where lie many of

Buried in the Yorba Cemetery, Senaida Zoraida Yorba De Botiller
was born in California in 1858 and died at age thirty-five from
consumption. Her parents were Jose Raymondo Dolores Yorba and
Concepsion De Serrano Yorba.
COURTESY LESA PFROMMER

Mrs. Carrillo's ancestors. . . . Funeral services will be conducted at
9 a.m. tomorrow at the historic old Yorba Church in Santa Ana
Canyon near the site of the old Bernard Yorba Hacienda.

Audel, Jose, and Adelina Carrillo were laid to rest in the Yorba
Cemetery, all three resting "side by side."
COURTESY LESA PFROMMER

While the Yorba Cemetery remained in the family for years,
eventually it was donated to the Los Angeles Roman Catholic Arch-
diocese. The last burial took place in 1939, but the cemetery became
neglected, overrun by weeds and often vandalized. In 1967, the Arch-
diocese deeded the 200-square-foot cemetery to Orange County. In
recognition, the large plaque with the names of those interred in the
original cemetery was installed. The Yorba Cemetery is now operated
by Orange County Parks.

The Oldest City in Orange County

Anaheim is the oldest city in Orange County. It was founded by
a group of Germans who traveled south from San Francisco to
establish farms where they could plant vineyards. In 1857, they
formed a corporation known as the Los Angeles Vineyard Company. The Germans named their community "Anaheim," using the

German word for home, *heim*, and **Ana** from the Spanish saint's name and the nearby Santa Ana River. The first house in Anaheim was built in 1857, and the first hotel was built in 1865. For many years, the Spanish-speaking communities called the German community "Campo Alemán."

Construction was slow to occur, however, as lumber had to be hauled from Los Angeles, thirty miles away. Seeking a port that would accommodate boats rather than freight wagons, Anaheim Landing was built. It served the region until Southern Pacific Railroad set up a terminus in 1875.

Santa Ana Cemetery, now located at 1919 E. Santa Clara Avenue, Santa Ana, was founded in 1870 at the junction of Eighth and Ross Streets. Originally, it was known as the Masonic Cemetery, although the first burials were of two infants from the Jacob Ross family. In 1898, the decision was made to move the cemetery from the middle of town to a 100-acre location on the outskirts of Santa Ana. All of the bodies buried in the first location were exhumed and reinterred in the new (and present) location on E. Santa Clara Avenue. After a time, other groups began to purchase portions of the Santa Ana Cemetery. **Fairhaven Memorial Park** is actually composed of two-thirds of the original 100-acre cemetery, and it opened up to burials in 1911. Masons, Odd Fellows, Lutherans, and other groups bought up acreage for the burial of their own members as well.

Lysander Utt (1824–1890) was one pioneer laid to rest in the Santa Ana Cemetery. He had crossed the plains to California in 1849 where he tried his hand at mining, but failed. Instead, after marrying **Arvilla Emily Platt** (1834–1910) in 1865, Lysander took up ranching in Placer County. Then, in 1874, he sold out and moved his family to Tustin, in Orange County, and went into the mercantile business.

Charles Edward Utt (1866–1950) also called C. E. or Ed, inherited his father's mercantile business in 1891. He managed the store for only two years then purchased the Water Works from the Willard Brothers. In 1906, he entered farming and became one of Orange County's most progressive and enterprising producers. He raised lemons, Valencia oranges, and walnuts, and introduced planting beans, peanuts, and chilies between the tree rows. C.E. quickly became known as the "Peanut King." He passed away in 1951 and was buried in the Santa Ana Cemetery.

Benjamin Franklin Grouard (1819–1894) is also buried in the Santa Ana Cemetery. Born in New Hampshire, he left home at fourteen and went to sea. At some point, he converted to Mormonism and was baptized. He became one of the first Latter-day Saint missionaries to the Society Islands, which were part of French Polynesia. After landing on the island of Tubuai, Grouard sailed to Tahiti where he established a branch of the church and ministered to the people. He married a Polynesian woman, and in 1852, brought her and their children back to San Bernardino. Unfortunately, she despaired over leaving her island home and took two of the three boys and returned to the islands. Frank Grouard, the middle son, was left behind and taken in by the Pratt family in Utah.

Frank Benjamin Grouard

Much like his own father who ran away to sea at fourteen, young **Frank Benjamin Grouard** (1850–1905) ran away from the Pratts. He became a stage driver and express rider, but on one of his details was attacked by a band of Crow Indians. Stripped of his clothes and possessions, he was left to die but was discovered by a party of Sioux. Taken captive, it's been said that Frank was "adopted" by a member of Sitting Bull's band. He did finally escape and found himself working as one of General George Crook's scouts. He fought in a number of Indian campaigns, including the Battle of the Rosebud.

Not knowing his son had actually survived the attack by the Crow, when Benjamin Grouard heard of Frank's involvement with General Crook, he couldn't wait to find him. As it turned out, in 1893, only a few months before he passed away, Benjamin Grouard traveled to Wyoming to see his son Frank Grouard.

Benjamin Franklin Grouard passed away in 1894 and was laid to rest beside his second wife, **Louisa Maria Hardy Grouard** (1831–1892), the mother of five of his children, who passed away in 1892. Three of their daughters were also buried near Grouard in the Santa Ana Cemetery.

William H. "Uncle Billy" Spurgeon (1829–1915) has been called the "founder" or "father" of Santa Ana. After serving with the Oregon Mounted Volunteers, he was ready to settle down with his second wife, **Margaret Jane "Jennie" English** (1850–1935)—twenty years his junior and daughter of another early Southern California settler. Spurgeon helped lay out Santa Ana's streets and became its first mayor, postmaster, and "purveyor of the first artesian well." He ran a general store where "you could buy anything from a darning needle

While Frank's father, Benjamin, was buried in the Santa Ana Cemetery, Frank Grouard did not return to his family but was buried in Missouri.

to a Chicago ham." Finally, Spurgeon created a "new" cemetery, the **Fairhaven Memorial Park,** in Santa Ana. Spurgeon, his wife, and the rest of his family were all interred in Fairhaven Memorial Park.

William N. Tedford (1826–1905) was born in Tennessee. Near the end of the Civil War (April 1864), he set out for California. With one wagon and three yoke of oxen, thirty-eight-year-old Tedford and his family crossed the plains and arrived in California in October. The first stop was in Solano County, but two years later, the family moved to Watsonville, in Monterey County. One of Tedford's nearest neighbors was William H. Spurgeon; another was Isaac Williams. After Mr. Spurgeon and Mr. Williams visited Southern California and decided it was the place to settle, they invited Tedford to join them. In the words of Walter Tedford, William's son (born 1854):

> Both Mr. Spurgeon and Mr. Williams told my father of the wonderful country they had found, and urged him to come with them to this new country. Mr. Williams told him he could have any part of and as much as he wanted of the twelve hundred acres he had purchased, if he would move with his family on to the land and make it his home, and at the price he had paid for the land, namely, $12.00 per acre. Mr. Spurgeon (also) made my father a proposition to give him a lot in the new town site if he wanted to build a home there and live on it.

William Tedford preferred the ranching proposal, and, in September 1868, he and his family headed south. Tedford eventually carved out a trail from the coastline up to Newport, and his was the first white family to settle in the region. William Tedford passed away in 1905, at eighty. His wife and the mother of his ten children, passed away in 1919, at eighty-six. They were both buried in **Fairhaven Cemetery** in Santa Ana, California.

A daring and remarkable woman who was buried in Fairhaven was **Bessica Faith Medlar** (1875–1932), also known as **Bessica Raiche**. Born in 1875, in Wisconsin, she was definitely a woman ahead of her time.

A Dentist and First Female Aviator

Even at a young age, Bessica Faith Medlar Raiche engaged in activities few women dared to: she wore bloomers, drove an automobile, was a musician, painter, and even participated in swimming and shooting. By 1900, she was working as a dentist in New Hampshire. She married and she and her husband moved to New York, where they "built a Wright-type biplane in their living room and then assembled it in their yard." The airplane was constructed of bamboo and silk rather than canvas like the Wright brothers used.

On September 16, 1910, Bessica Raiche flew her biplane, making hers the *first* recognized solo flight by a woman in the United States. Another flier, Blanche Stuart Scott, had flown solo earlier in September, but her flight had been poorly documented. Bessica wrote, "Blanche deserved the recognition, but I got more attention because of my lifestyle." No doubt, her socially outrageous behavior had already drawn public attention to herself. In October 1910, the Aeronautical Society of America honored her as the "First Woman Aviator in America." Bessica and her husband went on to build two more airplanes, using lightweight materials.

By 1920, Bessica Raiche and her husband had moved west to Newport Beach where Bessie worked as a doctor. She was one of the first American female doctors to specialize in obstetrics and gynecology, and in 1923, served as the president of the Orange County Medical Association. Then, in 1932, at age fifty-seven, Bessica Raiche died of a heart attack. She was buried in Fairhaven Memorial Park, in Santa Ana.

In 1857, **Benjamin Dreyfus** (1847–1927) came to Anaheim to open a store. A native of Germany, he became a naturalized citizen in 1851. When he arrived in California, he also became the first Jew to settle in Orange County. He opened a store and then began to invest in other enterprises, particularly in wine and brandy cultivation and sales. According to the *Jewish Museum of the American West*, Dreyfus eventually owned 9,000 acres and became a renowned civic and business leader. In 1873, B. Dreyfus & Co. was cultivating some 200 acres of vines, which were producing 175,000 gallons of wine. By 1880, the company was shipping 2½ million gallons of both kosher and non-kosher wines around the world each year. Unexpectedly Dreyfus died in 1886 at the age of sixty-one. Originally he was buried in the **Anaheim Cemetery** then reinterred at the **Home of Peace Jewish Cemetery**, in Colma, San Mateo County, in 1889.

The Anaheim Cemetery, located at 1400 E. Sycamore Street, Anaheim, was founded in 1866. It is the oldest of Orange County's three public cemeteries and also home to the oldest community mausoleum in California, dating back to 1914. Although Mission San Juan Capistrano had a cemetery and the Yorba Cemetery served many locals, German residents wanted to establish a graveyard for themselves. The Anaheim Cemetery Association was created in 1866, which developed a sixteen-acre allotment with trees and lawns, giving the Anaheim Cemetery a park-like environment.

Born in Germany, **Augustus Frederick Langenberger** (1824–1895) was one of the original members of the Los Angeles Vineyard Society in Orange County. The son of a famous doctor and surgeon, as a student Langenberger learned to speak four languages, which helped him later in his career as a mercantilist. He immigrated to the United States in 1846, and then made his way to California. He opened a general store in San Gabriel, and it was here where he met and married **Maria Petra de Jesus Ontiveros** (1831–1867) in 1850. She was nineteen years old. After two years, August and Maria Petra moved to the Ontiveros ranch and, in time, Augustus became one of the largest cattle ranchers in the area. Though Augustus and Maria

Catherine Heyermann Backs (1854–1918) was laid to rest in the Anaheim Cemetery after succumbing to TB. Her father was Anaheim's first physician.

Petra had seven children, three died young: **John A. Langenberger**, in 1860, was less than one-year-old; **John B. Langenberger**, in 1867, was a month old and became the first official burial in the new Anaheim Cemetery; and **Theodore Edward Langenberger** was born in 1865 and died in March 1869.

Maria Petra, age thirty-six, passed away in September 1867, two months after John B. died, making son and mother the first two interments in Anaheim's cemetery. Maria Petra was not, however, installed in the Langenberger family mausoleum but was laid to rest in a plain grave with a simple wooden marker outside the crypt. That marker was eventually replaced with a plaque funded by the Mother Colony Household, in the 1970s. The question is how or why she was left outside the family crypt.

While August and Clementine rest inside the Langenberger mausoleum in the Anaheim Cemetery, Maria Petra Langenberger rests outside the tomb. Her wooden marker was replaced by a plaque in the 1970s.

Mrs. Clementine Schmidt and Augustus Langenberger

As family "stories" go, whether Augustus Langenberger's infatuation for **Mrs. Clementine Schmidt** (1841–1915) occurred before or after Maria Petra's tragic passing has never been confirmed, rumors alleging an affair did spread. Clementine's husband, Thomas Schmidt, tried to woo her back, but eventually he left California, and she filed for divorce in 1873. In 1875, Clementine and Augustus had twins, which raised another question:. Was there ever any record suggesting the pair were married? Whether yes or no, their combined household increased to eleven children.

Augustus passed away in 1895, at age seventy. Clementine lived another eighteen years. Both were buried inside the Langenberger Mausoleum in the Anaheim Cemetery. Outside the crypt is a plaque that reads: "In Loving Memory of Augustus and Clementine Langenberger—Pioneers." Interesting to note that, "Known for his generosity, when Langenberger passed away on April 3, 1895, his estate included promissory notes amounting to $2,000 owed to him by Anaheim families." However, while Augustus might have been generous to the many, the fact that Maria Petra lays outside the elegant family mausoleum is ironic. Add to that, Maria Petra de Jesus Langenberger is recorded on the U.S. Find a Grave Index as Augustus Langenberger's wife. There is no mention of Clementine (Schmidt) Langenberger as a spouse.

Of the fifty-six Civil War veterans interred at Anaheim Cemetery, **Lieutenant John Fenelon Marquis** (1841–1882) represents those who fought long and hard. At the age of twenty-one, Marquis enlisted in Company K of the Second Illinois Light Artillery as chief bugler. He saw action in a number of battles: Memphis, Tennessee; Clarkston, Missouri; and Vicksburg, Mississippi—where he served under General Ulysses S. Grant. Only a few weeks after the Confederates at Vicksburg surrendered to Grant on July 4, 1863, Marquis was able to marry **Neeta Jane Haile** (1846–1935). When he mustered out in 1865, he was brevetted to first lieutenant.

Another fascinating individual laid to rest in the Anaheim Cemetery was **Enid B. Williams Rimpau** (1892–1915). To this day, a mystery surrounds her sudden and unexplained death. In 1910, at age nineteen, she married Charles Stone of Glendale, California. Within a year, however, she filed for divorce and moved to Anaheim. She began working in 1913 and, by 1915, was engaged to **Robert Rimpau** (1882–1956), son of Adolph Rimpau, who has been credited with cofounding the town of Corona. Robert and Enid were married in July 1915 and immediately moved into a new home. Three months later, Enid was dead. Her death was ruled a suicide—although the suicide note was never confirmed to have been written by her, and those who had seen her earlier in the day recalled that she appeared happy and animated. In addition, only a small dose of poison was discovered to have been missing from its vial. The question remained: If Enid had been intent on dying, why had she not taken more to insure her death?

Death Left a Mystery

After Enid Rimpau's death, the Rimpau family eliminated any memory of her, even disallowing her burial in the Rimpau family mausoleum in the Anaheim Cemetery. Instead, she was interred in the cemetery's community mausoleum, in Section MA, Block D, Lot 57, Space 1.

Enid's story doesn't exactly end here: **Paul Clifford Whitice** (1887–1927) of Tennessee—after divorcing his first wife Alice—married Robert Rimpau's cousin, **Rosabelle Rimpau** (1860–1923), in 1916. He had a lovely home built for her, but a year later the bank foreclosed on it. In addition, he filed for bankruptcy. It was on a Sunday in July 1927, after playing golf, that Paul was found dead. The coroner declared that Paul had worn himself out, noting that he had suffered from heart issues for a while. There was also speculation that Paul and Rosabelle had exchanged heated words prior to his death. The most intriguing detail, however, is that a vial of poison was found in the bathroom. Whatever the details, the truth remains cloaked in mystery. Paul Whitice was buried at **Forest Lawn Memorial Park** in Glendale, Los Angeles County, in 1927. He was six days shy of forty years old.

Cayetano Castillo and A. Rivera Castillo rest side by side in the Yorba Cemetery in Yorba Linda, Orange County; while the date of A. Rivera's death is unknown, Cayetano passed away in 1926, at age 67 to 68.
PHOTO COURTESY OF LESA PFROMMER

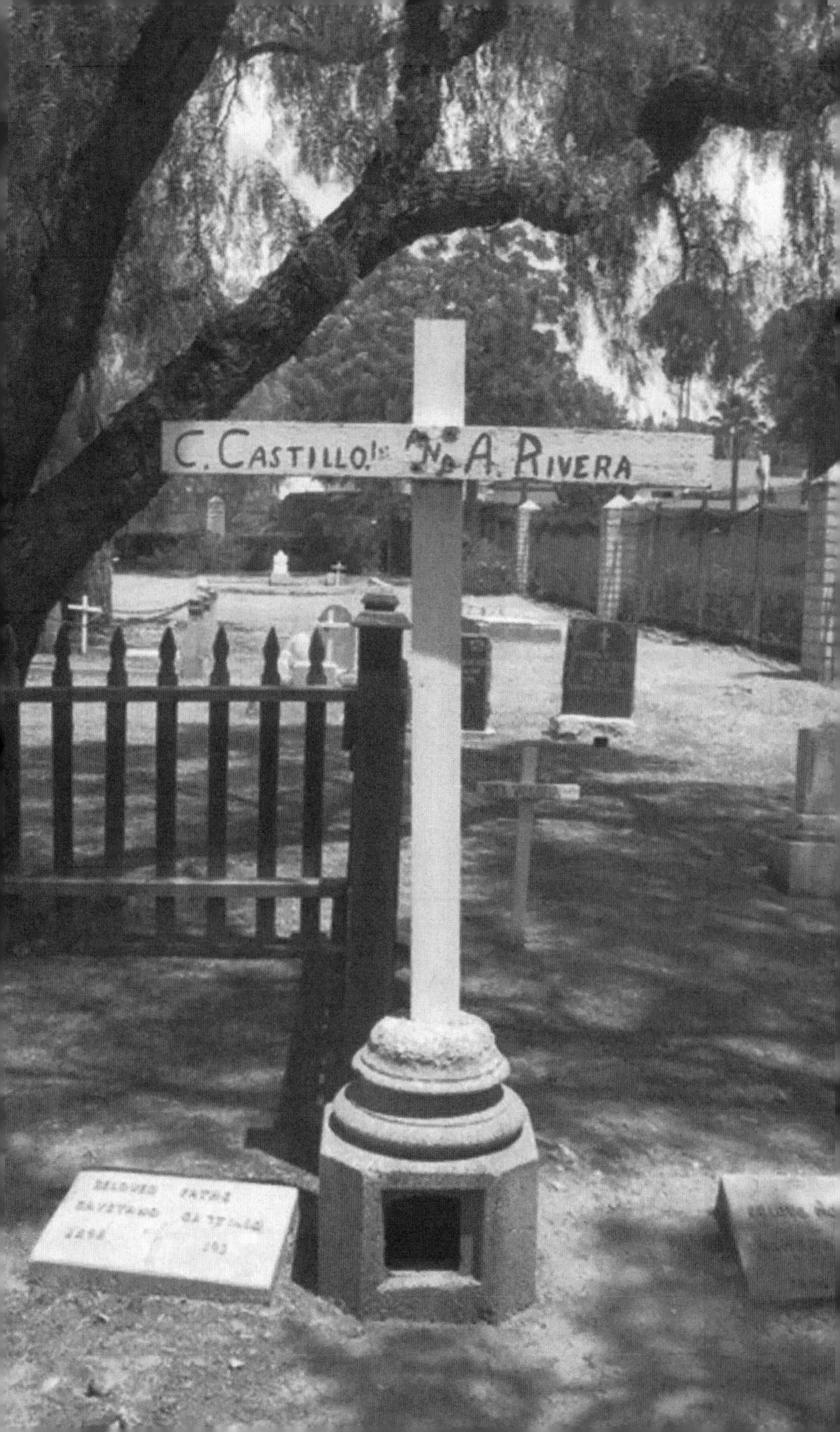
C. CASTILLO
A. RIVERA

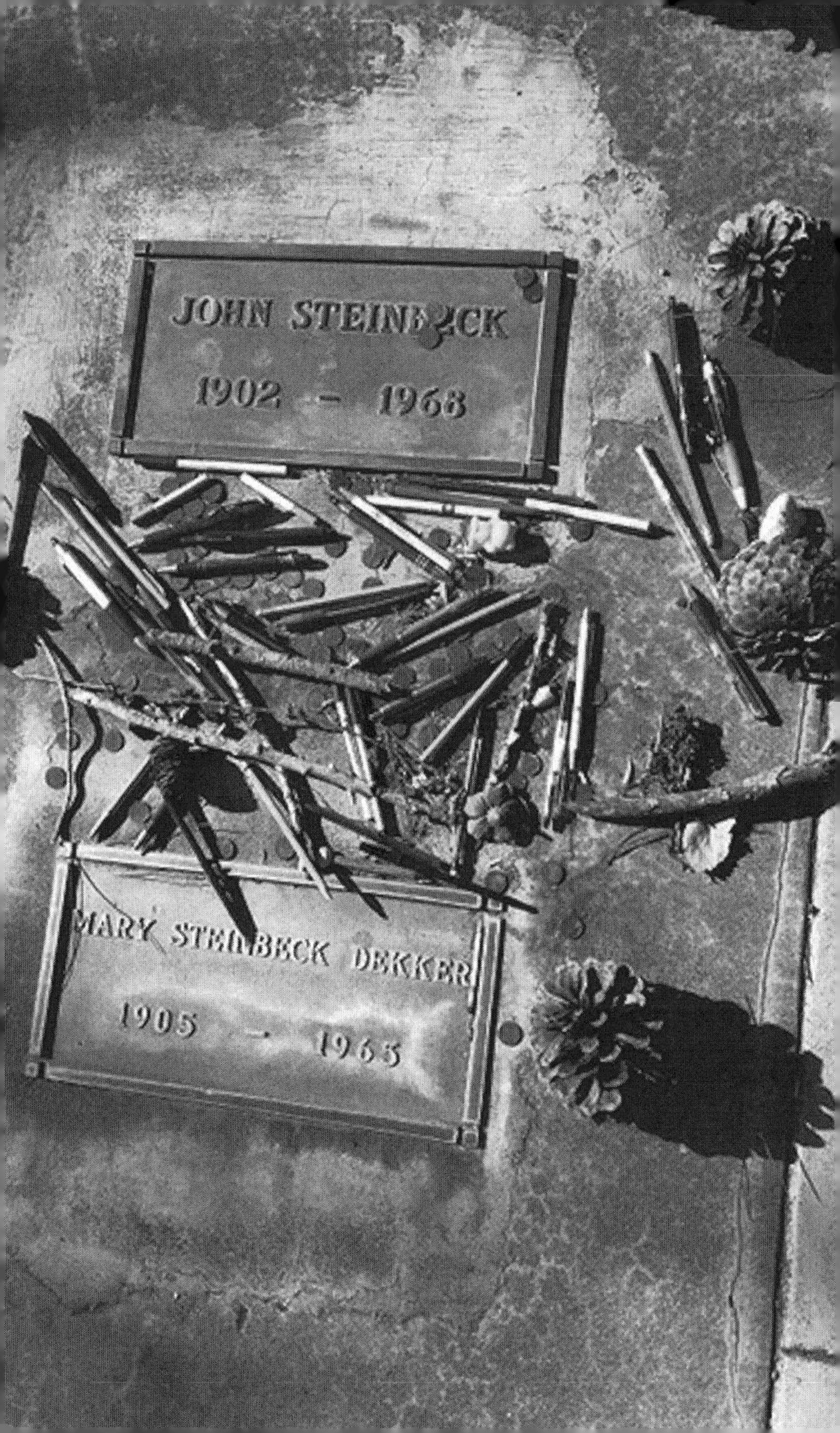

JOHN
1902 – 1968
MARY STEINBECK DEKKER
1905 – 1965

CHAPTER 3

LOS ANGELES REGION

The City of Los Angeles began as a Spanish colony, populated by the descendants of eleven families known as *los pobladores* (colonists), and little changed until the years following statehood in 1850. William Mason, the late California historian, wrote much about the rich history and diversity of early Los Angeles and the region. In a piece published in the *Los Angeles Times*, on September 4, 1975, he wrote, "Of the 44 original pobladores who founded Los Angeles, only two were white. . . . Of the other 42, 26 had some degree of African ancestry and 16 were Indians or mestizos [people of mixed Spanish and Indian blood]."

He continued, "Considering their tiny numbers, the early years of their little agricultural colony were remarkably productive. Within four years of its founding, Los Angeles was producing enough grain to enable the [regional] governor to halt imports from Mexico. By 1801, the settlement's grain surplus was large enough for Los Angeles to request permission to export to Mexico itself."

While there are reportedly twenty-seven established cemeteries in Los Angeles, the oldest cemetery is the original **San**

John Steinbeck's grave in Salinas, Monterey County, displays a collage of offerings from adoring fans: pens, pencils, pennies, pine cones, and more.

Gabriel Arcángel Mission Cemetery, also known as **El Campo Santo** (Holy Field). Located at 428 South Mission Drive in San Gabriel, it was the fourth of the twenty-one missions established by the Spanish in Alta California, founded officially on September 8, 1771. What is unique about this mission church is its "fortress-like" appearance.

Father Serra chose the location as a midway point between San Francisco and San Diego, and it became one of the wealthiest and most important missions. In spite of floods and two earthquakes, one in 1804 and one in 1812, it survived. The mission cemetery is the resting place for at least 6,000 neophytes, the Gabrieleño Indians who lived and worked as Catholic converts. As in most of the mission cemeteries, the majority of graves were not marked. However, one small

Mission San Gabriel Arcángel was the fourth of the twenty-one Spanish missions and was often referred to as the "Godmother of the Pueblo of Los Angeles."

stone marker marks the gravesite of **José de Los Santos** (1820–1921), the last Indian to be buried on the grounds in 1921, at the age of 101.

The First Gabrieleño Buried in the Mission Cemetery

The first Gabrieleño Indian to be buried in the mission cemetery was a man named **Antonio**. Neither his full name nor his birth date is known, but he died on October 20, 1778 and was buried in the Garden plot. A young Gabrieleño woman, **Adauta Maria**—born in 1779 in the Los Angeles area—was also buried in the Mission Cemetery in 1809 when she was just twenty-nine or thirty years old. Married to a Gabrieleño man, **Buenaventura**, Adauta gave birth to four children, although, for reasons not spelled out, three of the four died within the first month of life, while the oldest child, a daughter, only lived to be twenty-one.

Antonio Maria Lugo (1778–1860) was the seventh son of **José Francisco Salvador Lugo y Espinsosa** (1740–1805), a soldier, often called a "leather jacket," who came to Alta California with the 1774 Expedition. A man of commanding presence, Antonio Maria Lugo became one of the largest landowners in what is today San Bernardino County.

He married **Maria Dolores Ruiz** (1783–1829) in 1796, and together they had ten children. When she passed away in 1829, she was buried at the San Gabriel Mission Cemetery. Antonio Lugo then married **Maria Florentina de Jesus German** (1828–1863) in 1842 at Mission San Gabriel. They had several children. When she passed away at age thirty-five, she was laid to rest at the **Los Angeles Plaza Church Cemetery**, now defunct.

In 1810, Lugo received almost 31,000 acres in a land grant in recognition of his service to the Mexican government. His ranch was known as Rancho de San Antonio. From 1816 to 1819, he served as the alcalde of Los Angeles. He also served as *juez del campo*, or judge of the plains, from 1833 to 1834, making him responsible for settling disputes between the landholders and other ranchers. When he passed away in 1860, Antonio Maria Lugo was buried in the **Old Calvary Cemetery** in Los Angeles.

Once located on Bishops Road and North Broadway in Los Angeles, what remains of the Old Calvary Cemetery in Los Angeles now lies under the parking lot of Cathedral High School. Most—but not all—of those interred in the Old Calvary Cemetery were moved to the **New Calvary Cemetery** or other cemeteries. The New Calvary Cemetery was established in 1896 and lies east of downtown Los Angeles, on Whittier Blvd. A large upright monument commemorates the location of the original Old Calvary Cemetery. Attached to the upstanding monument is a large cement cross with an inscription below that reads: "Old Calvary Cemetery 1844–1929."

Hugo Reid (1811–1852) was another of those early settlers whose body was later moved from the Old Calvary Cemetery to the New Calvary Cemetery. Originally from Scotland, Hugo came to Los Angeles, via South America, sometime around 1832. He fell in love with a Gabrieleño woman, baptized at the San Gabriel Mission as **Victoria Bartolomea Comicrabit** (unknown–1868). Unfortunately Victoria was already married, with children. But when her husband died of smallpox, Hugo converted to Catholicism and married her. He also adopted her children, and they went on to have several more.

In 1840, Victoria received a land grant of the 13,319-acre rancho known as Rancho Santa Anita. She also received an adobe that went through restoration and is now part of the Los Angeles Arboretum. Today's Santa Anita Park was part of that original Rancho Santa Anita owned by Victoria and Hugo. It was **Elias J. "Lucky" Baldwin** (1828–1909), a multimillionaire and both breeder and racer, who later purchased the ranch. He built a racetrack adjacent to today's present site.

Elias J. Baldwin was a fascinating, but excessive man—and such an entrepreneur that it is hard to summarize all he did. He was born in Ohio, the fourth of fourteen children. He eloped with a local girl, **Sarah Ann Unruh** (1828–1872), then returned to the family farm to work, but more importantly, to train horses. Throughout his life, horses were his greatest love. In 1853, he loaded up several wagons with tobacco, brandy, and tea and hired drivers, and then he and Sarah and their six-year-old daughter Clara headed west. They joined a wagon train and after five months reached California. Rather than being a risky enterprise, Baldwin doubled his money on the journey, even selling brandy to Mormon leader Brigham Young's brother, in Utah. He did have two encounters with Native Americans: once he got lost and was rescued by a friendly band that returned him to his wagon train and once the entire wagon train fell under attack and he barely escaped with his life.

Elias Baldwin, Successful Entrepreneur

Seizing on opportunities in San Francisco, Elias J. Baldwin purchased a hotel on Pacific Avenue near the Battery for cash then sold it a month later, making a heavy profit. He became active in the San Francisco Stock Exchange, plus he opened up a brick-manufacturing plant, which provided bricks that were used to build the fort on Alcatraz Island and the U.S. Mint. He made money investing in various mines with the Comstock Lode in Nevada, even hauling timber that sold to those constructing mineshafts for a good profit. He received shares in mines in lieu of payment. Interestingly, Baldwin was considered a fair employer and gave equal opportunity to anyone who would work hard, including the Chinese, African Americans, Native Americans, and immigrants—though he did not pay them much.

Although he was lucky in his money ventures, Baldwin was not so lucky in love. He divorced his first wife and went on to have a number of relationships. In addition, he was married four times. It was said, "Baldwin didn't run after women; they ran after him." However, he had a penchant for young women, twice marrying sixteen-year-olds, and he was sued for breach of marital contracts four times. As if that should be enough to quell his wandering eye, he was the target of two pistol-toting women but escaped harm both times. He also escaped his own hotel fire just in time to spare his life. He moved to Southern California and bought over 63,000 acres of land, including the Hugo Reid adobe—which became a California Historic Landmark years later. He sold parcels of land or lots to those moving south. For a time he was the highest-paying taxpayer and landholder in the Los Angeles Basin. With the money he made, he began to breed and raise Thoroughbred horses;

several of his horses went on to win races on both the West Coast and East Coast, including the American Derby four times.

Ironically, Hiram Unruh, the nephew of Baldwin's first wife, became Baldwin's personal financial advisor and agent, serving him for the rest of his life. Hiram Unruh has even been credited with maintaining and increasing much of Baldwin's financial success. Another irony? When "Lucky" Baldwin passed away in 1909, the land in his estate was considered pretty worthless, until oil was discovered. The result: the Montebello Oil Fields ended up producing one-eighth of the crude oil in California, becoming one of the biggest oil fields in the West.

Lucky Baldwin was buried in the E. J. Baldwin Mausoleum at **Cypress Lawn Memorial Park Cemetery** in Colma, San Mateo County. Classic in design, it features two columns at the front entrance. Stepping inside, a black cross has been inlaid in the white marble floor. Others laid to rest here include: **Sarah Ann Unruh (Alden)** who passed away in 1872 at age forty-three; Baldwin's third wife, **Jane Virginia "Jennie" Dexter** (1855–1881), who lies alongside him (she passed away in 1881 from TB at age twenty-six); and his younger daughter, **Anita May Baldwin McClaughry** (1876–1939). Lucky's oldest daughter, **Clara Baldwin Stocker** (1847–1921) was interred in her own Stocker Mausoleum at the **Angelus Rosedale Cemetery** in Los Angeles.

The oldest "nondenominational" cemetery in Los Angeles is the **Evergreen Cemetery**, created in 1877. It is also the largest, with over 300,000 interments. **Biddy Mason** (1818–1891), who served the Los Angeles community for a number of years, was interred in this cemetery after passing away on January 15, 1891. Reading about all of her

BIDDY MASON

AUG. 15 | JAN. 16
1818 | 1891

FORMER SLAVE
PHILANTHROPIST
HUMANITARIAN

FOUNDING MEMBER
FIRST AFRICAN METHODIST
EPISCOPAL CHURCH
1872
LOS ANGELES, CALIFORNIA

Biddy Mason was not only kind and generous, even in hard times,
but she was also a successful entrepreneur. She was buried in
Evergreen Cemetery, Los Angeles.
COURTESY LARRY LUNA

grit and determination, it is easy to say she was a woman of uncommon integrity. Her great granddaughter, **Gladys Owens Smith**, wrote that Biddy was fond of saying, "If you hold your hand closed, Gladys, nothing good can come in. The open hand is blessed for it gives in abundance, even as it receives."

Born a Slave, Served Others

Biddy Mason was born a slave in 1818. Along with her three daughters, also slaves, she walked from Mississippi to California herding livestock for her master, **Robert Marion Smith.** When they arrived in California in 1851, they encountered a number of free blacks in San Bernardino. No doubt, Biddy hoped she and her girls might receive their freedom before long—but it appeared it might not happen especially when, in 1856, Smith decided they would travel to Texas, another slave state. Would she have to give up her dream of freedom? It was at this point that Biddy decided to risk all for the chance of freedom, especially for her daughters. According to Biddy, "I feared this trip to Texas since I first heard of it." So, assisted by a number of locals, including the sheriff, a group descended on Smith's camp in the Santa Monica Mountains and rescued fourteen slaves, including Biddy, her daughters, Biddy's sister, her nephews, nieces, and a grandchild. Enraged, Smith took his case to court, but lost. Even the local press, in the February 2, 1856 issue of the *Los Angeles Star* upheld the slaves' right to freedom. As a free state, Smith could not defend his "right" to keep them.

Biddy Mason quickly became known in Los Angeles, especially since she was an excellent nurse and midwife. During the smallpox epidemic of the 1860s, she nursed many people, both rich and poor, back to health. Dr. John S. Griffin even paid her $2.50 a day for her service in his practice. Biddy saved the money, and every time she accumulated $250, she purchased several lots in town for her and her extended family.

By 1872, Biddy Mason's home was the site of the first African Methodist-Episcopal Church in Los Angeles. In addition, after the floods of the 1880s, she purchased food and supplies for those affected—without regard to race. She also funded a day nursery and school. It is no wonder that when Biddy Mason passed away in 1891, "Los Angeles mourned her passing." Biddy's grave is located within the Chinese section of the cemetery, and at the top of Biddy Mason's upright black granite headstone is a cross. Below her name and the dates of her birth and death, it reads: "Former slave, Philanthropist, Humanitarian, Founding Member First African Methodist-Episcopal Church 1872 Los Angeles, California." Near the stone base of her grave, there is a small flat headstone that belongs to Biddy's great niece, **Gladys Owens Smith** (1895–1995) who lived to be 100 years old.

Dr. John Strother Griffin (1816–1898) was also buried at Evergreen Cemetery and has been considered one of Los Angeles's most outstanding medical pioneers. Originally from Virginia, he came from an amazing lineage: his uncle was William Clark, of Lewis and Clark; he was related to General, and later, President Zachary Taylor—which meant he was related to Jefferson Davis, whose first wife was Taylor's daughter—and he was related to President John Tyler. In addition, his brother-in-law was Confederate General Albert Sydney Johnston.

Dr. John Griffin came to California as a U.S. Army surgeon during the Mexican War of 1846–1848. After mustering out, circa 1848–1849, he purchased 2,000 acres of ranch land, and he began to invest in land around Los Angeles, which he sold in lots for $150 each. In 1856, he married **Louisa M. E. Hayes** (1821–1888), who had traveled west with her sister and niece, via Panama. She not only worked as a schoolteacher but also helped raise her nieces and nephews after two of her siblings' spouses died of TB. She and Dr. Griffin had no "other" children of their own. Louisa passed away in 1888, at age sixty-seven, and Dr. Griffin passed away ten years later, at age eighty-two. Both were buried in Evergreen Cemetery.

Also buried at Evergreen was **Dr. Charles Price Jones** (1865–1949), who was born in Georgia in 1865. His mother was a former slave, and his father was her slave master. A pastor and a composer, after Jones felt "called into the ministry," he served as a minister in Alabama and Mississippi before cofounding the Church of Christ (Holiness) and moving to California. Dr. Jones was also the author of over 1,000 gospel songs, including "All I Need," "Come Unto Me," and "Where Shall I Be When the Last Trumpet Sounds." He passed away in 1949 after serving as the bishop of his church in Los Angeles from 1928 until his death. After **Pearl W. Jones** (1893–1972) passed away on her seventy-ninth birthday, she was laid to rest beside Dr. Jones in the Evergreen Cemetery. Just below her name is written "Jesus Only," and across the bottom of their shared headstone is written, "Little Children Love One Another."

Another African American of great integrity and energy to be laid to rest in the Evergreen Cemetery was **Charlotta Amanda Spears Bass** (1874–1969). She was born in Sumter, South Carolina, to Hiram and Kate Spears. In 1901, she moved to Los Angeles and began selling ads for the *Eagle*, the longest-running African American newspaper. She then purchased the paper and changed the name to the *California Eagle*, which she published for nearly forty years.

Newspaperwoman and Activist

Charlotta Bass became well known through her writing, especially her personal column, "On the Sidewalk." In many ways, it became the vehicle by which she pushed for civil rights and political equality. In 1931, she even initiated a "Don't shop where you can't work" campaign. In 1912, she met **Joseph Blackburn Bass** (1863–1934), a teacher, businessman, and newspaper editor. Born in 1863, Bass had taught school for seven years. He then moved into the world of journalism, establishing *The Montana Plaindealer*, in Helena, Montana, in 1905. He was also an activist, and among the groups he helped organize were the Helena chapter of Booker T. Washington's National Negro Business League and the Afro-American Building Association.

On a trip to California, Joseph Bass visited Charlotta's newspaper office. She suggested he work for her as editor and he agreed. The couple eventually married in August 1914. He continued to hold the position of editor of Charlotta's *California Eagle* until his death in 1934. In a column dated April 2, 1937, Charlotta wrote, "My last visit Sunday was to the grave of the late editor of this paper, J.B. Bass. I did not lay a large bouquet upon the grave of him who sleeps beneath, but gardenias three in number, with their fragrance mild but sweet, conveying a message I cannot here repeat."

Etched into his headstone are the words "Loving Husband."

Charlotta Spears Bass, with Joseph Bass as her cohort, took many risks in her public outcry for civil rights; she even came under the surveillance of the FBI as she continued to represent those who had little or no voice statewide. In 1952, she became the vice presidential nominee for the Progressive Party, making her the first African American woman nominated to run for the second-highest office in the country. She died in 1969 from a cerebral hemorrhage, thirty-five years after her beloved Joseph Bass. Both Charlotta and Joseph rest in the Evergreen Cemetery in Los Angeles.

Chloe Phebe Wescott Canfield (1860–1906) was only forty-six when she was laid to rest at the Evergreen Cemetery in Los Angeles. The wife of oil tycoon **Charles Adelbert Canfield** (1848–1913), Chloe was shot to death by an embittered former coachman, Morris Buck. While her husband and two of their daughters were away, Buck appeared at the door, angry that a request for a loan had been ignored. When Chloe refused to give him money, he shot twice, killing her instantly. She was barely twenty when she married Charles Canfield in 1879. She had been a schoolteacher and Charles a struggling miner who would eventually make a fortune in oil. The couple had seven children, one of whom passed away at age nine.

When Charles Canfield passed away in 1913, he was laid to rest with his wife and their nine-year-old son. Buck Morris, who tried to escape after killing Chloe, was caught almost immediately. At his trial, he was found guilty of first-degree murder and sentenced to hang. He was executed on December 6, 1907, at San Quentin prison and buried in the **San Quentin Prison Cemetery.**

One of Orange County's first female doctors, **Willella Earhart Howe-Waffle** (1854–1924), was buried in the Evergreen Cemetery in Los Angeles after practicing medicine for thirty-eight years. She married **Dr. Alwin Howe** (1850–1904) and for several years taught school in Santa Ana, earning enough money to fund her own medical education at Hahnemann Medical College in Chicago. After returning to California, the couple moved into a luxurious 1889 Victorian

The Canfield Mausoleum was an elaborate Greek-inspired canopied monument.
COURTESY A.J. MARIK

House—which was ultimately saved from destruction in the 1970s and restored by the Santa Ana Historical Preservation Society. Today it is the Dr. Willella Howe-Waffle House and Medical Museum.

Because of the laws prohibiting abortion, Willella's husband was arrested, tried, but acquitted for performing one. Shamed and disgraced, however, he abandoned his wife and daughters and moved to San Francisco. Willella divorced him in 1897; he died seven years later. Willella then married **Edson Waffle** (1854–1935), a local rancher and livery stable owner. Always a devoted physician, Willella would drive her buggy through torrential rain to reach a patient, and sadly, she passed away at age seventy while tending a patient. She was buried at the Evergreen Cemetery, the same cemetery where her first husband Dr. Alwin Howe was also interred.

Vito Casino (1862–1892), originally from Italy, died in a terrible explosion in downtown Los Angeles while celebrating the "400th" anniversary of Columbus's "discovery" of America. According to one account:

(Los Angeles, Cal., Oct. 22)—The "Discovery Day" celebration here ended last night with a display of fireworks. Henry Wilson, who was in charge of the display, had arranged to fire what he called a salute of bombs for the last part. The bombs consisted of short lengths of cast iron pipe in which cartridges were exploded, the noise of the explosions resembling that of cannon. Two went off successfully, but the third one burst, doing all the execution of a bombshell; six persons were either killed outright, or died within a few minutes.

Wilson was quickly arrested, while Vito, also known as Victor (or *Vittorio*), was one of those killed outright. Ten more people were injured, of whom three died later. A young girl, Lillian Rapp, died, as did a young boy, Gilbert Christian—who survived only a few hours. Ten-year-old Ed Griffiths had to have a leg amputated. Vito Casino was buried in the Evergreen Cemetery in Los Angeles.

James Herman Banning (1899–1933) was born and raised in Oklahoma. When he started school in 1907, he quickly demonstrated an aptitude for reading, mathematics, and mechanics. He also enjoyed repairing the equipment on his family's farm. By the time he was in high school James was an able mechanic and earned money repairing automobiles. While watching World War I newsreels, he became fascinated by combat flying machines.

James Banning, the First African American Licensed Pilot

James Banning, an African American, was accepted into an elite college in Iowa where he planned to study engineering. Once at school, he realized he wanted to do something else, so he dropped out in 1921 to open his own machine shop. He also began taking flying lessons with a World War I veteran pilot, Lieutenant Fisher. One day, after Banning and Lieutenant Fisher had finished their last flight—Banning watched as Fisher and another student took off, and that's when the unthinkable happened. The plane did not travel very far when it came down in a rush. Both men were killed instantly, and the crash affected James deeply. When he learned that the engine from the downed plane was actually intact, he decided to purchase it and put it back together, piece by piece. He knew his flight instructor would have approved.

In 1926, the U.S. Department of Commerce began issuing aviation licenses. When James Herman Banning received his, he became the *first* African American pilot to receive a pilot's license in the United States. A skilled but daring pilot, he quickly became a barnstormer and toured the country flying in expositions; he also flew mail routes from 1929 to 1933.

In 1932, James Banning and another flier, Thomas C. Allen, became the first black pilots to complete a transcontinental flight from Los Angeles to Long Island, New York, making the 3,300-mile trip in less than forty-two hours (aloft). The trip actually required twenty-one days to complete because each time they stopped to refuel, they had to raise money in order to keep flying. After landing, the pair was enthusiastically awarded the keys to the city of New York. Unfortunately, the pair crash-landed on their return trip and had to abandon their plane, but neither pilot was injured. Though they had to take a bus back to Los Angeles, Banning and Allen accomplished what they set out to do.

On February 5, 1933, Banning was seated in the front open cockpit (without controls) in a biplane, during a San Diego air show. The Navy pilot at the controls, in a careless maneuver, pulled the nose of the plane up into a steep climb. Suddenly the plane stalled and fell into a fatal spin in front of hundreds of horrified spectators. Investigators later suggested that had Banning been at the controls, he'd have been able to maneuver the plane successfully. James Herman Banning was buried in Los Angeles's Evergreen Cemetery. He was just thirty-three years old.

John Gregg Nichols (1812–1898) arrived in Los Angeles before statehood. In 1850, he established the first English school in his own home. His son, **John Gregg Nichols, Jr.** (1851–1961), was the first *American* child born in Los Angeles, that is—as the child of an American citizen—on April 15, 1851. He moved to Guadalajara, Mexico, where he lived for fourteen years. He was buried at Panteon de Mezquitan in Guadalajara Municipality. His father, John Gregg

Nichols (Sr.), was laid to rest in 1898 in the now defunct **Los Angeles City Cemetery** and then reinterred at the **Angelus Rosedale Cemetery,** located at 1831 W. Washington Blvd., Los Angeles.

Also known as "**The Hill Cemetery**," the **Los Angeles City Cemetery** goes back to December 1847 when four unknown soldiers were interred there. Initially the cemetery had separate locations for members of the Redmen, Masonic, Independent Order of Odd Fellows (IOOF), Knights of Pythias, Societe Francaise, Soldiers or Firemen groups or associations. There was also an area designated for the Chinese, but as the town's limits expanded, the cemetery was closed to all future burials, and those already interred had to be exhumed and reinterred elsewhere.

Unfortunately, records for those early burials and removals were lost, and in 2006, the remains of eighty individuals were unexpectedly uncovered during a construction project. The remains were reburied in the **Angelus Rosedale Cemetery**.

Jacob Bell (1817–1870) was also laid to rest in the now defunct Los Angeles City Cemetery then reinterred at the Angelus Rosedale Cemetery. During an argument over water rights, Jacob was shot and killed by Michael Lachenais, who had already killed five or six men before being charged with the murder of two more men. The Los Angeles vigilance committee—which had not interfered before—decided it could not let Lachenais get away with another murder. On December 17, 1870, three days after Jacob's death, 300-armed men demanded Sheriff Burns release his prisoner to them. The sheriff refused, so the mob broke through two heavy doors, pulled open the jail's gate, and grabbed Michael Lachenais.

With no one to stop them, they hanged him. After being buried in the Los Angeles City Cemetery, Jacob Bell was also exhumed and reburied at the Angelus Rosedale Cemetery.

An African American notable who moved to the Santa Monica area, in Los Angeles County, was **John Ballard** (1829–1905). A former slave from Kentucky, John brought his wife and family to California in the 1850s. He and his wife **Amanda "Mandy" Ballard** (1840–1871) had eight children. She died in 1871, likely during the birth of her ninth child, and was interred at **Los Angeles City Cemetery**. When the city cemetery closed, Amanda was reinterred, probably at the **Angelus Rosedale Cemetery**, with husband John Ballard.

John Ballard, Founder of the First African American Church

Settled in the Los Angeles basin, John Ballard found work as a teamster and accumulated enough wealth to pursue a place in the frontier community. In 1869, he cofounded the first African Methodist-Episcopal Church. Unfortunately, racial conflict increased in the 1870s and 1880s and John's good fortune turned; with increased population came increased segregation and prejudice, which forced him to move his family once more. Ballard and his daughter were able to claim homesteads totaling 320 acres, along with 4,000 other former slaves and/or African Americans who had settled nearby. The property sat at the base of the mountain now called "Ballard Mountain" (renamed in the late nineteenth century). John Ballard was a man of great character and grit and brought a sense of leadership to the burgeoning community, in spite of attempts by many to expel him from his home. When he passed away, he was laid to rest in the **Angelus Rosedale Cemetery**.

Dr. Mary Stone (1873–1954), also known as *Shi Meiyu*, was born in China but brought to America to study medicine. After graduating from the University of Michigan, she returned to China and became a missionary doctor, inspired by medical missionary Dr. Kate Bushnell. Incredibly, Dr. Stone was the only doctor for 5 *million* rural Chinese. Still, she established a modern nursing school and founded the Women's and Children's Hospital JiuJiang, which she named the Elizabeth Skelton Danforth Hospital. Thankfully, Dr. Stone managed to return to California just before the Communist Revolution. She died on December 30, 1954, at the age of eighty-one, and was buried in the **Mountain View Cemetery and Mausoleum,** established in 1882, in Altadena, located at 2400 Fair Oaks Avenue, Altadena, in Los Angeles County.

Thaddeus S. C. Lowe (1832–1913), also known as Professor T. S. C. Lowe, was a pioneer in hot-air ballooning. A scientist and inventor—mostly self-taught—he has often been called the "father of aerial reconnaissance" after being selected by President Lincoln in 1861 to the position of chief aeronaut of the Union Army Balloon Corps.

As a pioneer in hot-air ballooning during the Civil War, Thaddeus Sobieski Constantine Lowe has also been titled the Grandfather of the U.S. Air Force.

Lowe Rises Above the Enemy

One of Thaddeus Lowe's notable achievements during the Civil War was when he ascended more than 1,000 feet above Arlington, Virginia. From that height he was able to locate Confederate troops more than three miles away. Sending the information down to the army on the ground, the Union forces were able to fire on the enemy without having to set eyes on them first. According to the Smithsonian National Air and Space Museum, Lowe "is noted for building one of the largest balloons ever constructed to cross the Atlantic Ocean (1859–1860), held flight endurance records for distance and altitude, and invented the first altimeter used without a horizon. . . . Serving under General George McClellan in this civilian post, Lowe constructed five balloons (for a total of seven) to be used to spy on the Confederate Army. Lowe not only was the first prisoner of the Civil War, but was considered 'the most shot at man' as well, due to his high profile while aloft."

In 1863, Thaddeus Lowe resigned his post and moved to Southern California, where he quickly became a millionaire as he worked on several patents and processes. He built a 24,000-square-foot home in Pasadena (supposedly the largest home in America for the time) and founded Citizens' Bank of Los Angeles. He then began to invest in a project constructing an all-electric scenic mountain railway above Pasadena, but the investment failed and he lost the railway to Jared S. Torrance. Lowe's fortune collapsed, and he spent the remainder of his life living at his daughter's home. He passed away in January 1913 and was interred in the Mountain View Cemetery in Altadena. While Lowe's achievements have been mostly forgotten, the idea of taking to the skies to collect intelligence has become one of the strongest missions of the U.S. Air Force today, in part because of Thaddeus Lowe and his creative inventions.

Joseph Newmark (1799–1881), born in Neumark, Prussia, was a different sort of pioneer. He arrived in New York in 1835, where he married **Rosa Levy** (his second wife) and went to work. Around 1846, he, with his wife and six children, traveled west. After residing in a few different locations, they moved to San Francisco. Then, in 1854, Joseph moved his family to Los Angeles. According to Maurice Newmark and Marco Newmark, "Joseph [Newmark] established the Los Angeles Hebrew Benevolent Society, which met for some time at his home and served as the first charitable institution in Los Angeles." The society helped preserve and promote Jewish traditions, whether for weddings or funerals, and it oversaw the maintenance of the first Jewish cemetery, which opened in 1855. Joseph also cofounded the Congregation B'nai B'rith, the oldest synagogue in Los Angeles, and he conducted the first Jewish wedding in California. When he passed away in 1881, he was buried in the Jewish cemetery. A second Jewish cemetery, located at 4334 Whittier Blvd., in Los Angeles, was established in 1902. Known as the **Home of Peace Memorial Park**, there the remains of the 360 Jews buried in the old cemetery were moved between 1902 and 1910. Joseph was also reinterred, this time being placed in the Newmark family mausoleum, a simple but classic stone block and cement structure. It was noted in the *Los Angeles Herald*, dated October 21, 1881, that at Newmark's funeral, there followed "the largest concourse of citizens we have ever seen in Los

Angeles. They thus testified their respect for the eminent virtues of the deceased."

Carl Laemmle (1867–1939) was also laid to rest in the Home of Peace Memorial Park. Born in 1867, in Baden-Württemberg, Germany, Carl dropped out of school at age thirteen and immigrated to Chicago in 1884. While trying his hand at various trades, he became fascinated by the crowds that gathered in front of storefront nickelodeons. In 1906, he managed to open up a cinema theater, known as the White Front Theater. Within three months, he opened a second theater. Laemmle was highly successful but soon found himself in competition with Thomas Edison's Motion Picture Patents Company, which was looking to monopolize the new, evolving motion picture industry. It took several years to resolve a lawsuit (to Laemmle's benefit), but in the meantime, Laemmle's company, the Independent Motion Picture Company (IMP), managed to debut its own films. IMP then merged with smaller producers to create the Universal Film Manufacturing Company, which became the film company we know today as Universal Studios.

From his film sales, Laemmle built the renowned 230-acre studio complex, Universal City, near Hollywood. Unfortunately, after the Great Depression and after Laemmle's son Carl, Jr. foolishly spent business money on lavish living, Laemmle was forced to sell his enterprise. He passed away in September 1939, at the age of seventy-two, and was laid to rest in the Chapel Mausoleum, in the Corridor of Love, at Peace of Home Memorial Park.

Forest Lawn Memorial Park, located at 1712 South Glendale Avenue in Glendale, is probably the most beautifully and artfully manicured cemetery in Los Angeles County. Not only is it a place of "eternal rest," Forest Lawn has hosted 50,000 weddings, including the wedding between Ronald Reagan and Jane Wyman. Nearly 336,000 individuals have been laid to rest here—including thousands of celebrities and famous people. It was founded in 1906, but in 1912, **Dr. Hubert Eaton** (1881–1966) took over its management. For many reasons he is considered the "Founder" of Forest Lawn, especially as it is known today. Until 1913, the cemetery totaled only fifty-five acres. Today it totals over 300 acres.

After touring Europe, "[Eaton] came back with a revolutionary idea: henceforth, above-ground monuments would be forbidden at Forest Lawn. In their place, the cemetery would provide occasional marble sculptures on authorized subjects like motherhood or valor. The very wealthy could purchase one of these pre-approved monuments as a grave marker. He restricted everyone else to a bronze marker set into the sod."

Eaton's dream was to create a memorial garden with trees and wide expanses of lawn and selected statuary and art. "'I believe in a happy eternal life,' Eaton wrote in the Builder's Creed that is chiseled in stone at the park. 'I therefore prayerfully resolve on this New Year's Day, 1917, that I shall endeavor to build Forest Lawn as different, as unlike other cemeteries as sunshine is to darkness, as eternal life is unlike death.'"

Besides the illustrious and famously rich individuals laid to rest at Forest Lawn, there are some lesser-known, but fascinating and significant individuals, as well, including **Tatzumbie DuPea** (1849–1970) who was born in Diamond Wash near Lone Pine, Inyo County. A Paiute woman, she was raised by her grandmother, taken as an infant after her mother was killed in a massacre and her father retreated into the Purple Mountains to live. The pair lived in Death Valley until Tatzumbie's grandmother passed away. The old woman told Tatzumbie, who was then about twenty-five years old, to travel to the "Purple Mountains" and find her father.

A New Life for Tatzumbie

Tatzumbie DuPea set out on foot in the direction of the Purple Mountains. She could not speak English so that when she found herself wandering into a white settlement, she was afraid. A woman gave her bread, butter, and water. That night she slept in a haystack and in the morning, stumbled onto some watermelons. Not understanding that they were not there for the taking, when a white man caught her, she did not struggle or fight back. She remembered that her grandmother had warned her to never resist, that the whites would release her if she didn't fight. So she let the man lead her back to his home where she saw the very woman who had given her the bread and butter. This time the woman brought her some soup. She then cut Tatzumbie's tangled hair and took her upstairs where she gave her a bath, washed her hair, and gave her clean clothes. The woman's blonde hair and blue eyes fascinated Tatzumbie. "I thought there was something wrong with her. . . . I thought she was sick," she explained years later.

Tatzumbie lived with the family for four years where she learned to speak and read and write in English. Tatzumbie then trained to become a nurse. In the next few years, she married twice; her first husband died in a railroad accident. She had a daughter by her first husband and a son with her second husband. It was at this point a movie company hired her, and Tatzumbie appeared in several iconic movies, like *Cimarron* and *Across the Wide Missouri*, with Clark Gable.

Many of us have seen this Weeping Angel in various cemeteries as she is so beautifully sculpted and speaks directly to the grieving. This Weeping Angel is located at Inglewood Park on Dr. Mary Ertl's monument.

When Tatzumbie passed away, there was disagreement about her actual age. Some insist she was ninety years old, but others say suggest she was actually 120 years old. It will remain a question without an answer. She was buried in the Eventide Plot at **Forest Lawn Memorial Park.** Her headstone is a flat bronze marker with a raised rose on the left edge, a fairly simple marker for a rare woman of fortitude and character.

Another woman interred at Forest Lawn Memorial Park of unique character was **Dr. Mary S. Ertl** (1855–1931), who is considered to be the first female medical practitioner of Los Angeles. While Dr. Ertl's actual interment is located inside her mausoleum at Forest Lawn, there is also a sculpture dedicated to her at **Inglewood Park,** northeast of Los Angeles. Large lawns and palm trees characterize Inglewood Park; reportedly, there are more than 35,000 palms in the cemetery. It's easy to navigate the park as the names of the various plots are painted along the curbs, and there are numbered markers indicating individual graves. Located on the "Sunny Slope" section is a beautiful statue of a Weeping Angel.

Mary's name, "Mary S. Ertl, M.D.," is inscribed across the upright stone of the angel. This monument replaced an earlier one that featured Dr. Ertl, seated, with her doctor's bag, ready to attend a patient, which was damaged in the 1920 earthquake. After repairing the original statue, it was moved and now sits inside Dr. Ertl's mausoleum at Forest Lawn Memorial Park. Dr. Ertl passed away in 1931, and she was laid to rest alongside her husband inside their mausoleum.

Captain William Goodwin Dana sailed into Santa Barbara in 1828, where he married Maria Josefa Carrillo. Both William and Maria Josefa were buried in the Old Mission Cemetery in San Luis Obispo, San Luis Obispo County. Maria's smaller headstone sits to the side of Dana's enormous obelisk monument.

CHAPTER 4

Inland Region

San Bernardino County was created in 1853 from portions of Los Angeles, San Diego, and Mariposa Counties, while Riverside County was created from parts of San Diego and San Bernardino Counties. However, as with the entire Southern California region, the recorded history stretches back to the Spanish reign and early mission period.

In 1841, Agua Mansa was the first town established in San Bernardino County, settled by Mexican immigrants from New Mexico. These immigrants brought with them much of the culture of the Southwestern Indians. The town of San Bernardino, however, was settled in 1851 by Mormon colonists who purchased the land from Don Antonio Maria Lugo (1778–1860). In 1857, the Mormons were ordered to return to Utah, though a number of them stayed behind. Today, San Bernardino County is the largest county in California by size.

The community of Agua Mansa thrived until January 1862, when a flood overflowed the Santa Ana River's banks and destroyed it, leaving only the **Agua Mansa Cemetery**, the chapel, and Cornelius Boy Jensen's store, built in 1854. Most of the homes in nearby La Placita were also damaged or destroyed. Both of these communities had been the first "non-native" settlements in the San Bernardino Valley and were the largest communities between Los Angeles and New Mexico during the 1840s.

The first burial at the Agua Mansa Cemetery took place in 1852, while the last one took place in 1963. Located at 2001 W. Agua Mansa Road in Colton, the Agua Mansa Cemetery's burial ground and a replica of the original chapel is all that exists today. Vandals destroyed and/or damaged much of what was left of the cemetery, so in 1955 a group was formed to restore and improve it. Wooden crosses had marked many of the original graves, but there were few, if any, crosses left. In 1967, the site was taken over by San Bernardino County and made part of the San Bernardino County Museum. I found this cemetery fascinating with its randomness and obvious history.

One of those buried in the Agua Mansa Cemetery include **Cornelius Boy Jensen** (1814–1886), born in Denmark. A sailing captain who made a number of trips around Cape Horn, when his crew abandoned ship in the San Francisco Bay in 1848, he traveled to Sacramento. Rather than mining gold, he chose to open a store. Then in 1854, he traveled south and opened a new store in Agua Mansa. He married **Mercedes Alvarado** (1837–1914), daughter of Francisco Maria Alvarado and Juana Maria Abila de Alvarado.

When the 1862 flood destroyed much of the town, including the store, Cornelius and Mercedes purchased land from **Louis Robidoux** (1796–1868). They developed orchards and a vineyard and quickly established one of the first commercial wineries in Southern California. Their brick home was later listed on the National Register

Agua Mansa Pioneer Memorial Cemetery was established in 1854, but after the flood of 1862, the cemetery was one of the few local, surviving landmarks.

of Historic Landmarks. Cornelius Boy Jensen passed away in 1886 and Mercedes passed away in 1914. They were laid to rest side by side in the Agua Mansa Pioneer Cemetery.

Louis Robidoux was born in Missouri. His father, a merchant in St. Louis, helped outfit the Lewis & Clark expedition. On his way to California, Louis supposedly won enough money in a card game to finance his investments in San Bernardino County. He became one of the first non-Hispanic landowners to settle the area. He married **Guadalupe Garcia de Noriega** (1812–1892), the daughter of Pedro Antonio Garcia de Noriega and Maria Gertrudis Ortiz, and together they had ten children, although three-year-old **Mariano**, born in New Mexico, died on the trail to California.

Robidoux built up one of the largest livestock operations in Southern California, in addition to orchards and vineyards and the first gristmill for grinding wheat. In fact, in 1860, Robidoux was one of "the highest paying taxpayers in California." He also served on the first Board of Supervisors. He died at seventy-two. His wife Guadalupe died in 1892. Both were buried in the Agua Mansa Cemetery.

Another cemetery located in San Bernardino County is the **Mountain View Cemetery**, also known as the Mountain View

Made of rough sandstone or a kind of clay, Robidoux's original gravestone in Agua Mansa's Pioneer Cemetery was written by hand.

Mortuary and Cemetery. Established in 1907, it's located at 570 East Highland Avenue in San Bernardino and has more than 40,000 memorials.

One early pioneer to be interred at Mountain View Cemetery was **Dr. Ben Barton** (1823–1899). Born and raised in South Carolina, Barton obtained his medical training in Kentucky then traveled to Alabama and Texas where he began his practice. In Texas he married **Eliza Brite** (1827–1920), and in 1854, they traveled to California. Two sons were born to them, **John** and **Hiram** in 1855 and 1856. Later they would have three daughters, of whom one died in infancy. In 1857, Ben had an opportunity to purchase a substantial amount of land when the Mormons were called back to Utah. According to historian Leo Lyman, Barton bought "a piece of land from Mormon elders Amasa M. Lyman and Charles C. Rich that was part of the original Rancho San Bernardino. . . . The purchase included the old mission buildings at the site of today's Asistencia on Barton Road in Redlands."

Barton became an important man in the community. He was appointed county superintendent of schools and served in the California State Assembly in 1861–1862. After his death, both of his sons continued to grow the enterprises he had initiated. Eliza passed away in 1920, at age 93. Both Ben and Eliza were laid to rest in Mountain View Cemetery Park.

There is always curiosity concerning the West's famous and infamous figures. Two frontier heroes buried in San Bernardino include two of Wyatt Earp's brothers—James Cooksey Earp, who's buried in the Mountain View Cemetery and Morgan Seth Earp who's interred at **Hermosa Gardens Cemetery**.

James Cooksey Earp (1841–1926) was the oldest brother of Virgil, Morgan, and Wyatt Earp. Born in Kentucky, he enlisted in the Union's Seventeenth Illinois Infantry and was badly wounded in the battle at Fredericktown, Missouri, in October 1861. After the war, he headed to Dodge City where he worked for a time as deputy sheriff. He married a former prostitute (known also as a "Sporting Woman"), **Nellie "Bessie" Ketchum** (1840–1887) in 1873; she was a strong woman and James called her his "Beautiful Brunette." Though they joined his more famous brothers in Tombstone, Arizona, James did not participate in the gunfight at the OK Corral. When Morgan was killed, however, James did travel to Colton, California, with Virgil and the Earp women. He later engaged in mining in Idaho before returning to Southern California, where he retired. He died of natural causes in 1926 and was interred at Mountain View Cemetery.

Morgan Seth Earp (1851–1882) was only thirty years old when he was murdered while playing pool at Campbell and Hatch's Saloon in Tombstone, Arizona. The youngest of the "Fighting Earps," he married **Louisa Houston** (1855–1894) in 1875. They moved to Tombstone in 1880 where Morgan served as a policeman under Virgil Earp, Tombstone's city marshal. After he was shot, Virgil and James took Morgan's body back to their parents' home in Colton, California. Morgan was first buried at **Slover Mountain Cemetery**, but that site was destroyed by mining operations, so his body was exhumed and reinterred at **Hermosa Gardens Cemetery**.

Elizabeth Flake (1825–1905), a North Carolina–born slave owned by Mormons **James M.** (1815–1850) and **Agnes Flake** (1819–1855), was buried in San Bernardino's **Pioneer Memorial Cemetery.** In 1848, when her owners left Nebraska for the Salt Lake Valley, fifteen-year-old Elizabeth, most often called "Lizzy," accompanied them on their journey, walking all 1,100 miles. In 1851, Elizabeth set out again in the 150-wagon Mormon expedition from Utah to Rancho San Bernardino in California. She was responsible for driving the cattle and two yoke of oxen across both mountains and desert. She did, however, meet her future husband, **Charles H. Rowan, Sr.** (1808–1905), on the trek.

California Freedom

Charles Rowan came to California as a free black man, and Elizabeth became a free woman when she crossed into California. After she and Charles were married in 1860, he continued to work as both a teamster and as a barber in the Southern Hotel, and she worked as a laundress. The couple became known in the area's African American community as they continued to work for an end to slavery. Elizabeth Flake Rowan died in 1903 at age eighty-three, while Charles lived to be ninety-six or ninety-seven years old. Both were interred in the Pioneer Memorial Cemetery. Their daughter **Alice Rowan** (1868–1912) married **Frank Hanibal Johnson** (1869–1956) and became one of the first African American students to graduate from college in California. She then became a teacher in Riverside, and it's been said that she was the first black teacher to teach white students. Both Alice and her husband were buried in **Olivewood Memorial Park**, located on 3300 Central Avenue in Riverside, which was established by pioneer families in 1888.

Mission San Luis Rey, established in 1798 and completed in 1815, was known as "King of the Missions."
LIBRARY OF CONGRESS

Temecula is one of the most historic settlements in Southern California. The hills were homeland to bands of *Temecula*. From the hills to the ocean, the Native Americans living here became known as the **Luiseño**, named by the Spanish missionaries who established control through **Mission San Luis Rey.**

The Temecula Massacre

One of the most significant events to occur in Temecula was the Temecula Massacre, which took place during the **Mexican American War** on the heels of the Battle of San Pasqual (where Californios defeated General Kearny and his battalion). According to various accounts, a number of Californios traveled to a rancho in Pauma Valley after the Pasqual battle, where a group of

Luiseños who were sympathetic to the American cause and under the leadership of Manuelito Cota and young Pablo Apis captured and killed eleven Californios.

The retaliatory ambush came in January 1847 when a party of *Cahuilla* Indians, led by Juan Antonio, traveled to the Temecula Valley and killed 100+ of the warring Luiseños warriors. As the Luiseño were burying their dead, the Mormon Battalion arrived from their trek to California, and on January 25, 1847, they assisted in burying the dead in the half-acre graveyard known as the **Pechanga Tribal Cemetery**, which is even now protected by a six-foot wall.

Historian Horace Parker wrote of a letter penned by a priest to his bishop in 1867 regarding the Pechanga Tribal Cemetery in Temecula. "They have fenced the cemetery which will be five or six hundred feet square, with a wall of adobe, well boarded door and all arranged nicely. I would wish that your Excellency would grant me the authority to bless it, if you would judge it opportune. They have many and great desires to have it blessed, and I believe that it is suitable because it is in reality worthy of it."

Today there are no identified Indian headstones within the Pechanga Tribal Cemetery and only seventeen identified "graves," but it's believed that others, whether Luiseño or not, are still at rest here, many buried before and after the massacre. The cemetery is located on Pechanga Road off County Road S 16, Temecula, in Riverside County. One tombstone has remained untouched. It is inscribed as belonging to "**George Cuishman** (1826–1882), Died April 20, 1882, Aged 56 years."

Historian Gordon Johnson has written that George Cuishman was married to a Temecula Indian woman, and his descendants live at Pechanga. Two others listed as having been buried in the Pechanga Tribal Cemetery include **Felipa Magee** (unknown–1918), who died at the **Sherman Indian School**, and **Louis Moren** (unknown–1918), who lived with his uncle **Ed Garcia** at Pechanga. Both Felipa and Louis died of the Spanish influenza during the great pandemic of 1918.

Louis Wolf (1833–1887), often dubbed the "King of Temecula," came to the Temecula Valley around 1857—reportedly to evade religious persecution. Born in Alsace, on the French German border, Wolf became more than just a shopkeeper. In partnership with John Magee, the two men ran the first store in Temecula. Their store was located at the junction of the southern Emigrant Trail and a north-south road between San Diego and San Bernardino. When their store burned down, Wolf built a second one, which served as a stable, school, stagecoach stop, post office, and courtroom. He also served as postmaster and justice of the peace.

In 1862, Louis married **Ramona Place** (unknown–1894), whose father was from the Caribbean-West Indies and whose mother was *Chumash*. Louis was twenty-nine and Ramona was sixteen. The couple had at least eight children, and, according to one account, author Helen Hunt Jackson stayed with the Wolf family in 1882. Ramona Wolf may well have been the inspiration for Hunt's main character in her novel *Ramona*.

What is really intriguing, however, is Louis Wolf's tomb. It stands on the highest hill overlooking the valley, alone, on a cul-de-sac off Linda

Loma Road. It's a substantial white sarcophagus highlighted by a tall, pillared monument—encircled by a wrought iron fence. Reportedly, Wolf designed it himself. Unfortunately, the tomb fell into disrepair over several decades, so the Temecula Valley Historical Society took on its restoration in 2002. The tomb weighed 17,000 tons and the above-ground sarcophagus had to be raised and leveled out.

Wolf died a wealthy man in 1887 and was buried; however, it has been suggested by some that he may not actually be inside the tomb's sarcophagus (above ground), but that he was buried underground instead. No one has figured out the mystery yet. Ramona Place Wolf died in 1894 and was buried at the cemetery at Mission San Luis Rey in Oceanside. Three of Wolf's children were interred with him.

The **Sherman Institute Cemetery**, also known as the Sherman Indian School Cemetery, is located on the 12891 block of Indiana Avenue in Riverside. In 1892, the first Indian school in Southern California was opened in Perris, California. Within a few years, it was clear that a new school needed to be built, so James S. Sherman, chairman of Indian Affairs, appealed to the Congress for funds to build a new facility in Riverside.

Congress authorized $75,000 for the construction of the Sherman Institute and the school opened in the fall of 1902. By 1912, there were 631 students from twelve states, representing fifty-five tribes. One aspect of the school's curriculum was a 400-acre farm where students raised produce for themselves. Life at the school, however, was radically different and difficult. Students traveled long distances and were separated from their families, their communities, and their culture;

some could not return home for years at a time. A number of Sherman's students fell ill and died while attending school, and others died from accidents. Many struggled to overcome loneliness. Those who passed away were often interred in the Institute's cemetery. Three names from Sherman Institute's Cemetery include the following: **Frank Beatty** (1896–1912), a native Paiute from Beatty, Nevada, who died on August 24, 1912 at fifteen or sixteen years old; **Elizabeth Chi-Nup-pa** (1908–1921), who died on April 17, 1921; she was only twelve or thirteen years old; and **Jose Juan Chico** (1898–1920), who died on November 13, 1920; he was twenty-one or twenty-two years old.

Ulysses S. Kaneko, born in 1860, was buried in Olivewood Memorial Park in Riverside, in 1918—along with Mary Chiye Kaneko and Wilson Masao Kaneko, all very likely from the 1918 influenza pandemic.

CARL
JULY 7, 1818
APRIL 18, 1828

D'ALFONSO

CHAPTER 5

SOUTHERN SAN JOAQUIN VALLEY REGION

Because the Spanish Missions were located along the Pacific coastline of California, most settlements were centered near or around them. The road Californians still know as *El Camino Real*, "the Royal Road" linked the twenty-one missions, but the need to travel more directly to San Francisco from Los Angeles led to the construction of the road known as *El Camino Viejo*, "the Old Road." This road was used as early as 1780, but as more and more settlers made their way into California, they began to explore the edges of California's great valley. The interior of California, however, remained somewhat remote. Travel into sections of the San Joaquin Valley was difficult, at best.

All that changed after the **Mexican American War** of 1846–1848 and the discovery of gold in 1848. With the rush to the gold mines, California opened up to discovery and settlement. By 1853, gold claims were even being made along the Kern River and other points south and east.

Colonel Thomas Baker (1810–1972), after whom Bakersfield was named, settled in Kern County around 1863. Born in Ohio,

This monument at Calvary Cemetery honors architect and designer Alex D'Alfonso of Santa Barbara County, in addition to young Carl D'Alfonso, who was only ten years old at his passing.

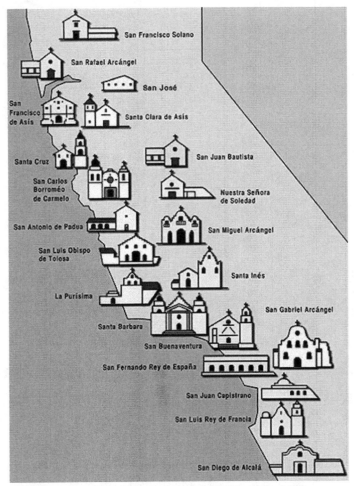

This map shows the route undertaken by the Spanish as they established the chain of California missions.
WIKIMEDIA COMMONS

he became a student of law and surveying and, at nineteen, was appointed a colonel in Ohio's militia. After moving to California, he was able to negotiate with the California legislature over thousands of acres in Kern and Fresno counties. Baker was appointed to survey the site selected for the city of Bakersfield. He retained eighty acres of land within the proposed city limits. Unfortunately, he had counted on the railroad to set up a station in Bakersfield, but that did not materialize. One of Baker's successful enterprises involved setting up a gristmill for grinding wheat and corn; he even permitted local farmers to grind their own grain at no cost. A second successful enterprise was the construction of a toll road between Bakersfield and Havilah known as "Baker Grade."

Baker continued to work for the community until his death in 1872 when he contracted typhus fever in an epidemic that swept the area. He was the first to be buried in Bakersfield's **Union Cemetery**, which later became the resting place of thousands of pioneers and settlers. He was also honored with a memorial sculpture that sits in front of the Bakersfield City Hall at 1501 Truxton Avenue.

David S. Coverdale (1835–1905) was also laid to rest at the Union Cemetery. The eldest of six children, born in 1835, he tried his hand at various jobs. When war broke out, he enlisted in Company K, Second Minnesota Volunteer Infantry. He was quickly promoted because of his "meritorious service." He entered as a corporal and was brevetted four years later as a captain.

Pioneer of Kern County

David S. Coverdale was an imposing man at six feet three inches and quickly earned the respect of his superiors in the army. He fought in a number of Civil War campaigns, including Stone River, Fort Donelson, Chickamauga, Missionary Ridge, and Lookout Mountain. During the battle of Chickamauga, he was wounded in

The veterans' section of the Bakersfield Union Cemetery is home to generations of veterans.
COURTESY DEAN HIRST

the right thigh and left on the battlefield for three days without food or water. He was then taken prisoner by the Confederates, but he managed to escape at night by crawling for miles on his hands and one knee. Recovered, Coverdale led his men into battle at Missionary Ridge and Lookout Mountain even with a cane. He continued to engage in battle after battle, at places like Kenesaw Mountain, Marietta, Atlanta, Pine Ridge, and more. He traveled with Sherman in his infamous march to the sea and witnessed the final surrender of the Confederate Army.

After the war, Coverdale married **Nellie Gould** (1850–1912), and they had one daughter. In 1887, they moved to California and settled in Kern County, where he soon established himself in real estate and other enterprises. He served as a judge and justice of the peace, a notary, and president of the board of trade. He died in 1905 and was buried in the Union Cemetery in Bakersfield in the veterans' section. Nellie died in 1912 and was buried with her husband in the Union Cemetery. On her headstone it was written, "Answered the Call."

After Ng Hon Kim, often called "Jesus Kim" because of his Christian faith, was murdered, he was laid to rest in the Union Cemetery.
COURTESY DEAN HIRST

Charles Averill Barlow (1858–1927) was another early pioneer in Kern County. He was born in Ohio in 1858 and then moved to California in 1875. He began farming and was selected as a member of the California State Assembly from 1892 to 1893. He also served as chairman of the People's Party at the California State Convention in 1896 and was elected as a populist to the Fifty-fifth Congress where he served until 1899. He married **Lizzie McDonnell** (1867–1914) of Ventura, California, and the couple moved to Bakersfield in 1901. In 1914, Lizzie passed away after a long battle with TB. Charles later married **Julia Lillis Caldwell** (1878–1971), who had moved to Bakersfield as a nurse. Though Charles was not re-elected to Congress, he did act as a delegate to the 1912–1920 Democratic National

Conventions. When he passed away in 1927, he was buried in the Union Cemetery in Bakersfield. Julia was buried there in 1971.

Bakersfield's **Chinese Cemetery** was the resting place for a number of local Chinese—but not all. Many were interred in the Union Cemetery in Bakersfield, like **Ng Hon Kim** (1852–1917), aka **Ah Kim**, who first immigrated to Australia and then to the United States in 1883. He married Chin Mooie, a former slave child. They raised ten children. Sadly, Ah Kim was murdered, though the case was never solved.

Kern County's Chinese Cemetery

The Chinese Cemetery was established sometime in the 1870s, described by the *Kern County Gazette* in 1878 as located on a "high, barren, dry, forbidding knoll of ground, the elevated position of which can never be irrigated in the midst of low surrounding." Because many Chinese immigrants hoped to have their bodies returned to China, family and/or friends were required to remove the deceased's bones after a period of time and ship them back to the homeland. That left the cemetery with far fewer grave markers or reminders as time passed, leaving behind a myriad of depressions where graves had been located. By the 1930s, the Chinese Cemetery had become so overgrown and desolate that in 1956, more than 300 fragile graves were moved to the Union Cemetery, located at East 6th and Tulare Streets.

According to *The Bakersfield Californian* on August 25, 1956, "The Chinese have a remarkable method of preserving identity of their dead. Into each grave went a bottle with a cloth marked in Chinese with the name and age of the occupant. The work of identification is being done by Jack Chow Wong, 77. . . who is re-inscribing the names in a book of Chinese."

In spite of the prevalent racism and prejudice against the Chinese, some area newspapers did report on the life and death of key individuals. Arthur A. Moore III, who grew up in the area, collected stories about a number of those buried in Bakersfield's Chinese Cemetery, including **Chee Ye**, whose death was announced on August 14, 1894, and whose funeral was described in detail in the *Bakersfield Daily Californian*. Chee Ye left behind a wife in China, as well as one brother, **Chee Li**—a local Bakersfield Chinese butcher, in addition to five other brothers living elsewhere in the United States. A well-known merchant, Chee Ye had amassed a "fortune," and thus his funeral was quite a celebration:

His body was placed in a fine cloth-covered casket, beneath a large canopy in front of (his) store. A grand feast consisting of four fat pigs and a sheep, roasted brown, and many dainties dear to the palates of the Chinese, was spread at his feet. Incense was burned and a large corps of hired mourners were gathered around. When the funeral procession started, two Chinese with gongs headed it. The members of a secret organization followed, bearing banners of gaudy hues. Following the hearse were about twenty women, wearing white mourning hoods. Then came busses loaded with friends of the deceased, prominent Chinese merchants and visitors from neighboring towns. A wagon loaded with dainties, intended as a feast for the departed on his way to the better land, followed the procession. All in all it was a grand funeral.

Ko Chow, a laborer in Bakersfield, passed away in 1903, and an article in *The Bakersfield Californian* on April 7, 1909, reported that his bones would be shipped back to China, their removal supervised by "five aged '*Celestials*,'" (a frequent descriptive of the Chinese). The bones were "transferred to tin boxes about the size of cracker boxes. The bones, divided into convenient sections, and each wrapped in cloth and labeled, were placed in their receptacles." According to the report, the boxes "are hermetically sealed" and made ready "for their long journey across the seas to Canton where they will be re-interred, never again to be disturbed." Ko Chow's daughter had passed away earlier than 1903 so her bones had already been returned to China where they were "at rest beneath the sod in the Flowery Kingdom . . . and those of her father will soon lie by her side."

While most Chinese in California worked as laborers, domestics, or merchants, **Unh Chew** was a rancher. Born in China in 1849, he arrived in California around 1870. As reported by *The Bakersfield Californian* on October 27, 1911, "He (Chew) had been a rancher and was one of the pioneer 'Celestial' residents of the county." Unfortunately, he fell ill and moved into a Chinese hotel only a week or two before he passed away.

Visalia Public Cemetery, Tulare County, dates back to 1850–1852 with the death of twenty-five-year-old **David Whitfield Russell** (1824–1852) from Lincoln County, Tennessee. Searching for his fortune, he came west with at least two, maybe three, of his brothers, including one **John Cowan Russell** (1822–1893) who died in Calaveras County and was interred in Visalia. After his death his remaining brothers remained in California.

Mary Ann Graves Clark (1826–1891) also rests in the Visalia Public Cemetery. As one of the last survivors of the **Donner Party** tragedy, her life was certainly haunted by death. She was the daughter

Donner Memorial State Park is located near Donner Lake. The immense memorial stands twenty-two feet upon which stands three bronze statues of settlers peering west and is located on the site of one of the cabins of the actual **Donner Party**.

of **Franklin Ward Graves** (1789–1846) and **Elizabeth Cooper Graves** (1800–1847). Originally, the Graves were traveling with the Smith Company wagon train, but after overtaking the Donner Party on the trail, they joined the Donner group. In an unfortunate argument earlier on the trail, Mary Ann's intended was killed with a knife. The killer was then banished.

When the members of the Donner party became caught in the deep winter snow after failing to make it through the mountain pass, Franklin Graves built a cabin near Truckee Lake for his wife and children. He then joined the rescue group dubbed "The Forlorn Hope," along with daughters Mary Ann and Sarah and Sarah's husband, Jay Fosdick. They all made snowshoes from oxbows and cowhide in order to tramp through twelve- to twenty-foot snowdrifts. Within days, however, the exhausted group ran out of food and became trapped in a blizzard.

Death Fills Mary Ann Graves's Life

Neither Franklin Graves nor Jay Fosdick survived the Donner rescue party's journey, though both of Franklin's daughters, Mary Ann and Sarah, did. Tragically, their mother and young brother Franklin also froze in the snow between the first and last rescues, and—like Franklin and Jay Fosdick—their bodies were never recovered. Incredibly, the losses for Sarah and Mary Ann continued when their next two youngest siblings, Jonathon and Baby Elizabeth, died at Sutter's Fort in Sacramento, after being rescued.

In 1847, Mary Ann Graves married **Edward Gant Pyle** (1824–1848), a twenty-three-year-old who had also been a member of the **Donner Party** relief expedition. One year after their marriage, he was mysteriously found murdered in San Jose. In 1851, Mary Ann married for the second time. She and **James**

Thomas Clarke (1852–1925) had seven children—but four (possibly five)—passed away before her own death from pneumonia in 1891, at sixty-four. Interestingly, Mary Ann's headstone in the Visalia Public Cemetery is a simple, flat, marbled granite block, inlaid with black print, with no lengthy epitaph. In fact, there is only one line, which reads, "Mary Graves of the Donner Party." Having experienced so much grief, wasn't there more Mary Ann Graves might have wanted to say?

Edmond Edward Wysinger (1816–1891) was likewise buried in Visalia's Public Cemetery. Though we hear little about him, his accomplishments have clearly reverberated beyond his own immediate life. His mother was a slave and his father was *Cherokee*. While his Cherokee name was *Bush,* Edmond adopted his plantation owner's last name. Edmond was actually one of the first African Americans to migrate to California from the South.

Edmond Edward Wysinger Breaks the Mold

What Edmond E. Wysinger managed to do, in spite of so many obstacles, was to break the mold of what was expected of a black man at this time. At the age of thirty-two, he came west with his owner by ox team. They arrived in Nevada County in October 1849. Edmund then joined a group of black miners and worked in places like Grass Valley and Placerville and Diamond Springs in El Dorado County. After a year of working various mines, he bought his freedom for $1,000. He then met and married **Pernesa Wilson** and the couple moved to Visalia where Edmond continued to work at various jobs. He was also a preacher who taught that education was of great importance.

In 1888, as Edmond walked his son Arthur to Visalia High School to enroll him, he was told he had to take his son to the "colored" school. The teacher explained that the district had provided separate but equal schools for black and white children. Edmond refused, however, declaring that the schools were anything but equal. This led to a two-year struggle, and Edmond's case eventually ended up in California's Supreme Court where, incredibly, he won his battle for equality.

As historians have noted, "Wysinger's case eliminated one of the last vestiges of school discrimination in 1890" and paved the way for future civil rights. This man of incredible courage passed away in 1891, at the age of seventy-five, and was laid to rest in the **Visalia Public Cemetery**.

Two Tulare County men who became well known, but not for their integrity, were **John Sontag** (1862–1893) and **Chris Evans** (1847–1917). Both men carried grudges against the Southern Pacific Railroad—Chris Evans because he'd lost his property to the railroad as it laid track, and John Sontag because his brother George had suffered an accident as a railroad employee. They successfully held up a train and were able to stay on the run for ten months. The reward for their capture rose to $5,000 each, dead or alive, after two posse members were killed in one encounter. Finally, John Sontag was wounded, captured, and died in jail. He was buried at **Calvary Cemetery** in Fresno, Fresno County, in July 1893. Sometime later, Evans was betrayed by a friend's son and ended up in jail in Fresno County.

Though sentenced to life behind bars for murder, Evans was able to escape from jail with the help of a friend, **Ed Morrell** (1868–1946). At this point, Evans was able to reunite with his family, but not for long. The house was surrounded and the two men captured. Along with John Sontag's brother **George Contant Sontag** (1864–unknown)—who had helped out in the original train robbery—the three men were convicted and sent to Folsom Prison. Evans was paroled in 1911 and died in 1917. Having relocated to Portland, Oregon, he was buried at **Mount Calvary Cemetery** in Multnomah County.

Inyo County is the second-largest county in California, situated between the Sierra Nevada Mountains and the Nevada border. While it is 10,000 square miles in size, it has only forty-six square miles of water. It is the setting for Mount Whitney, the highest point in the lower forty-eight states, and Death Valley, sitting at 282 feet below sea level. It is also home of Owens Valley, a high desert landscape, and home of the *Coso, Mono, Timbisha, Paiute-Shoshone,* and *Kawaiisu* tribes. The county's borders were established in 1866 from parts of two counties, but it increased in size in 1870 and 1872.

It was in 1861, however, that **Charles Putnam** built his cabin in what is now Inyo County. It served as his home as well as a trading post, hospital, and even as a fort for the first travelers into the region. Five years later the site was renamed Independence. It is the county seat of Inyo County.

Death in the Line of Duty

Independence was a rough and tough community during its early years of settlement. A number of law officers were gunned down. **Thomas Passmore** (1866–1885) was the third man to serve as

---

the sheriff of the county and the first killed in the line of duty. On Sunday, February 10, 1878, he was shot as he entered a saloon to arrest a man who had murdered another man earlier in the evening. As recorded, however, the event triggered a huge response by the citizens of Independence:

> It's said that Sheriff Passmore was not cold yet when outraged townsfolk put out the hue and cry and then took arms. Soon the town's citizens gathered and surrounded the saloon. Then they opened fire on the saloon. They fired hundreds of rounds into the building wounding many inside. At one point the citizens saw the saloon owner trying to make a run for it. His attempt to escape out the back door of the saloon was cut off. He was stopped when he was caught. He was immediately shot to death by the citizens. The killer that Sheriff Passmore was after also tried to make an escape, he too was caught and shot to death by over a dozen citizens.

Passmore was only eighteen when he was killed. His body was returned to Llano County, Texas, for burial. On his headstone, there is a dove motif and the words: "T. Passmore, Born July 7, 1866, Died Mar 1, 1885. Blessed are the dead, who die in the Lord."

After Passmore's death, **William Lafayette Moore** (1828–1879), who had served as sheriff before Passmore, was asked to return to the job. Unfortunately, he, too, was gunned down—only sixteen months later—on July 4, 1879. Standing outside a saloon, he rushed in when he heard a gunshot but got caught between two men fighting. After he was shot, the citizens of Independence again wanted to take justice into their own hands, but violence was averted. The two men involved in the fight were convicted of murder and sentenced to San Quentin. Sheriff Moore was only fifty-one years old when he was laid to rest in the **Independence Cemetery**. On his tombstone, it was written, "In Memory of Our beloved Brother."

Henry Levy (1849–1925) was born in Prussia and immigrated to the United States as a teenager. He moved first to San Francisco, but by 1874, he had moved to Independence in Inyo County and built the Independence Hotel. **Hulda Levy** (unknown–1876), Henry's first wife who died in childbirth, was the first to be buried in what became the only **Jewish Cemetery** north of Independence, in February 1876. Henry then married sixteen-year-old **Mary Joseph** (1860–1953) a few months later, and the couple went on to have eight children, although two sons died young: **Mark Levy** (1870–1877) at seven years old from whooping cough and **Joseph Levy** (1883–1900) drowned in the Owens River after his horse threw him into the water. His friend, Johnny Ruiz, tried to rescue him but was drowned as well. Their bodies were not found for four days, and both boys were buried in the Jewish Cemetery.

Lone Pine, located about fifteen miles south/southeast of the Inyo County seat of Independence, is the site of several intriguing pioneer cemeteries. **The Pioneer Cemetery**, or **Lone Pine Pioneer Cemetery**, is located on Sub Station Road and is the oldest of the local graveyards. The Lone Pine Cemetery was the only burial site until 1884, but remained in use until 1914. The oldest graves include the grave of a woman, **Mrs. McGuire**, and her young son, **Johnny McGuire**, as described in the memorial placed at the cemetery. Encircled by a white picket fence, the plaque dedicated in 2008 by E Clampus Vitus reads:

This cemetery was established in 1865 when Mrs. McGuire and her son were killed on Jan. 1, 1865, during the last battle of the 1860's Owens Valley Indian Wars. Those buried here were the Town's founders, including C. Begole and A. Johnson, who along with J. Lucas were the first to climb Mt. Whitney. Some members of the Diaz family are also buried here. Diaz Lake is located on then site of their 1870's ranch. The last burial here was in 1905. It is now managed by the Mt. Whitney Cemetery District, a special district of Inyo County.

Dedicated June 21, 2008
Slim Princess Chapter 395
E Clampus Vitus

A second cemetery in Lone Pine was the **Depot Cemetery** but graves here were generally temporary, and bodies were moved in the springtime to the Pioneer Cemetery. The water and conditions of the soil made permanent interment difficult. The oldest marked grave, however, belongs to **Josefa Canes DeAlday** (1841–1882), born in Sonora, Mexico. An inscription reads: "Josefa C. of Alday Born to Magdalena Sonora /Born on the of 13th of March 1841/ Died on the 5th of February 1882 In Lone Pine, Cal." Though the stone has been broken across the middle and lays flat on the ground, there is a wooden cross that stands at the head of the stone.

Lone Pine Indian Cemetery is located in a narrow desert canyon of the Alabama Hills, eighteen miles south of Independence. It has approximately eighty known graves, many identified by rocks and simple crosses, but it is still an active cemetery. Entry is through a barbed wire gate. To say the least, it discourages visitation. The earliest known grave here dates back to 1924 and belongs to **Bill Chico** (1839–1924), also known as "Old Bill." A farmer, Bill's first wife was **Jinie, or Jenny** (1829–1911), and a son, **Frank Chico** (1863–1920), preceded him in death, but while Bill and Jinie are buried here, Frank and his children were buried in the **Onyx Indian Cemetery**, in Kern County.

Located at 1435 North Main Street (also known as U.S. Highway 395), in Lone Pine, is the mass burial site for the victims of the **1872 Owens Valley/Lone Pine Earthquake**. There is a monument dedicated to the twenty-seven known individuals killed in the 8.3 earthquake. In all, fifty-two of the town's more than sixty buildings

In addition to the twenty-seven killed in the earthquake, sixteen unidentified individuals were buried together in a common grave.
COURTESY JULIA BASKIN GREEN

were leveled. The plaque on the monument reads: "On the date of March 26, 1872, an earthquake of much proportions shook Owens Valley and nearly destroyed the town of Lone Pine. Twenty-seven persons were killed."

Some of those buried together included the following victims: **Alice Meysen** (1861–1872); **Ignacio Cordova** (1825–1972), a local miner; **Antonia Montoya** (1846–1872); **Maria Cordova Tarrazona** (1850–1872) and her children, **Antonio Tarrazona** (1870–1872), **Delores Tarrazona** (1864–1872), and **Louisa Tarrazona** (1865–1872); Lucy "Unknown"(1837–1872), known locally as Miss Lucy; **Francisco Lopez** (1837–1872), a farmer, from Chile; **Lorenzo Mesa** (1818–1872), also a farmer, from Mexico; and four other children: **Alberto Henriques** (1870–1872), **Philomel Henriques** (1868–1872), **George Joslyn** (1868–1872), and **Baby Munzinger** (1870–1872). The details around Antonia Montoya's death were tragically outlined. It seems she had "on the fearful night shared her couch with a paramour. . . . The shock startled them out of their sleep—the woman to scream and pray, the man to bound out of bed and at once leap clear of the building with its treacherous roof and crumbling walls." Sadly he left her behind and "in his mighty selfishness the craven creature fled alone, leaving the poor woman to perish miserably in the ruins." Antonia was not even twenty-six years old.

Mount Whitney Cemetery is now the principal cemetery for the area, but it does date back to 1884 when several local ranchers donated a piece of land for a burial ground. Located on California

Highway 395, Lone Pine's Knights of Pythias was the group in charge of its original development, but today the Lone Pine Cemetery District administers the cemetery. One of those buried at Mount Whitney Cemetery was **Jean Pierre "Pete" Augereberry** (1874–1945). Born in the Basque region of France in 1874, Jean Pierre came to California and became a prospector in Death Valley. He mined for over forty years and, along with his partner **Frank "Shorty" Harris** (1856–1934), struck gold at Harrisburg Flats in 1905. Their claim became known as the Eureka Mine, a mine Jean Pierre continued to work until his death in 1945. Frank Harris passed away in 1934, at seventy-seven. Rather than be buried in the Mount Whitney Cemetery, however, his burial site is at the **Dayton Harris Grave Monument**, in Inyo County. A rocky shrine contains "Shorty" Harris's and **James Dayton**'s graves, each covered by layers of rock, and an aged bronze plaque placed on a raised rocky mound between the two graves: "Bury me beside Jim Dayton, in the valley we loved. Above me write 'Here Lies Shorty Harris, a single blanket jackass prospector.'—Epitaph Requested by Shorty (Frank) Harris Beloved Gold Hunter. 1856–1934. Here Jas. Dayton, Pioneer, Perished, 1898. To These Trailmakers Whose Courage Matched the Dangers of the Land, This Bit of Earth is Dedicated Forever."

Similarly, Jean Pierre hoped to be buried at the top of the road he built up to Augereberry Point, a point that overlooks Death Valley, but his request was denied. Instead, he was interred in the Mount Whitney Cemetery.

Tombstone Materials

While slate was a material used for tombstones in the East, it was not used much in the West. Wood, of course, or rock, was often used when nothing else was available; we still see graves with wooden crosses or flat boards, but their use decreased as other materials were located. Metal markers, though used less often, were often made of zinc and the inscriptions were applied to their surface; these markers actually wear well over time. For larger monuments, cement or rock was often used as a base or as the headstone itself.

Field stones, soapstone, and sandstone (often bluish gray or brown) were used in early cemeteries as well, especially since they could be carved fairly easily, although inscriptions faded or washed away over time.

In most California's cemeteries, we see various kinds and colors of granite and marble headstones. Occasionally marble does discolor, depending upon other environmental conditions. Some marble was shipped in from locations like Vermont, Georgia, even Italy, especially before regional quarries were established. Granite, too, was imported, often from Vermont or even Scotland, until company quarries were founded up and down the state. With improved cutting technology, the ability to shape and cut was made easier. A few California named quarries included: Rocklin Granite Quarries; Winters Sandstone Quarry; Folsom (Prison) Quarry; Combs Quarry; Indian Diggins Marble Quarry; Porterville Granite Quarries; Oro Grande Granite Quarries; and more. Inyo County was the site of some important quarries in Southern California, one being the Inyo (Dolomite) Marble Quarry, located in the eastern foothills of the Owens Valley near Lone Pine. Some of the sandstone used in northern California's cemeteries came from quarries at the Benicia Arsenal grounds.

According to *The Structural and Industrial Materials of California, Bulletin No. 38*, California, State Mining Bureau, San Francisco, California, 1906: "Besides the use for paving stone, the Corona granite (quarried near Corona, Riverside County,

California) is used to some extent for building stone, and in considerable quantities for monuments, in Los Angeles, Riverside, and other places in southern California. The monument dealers in the different towns nearly all speak highly of the Corona granite for monuments, thus giving it a growing reputation in that field."

In addition, there were various stonecutters and marble works companies established in cities like Sacramento and San Francisco. It is not easy to discern the signatures (occasionally located on an edge of the headstone) of these cutters when headstones have weathered or worn, but in examining old newspapers and scanning the Internet, you can find references to some cutters, including: Q. Battin; Arrigo Fantozzi Marble and Granite Works; A. Taylor & Son; Blanchard & O'Neil; Hugh Coyle; G. Griffith.

It's interesting to note that as Americans gained more financial security, one area where prosperity was demonstrated was in cemetery art and ornamentation. Most followed one of these stylistic conventions: Egyptian; Greek; Roman; Celtic; Gothic; Renaissance; or Colonial. Examples of design and/or ornamentation in each of these categories included such images or shapes as the obelisk; occasionally a pyramid, with illustrations like the lotus or water lily; sheaves of wheat or palms, or graphics that might be seen on the walls of Egypt; the vine, whether grape or ivy; laurel wreaths; the acanthus (similar to a thistle); the head of a lion or sheep; columns and graphics involving fretwork and angles as in Greek tradition; Roman images, which evolved from the Greek and Egyptian motifs, though sometimes a bit more refined in design. These included images like swags or garlands, vines, columns, vases, heads (with horns), even human forms.

Moreover, cemetery vaults frequently employed Roman architecture, with barrel vaults or domes; Celtic design—generally devoid of plants or vines or human forms—was characterized by lines and shapes, intriguing interlapping of swirls or shapes; or Gothic designs characterized by shapes like the pointed arch and window "tracery" often projecting a Biblical relief. Renaissance stylization included lots of indulgences and embellishments; and Colonial design, which was understated, was represented by fruit, vines, festoons and flowers, the increased use of urn shapes, fence posts, scrolls, and images of pineapples or acorns, even the graceful curves found in carved furniture.

This unique pyramid tomb belongs to the Sahlberg family of Santa Barbara and is representative of an Egyptian style of architecture.

Keeler Cemetery is located outside the town of Keeler on the north side of Owens Lake, along Highway 136. It is one of Inyo County's older and sadly forlorn cemeteries. It was named after **Julius Keeler** (1823–1890), who settled in the Owens Valley in 1879. The town became a terminus for ships that crossed the lake. Unfortunately, fewer than half a dozen graves are marked in the cemetery and many more lack identification. There are reportedly forty-nine known graves in Keeler's Cemetery. Two graves with carved headstones include those of **John Russell Bean** (1857–1916) and **Luna Fidella Bean** (1868–1909). Their graves are laid out side by side, each one bordered by rocks. Luna passed away in 1909 from TB, augmented by grippe (influenza). And John's widowed mother, **Martha Jane Barbee Bean** (1825–1915), died at age eighty-nine from chronic kidney disease, possibly complicated by alcohol consumption. She was buried with Luna, and John—who died a year later.

Mary Smith (unknown–1914), an Indian "washwoman," is one of those buried without a headstone or marker. According to the Inyo County Death Certificate, Mary, aged fifty, died tragically, "presumably by being burned to death." There is no other information available to explain this terrible tragedy, but one wonders how it might have happened. Too often there are only vague details regarding Indian men and women's deaths. In similar fashion, a **Male, Unknown** (unknown–1907), labeled as a Japanese laborer, died tragically after falling from a train and being run over. With no marked grave and no identity provided, his story is lost forever.

CHAPTER 6

CENTRAL COAST REGION

The Central Coast, also known as California's Golden Coast, extends from the northwest edge of Los Angeles County north to the southern edge of Santa Clara County. Among the original settlers were the *Chumash*. The Chumash were one of California's larger tribes and likely numbered from 10,000 to 18,000 in 1770, but today there are fewer than 1,000 members of the Santa Rosa Band.

In 1769, as Gaspar de Portola traveled north on the way to the Bay of Monterey, he moved through the San Luis Obispo County area. Father Serra, after sending a hunting expedition into the region, decided it would be a good location for another mission. In September 1772, a cross was erected near San Luis Obispo Creek where Serra celebrated a first mass. **Mission San Luis Obispo De Tolosa** became the fifth in the chain of missions. Unfortunately, the first burials conducted at the **San Luis Obispo Old Mission Cemetery** were not documented. Burials took place within the mission's quadrangle and on nearby Chorro Street, but until 1859, there was little about them recorded. Only after the *second* **Old Mission Cemetery was established**, located near

This large white cross stands as a memorial to two Warm Springs warriors who acted as scouts for the U.S. Army during the Modoc War of 1872–1873. They were killed during the final battle of the war, known today as the Battle of Dry Lake, in 1873.

Higuera Street, were any records kept on interred individuals. In 1877, however, the City of San Luis Obispo condemned the second Old Mission Cemetery—so the cemetery was moved yet again.

This *third* location is also known as the **Old Mission Cemetery** (or **Old Catholic Cemetery**). According to an article printed in October 1888 in the *Daily Republic*, "Work was commenced last Tuesday on the removal of all bodies from the Old Catholic Cemetery. The work will be pushed forward until all the bodies are removed to the other cemeteries." It would take a couple of years for all the graves to be exhumed and then reinterred.

One early burial at Mission San Luis Obispo de Tolosa took place in 1772 for a young Chumash boy whose only recorded name was his Christian name **Francisco** (1763–1772). His parents brought him to the mission to be baptized because he was near death and they wanted him baptized before he passed away. The Corporal of the Guard, Antonio Alexo Gonzales, stepped in to serve as Godfather. Three days later Francisco died and was laid to rest in the Old Mission Cemetery on October 4, 1772.

Another early burial at Mission San Luis Obispo de Tolosa was that of **Petra Maria** (1761–1774). Aged twelve or thirteen, neither her nor her mother's Chumash names were ever recorded. She was a resident of Rancheria Chiguegua, along with her parents, both neophytes of the faith. When Petra passed away in 1774, she was laid to rest in the Old Mission Cemetery.

Cabo (Corporal) Nicolás Beltrán (1736–1781) was a soldier who was transferred to Alta California in 1775 and served at the

Presidio in San Diego beginning in January 1775. While the Quechan revolt at Yuma was taking place, Beltrán was responsible for delivering mail pouches, and Beltran was killed at the Yuma Crossing on July 17, 1781. According to a report written by Padre Cavaller, Beltrán "died in the Santa Barbara Channel going for mail and was buried there.... Sometime afterward some 'leather jackets' unearthed his bones and brought them here." Beltrán's remains were buried at Mission San Luis Obispo's **Old Mission Cemetery** between February 26 and April 19, 1784. He was either forty-four or forty-five years old.

Miguel Antonio Avila (1796–1874) was the son of **Jose de Santa Ana Avila** (1770–1806). Born in Santa Barbara, he enlisted in the Presidio Real de Monterey Company in 1816. By 1824, he was corporal of the guard at Mission San Luis Obispo de Tolosa. He married **Maria Encarnacio Inocenta Pico** (1803–unknown) in 1826, and they had fourteen children. Miguel received a land grant known as Rancho San Miguelito—which we know today as Avila Beach and environs. Miguel Antonio Avila was a grandson of **Cornelio Avila** (1745–1800), the patriarch of a large and famous Southern California family. Miguel Avila passed away at age seventy-seven, in 1874.

Captain John Charles "Juan" Wilson (1798–1860), a sea captain born in Scotland, arrived in Alta California in 1837. That same year he met and married **Maria "Ramona" Carrillo de Pacheco** (1812–1888), the widow of Jose Antonio Romualdo Pacheco who was killed in the battle in 1831. Her family was a most prestigious family in Alta California's history. Of her twelve siblings, one sister, Josefa Maria

Miguel Antonio Avila was interred in the San Luis Obispo Old Mission Cemetery.

Antonia Carrillo, married Captain Henry Delano Fitch in San Diego; another sister, Francisca Maria Felipa Benicia Carrillo, married General Mariano Guadalupe Vallejo—who would become the most important Mexican military commander in Alta California and played a major role in the transfer of California from a Mexican territory into a state.

A third sister, Maria de la Luz Eustaquia Carrillo, married General Vallejo's brother, Jose Manuel Salvador Vallejo.

In 1837, Ramona was given a 48,834-acre Mexican land grant. Following that, she and her new husband built the first two-story wood frame house in San Luis Obispo, across from the mission. Today it is the site of the San Luis Obispo County Historical Museum. In addition, Ramona and Wilson and his partner received a 3,167-acre land grant in 1845 from the then Governor Pio Pico; it included land

Maria Ignacia de Pujol was only twenty-six years old when she died.

that extended from Morro Bay to San Luis Obispo along the north bank of Chorro Creek.

When John Wilson passed away at age sixty-three, in October 1861, he was buried in the Old Mission Cemetery at San Luis Obispo. His headstone, a marble obelisk, was inscribed to read: "Sacred to the memory of John Wilson/ A native of Dundee, Scotland/ Born 1798 Died Oct. 13th, 1861/ Aged 63." Ramona and John Wilson's only daughter, **Maria Ignacia Felipa Wilson y Carrillo de Pujol** (1840–1866), passed away five years after John Wilson. She, too, was buried in the Old Mission Cemetery.

The San Luis Cemetery's Veteran Section

San Luis Cemetery has a large section devoted to war veterans. One Civil War veteran interred here was **Dr. Joseph H. Seaton** (1836–1908). Born in Wayne County, Indiana, he obtained his medical degree in Louisville, Kentucky, and became resident surgeon at the Louisville City Hospital. During the Civil War, he served as surgeon with the Twenty-First Missouri Infantry, from 1862 to 1865. The regiment's first notable action was at Shiloh where it served as part of the reconnaissance, which opened the battle. The regiment held the line "until it fell back when ordered to do so." The regiment also fought in a number of other battles, including Tupelo, Nashville, Mississippi, and Alabama—where it suffered severe losses and injury. After the war, Seaton traveled to California and settled in San Luis Obispo in 1877. In 1879, he married **Josephine B. Blunt** (1855–1941), who was nineteen years younger than he. When Dr. Seaton passed away in 1908, he was buried behind the "Big Bill" Cannon displayed in front of the rows of veteran headstones. His granite headstone is a flat, speckled granite marker, and below Seaton's name and dates are inscribed,

"United States Surgeon During the Civil War." Josephine passed away in 1941, at the age of eighty-five, and she too was laid to rest in the San Luis Cemetery.

Another Civil War veteran interred at the San Luis Cemetery was **Captain Francis Hubbard Cooper** (1833–1900). Born in New York, he ended up in Iowa where he was appointed Captain of the Seventh Iowa Cavalry in 1861. Rather than fighting in the

Although a cavalryman during the Civil War, Captain Cooper was assigned to the Western Front rather than the eastern theater.

eastern theater, the Seventh was assigned to fight Indians in the western territories. He was honorably discharged in 1865 and then he married **Marie Louise Mead Brier** in San Francisco in 1888. She was a widow with three sons who was twenty years Cooper's junior. Sadly, Cooper battled stomach cancer and traveled to San Luis Obispo only days before he passed away. He was buried in the G. A. R. (Grand Army of the Republic) section of the San Luis Cemetery.

In 1866, **Dr. William Williams Hays** (1837–1901) arrived in San Luis Obispo with his wife **Sarah Susan Parks Hays** (1840–1910). Sarah was the first English-speaking woman in the city and only the second one in the county. At this time, the town was a rough community. Between gunfights, typhoid, and other illnesses and accidents, the locals welcomed the doctor and his wife. Hays became well known for his care and concern, rarely charging those who had little money, helping to build the Episcopal Church and establishing the County Medical Society. Dr. Hays had served in the Civil War as a Union Army assistant surgeon, but the memories seemed to haunt him. After the war, he was anxious to find a new place where he could settle, San Luis Obispo provided the opportunity. As the only medical doctor, however, he was called out all hours of day and night to all parts of the county. After their only son, **Eric Bligh Hays** (1874–1896) died at age twenty-three, Dr. Hays began to fight his own malady—grief buoyed by alcoholism. As a result, his wife left him and he continued to struggle until he passed away in 1901. He was buried with his son in the Odd Fellows Cemetery, often called the **IOOF Cemetery** or

Sutcliffe Lawn Cemetery, which today is known as the San Luis Cemetery. The Hays' shared headstone—a marble cross—sits atop two flat stair-stepped stones that carry the names of both men.

The **Santa Barbara Mission**, in Santa Barbara County, was established on December 4, 1786, with the Feast of Saint Barbara. It was the tenth of the twenty-one missions. Often called the "Queen of the Missions," it overlooks the Pacific Ocean. The first recorded burial was for an Indian, **Isaya,** on August 8, 1787. After that the first mention of a cemetery was for the burial of the Indian named **Cristobal**, a man of about sixty years old. He had come from the Rancheria Saxpilil, otherwise known as Goldeta. He was buried on May 7, 1789, the same year a new church was constructed. The first non-Indian to be buried at the mission was a child, on December 18, 1789. The first of the laymen (not friars) to be buried in the **Santa Barbara Mission Cemetery** was **Captain Jose Francisco Ortega** (1734–1798); however, where specifically he was buried has not yet been discovered. Ortega had been a scout during the early Portola expedition. He also served as commander at the San Diego Presidio for eight years then moved north to Santa Barbara and, finally, he served at the Monterey Presidio from 1787 to 1791. He married **Maria Antonia Victoria Carrillo y Millan** (1741–1803) and they had eight children, although their youngest daughter passed away at less than a month old and was buried in the **San Gabriel Mission Cemetery** in Los Angeles County.

Jose died at his ranch unexpectedly in 1798, at age sixty-three. Maria passed away five years later, but while Jose was buried in the

Old Mission Cemetery, Maria was buried in the Presidio Chapel. Her name has been listed on the dedication plaque on the mission church's wall that indicates who was buried under the floor of the chapel.

The Santa Barbara Mission Cemetery

It has been estimated that though the **Santa Barbara Mission Cemetery** area is not overly large, at least 4,000 people were buried there from 1789 until the end of the Spanish-controlled mission era. According to Maynard Geiger in his booklet, *God's Acre at Mission Santa Barbara*, there is a description of where and how Indian burials were handled; this description came from Thomas Jefferson Farnham who visited the mission in 1840. He wrote,

The cemetery at the Santa Barbara Mission includes this grave of Daniel A. Hill, who came to California in 1823 and married María Rafaela Sabina Luísa Ortega y Olivera and with whom he had fifteen children. He passed away in 1865.

COURTESY CAROL HIGHSMITH/LIBRARY OF CONGRESS

"Walls of solid masonry, six feet apart, are sunk six feet deep to the level with the surface. Between these the dead are buried in such a manner that their feet touch one wall and their heads the other. These grounds have long been filled. In order, however, that no Christian Indian may be buried in a less holy place, the bones, after the flesh has decayed are exhumed and deposited in a little building on one corner of the premises."

In addition to the burial of Indians, many locals, whether Spanish soldiers or Mexican landowners, were also buried in the consecrated holy ground of the mission cemetery. The more prestigious among them built vaults of brick plastered over with cement, just inside the walls or scattered around the cemetery. While in-ground burials ceased within the cemetery circa 1872, burials inside these family vaults continued for many years.

Eventually the gateway to Santa Barbara's mission cemetery was closed off by sandstone blocks so that no more burials could take place within or around the cemetery grounds. In 1837, the then Mexican governor, **Juan B. Alvarado**, granted 16,955 acres in the Arroyo Grande Valley to **Francis Ziba Branch** (1802–1874), who was born in one of New York's well-known pre-Revolutionary families. Because his father died when he was an infant and his mother was destitute, Francis and his siblings were raised by various relatives. At eighteen, Francis joined a pack train headed to Santa Fe, New Mexico.

Once in Santa Fe, Branch joined a fur company expedition led by **William Wolfskill** (1798–1866). The company was headed to California to seek new trapping and hunting opportunities, but weather and terrain hindered them. At one point, Wolfskill's men had to eat their oxen to stay alive, but they continued to push on. The result? After nearly a year, Wolfskill and his men had carved out a new trail between Santa Fe and Los Angeles, soon to become known as the Old Spanish Trail.

William Wolfskill

While residing in New Mexico, William Wolfskill was granted Mexican citizenship, which allowed him to own land in California. In 1831, he met and married **Magdalena Lugo** (1804–1862), who was from a prominent Mexican family. Already a Mexican citizen, he was baptized into the Catholic Church and adopted the name Jose Guillermo Wolfskill. He is recognized now as one of the earliest settlers in Southern California and a pioneer in developing farmland. He is also credited with opening one of the first—if not the first—"American" school. As he developed his land, Wolfskill became quite rich, investing in and cultivating a variety of citrus fruits, nuts (in particular, the English walnut), and vineyards. In fact, he was the first to produce oranges on a commercial level, and at the time of his death, his vineyards were producing more than 50,000 gallons of wine each year. Historians have named Wolfskill one of "the three most important men in the history of California viticulture."

Both Wolfskill and Magdalena were buried in Los Angeles's **Calvary Cemetery** also known as the **New Calvary Catholic Cemetery,** located at 4201 Whittier Blvd., Los Angeles. Near the cemetery roadway stands the Wolfskill towering monument, which has a cross on each of its four concave sides, and under his name it's written, "He walked with God." Atop the monument stands a robed, winged marble angel with a trumpet in his right hand, his eyes looking heavenward. Below him and around the monument rest small flat headstones, representing Wolfskill's extended family and descendants.

In 1835, Francis Ziba Branch met and married **Maria Dominga Manuela "Corlona" Carlon** (1815–1909), in Santa Barbara, and was baptized into the Catholic Church. When he and Maria received a land grant from Governor Alvarado in 1837, the couple rode from Santa Barbara to their newly acquired Arroyo Grande property by horseback. Manuela carried their two small children on her horse. Eventually the couple had eleven children, although when Manuela passed away, she had already outlived all but four of her children (three of whom were buried in the family cemetery, most likely having died from some kind of epidemic); she also had thirty-eight living grandchildren and thirty-two great grandchildren. Having managed to survive so long—even after the heartache of losing so many children—is a testimony to the kind of woman Manuela had to be.

In addition to the land grant of over 16,000 acres, Francis Branch eventually owned 37,000 acres in the San Luis Obispo area, and he managed over 20,000 head of cattle. Civic-minded, he also worked to improve his community, even allowing his ranch house to be used as a school. He died at seventy-one after suffering from bronchitis. Francis Ziba Branch was interred in the **Branch Family Cemetery** in the Arroyo Grande Valley in 1874. Manuela lived to be ninety-four and was then buried with Francis in November 1909.

Governor Jose Figueroa (1792–1835) was the first Mexican-born governor of Alta California and the sixth to serve, from 1833 to 1835. He died on September 29, 1835 after a lengthy illness, and he was the first to be buried in the new crypt built beneath the sanctuary at the Santa Barbara Mission. Figueroa came into prominence during the Mexican Revolution and was famous for having worked to secularize the Spanish missions in California. The burial crypt inside the church under the sanctuary was built between 1815 and 1820 and used for the burial of the friars and some of the community's prominent citizens. On the floor of the church, just in front of the altar railing, there are two large brass plaques (that replaced the original tile plaques), listing the names of those who were entombed within the mission crypt. The first plaque lists the missionaries; the second plaque lists the names of "laymen." Some of those whose remains have been identified include: **Reverend Jose Maria Alsina** (1834–1863); **Reverend Buenaventura Bannon** (1846–1876); **Maria Antonia Carrillo De La Guerra** (1786–1843); and **Jose Antonio De La Guerra y Noriega** (1779–1858).

According to Santa Barbara county records, at least 100 burials took place in the **Santa Barbara County Hospital Cemetery**, located on South Salinas Street. The first interment took place in July 1892 and the last one took place in April 1904. Sadly, a number of headstones have been vandalized and thrown to the side of the cemetery, and others have been defaced, but some are decipherable. According to the records, ninety-five graves belonged to men or boys and five belonged to women or girls, with ages ranging from a stillborn infant to a man of 102.

In 1915, the County of Santa Barbara began negotiations regarding the sale of this property. The graves were then transferred to the "new" Hospital Cemetery. Surprisingly one anecdote is rather interesting: horses once owned by the Billings Stables were also buried in the original graveyard; however, I could not find an answer to the question:

Were the horses' graves moved to the new cemetery along with the human graves? The Santa Barbara County Genealogical Society has invested a tremendous amount of energy in gathering information on these Hospital Cemetery graves. These are just a handful of those whose names have been documented: **Luigi Avenatti**, age nineteen, died May 4, 1901; **Antonio Arica**, age thirty-three, died October 31, 1892; **Severo Burola**, age eighty-five, died February 18, 1901; **W. J. Wallace**, age forty-seven, died February 16, 1902; **Bert Ellesson**, age twenty-five, died February 12, 1893; **John Sanford**, age 102, died March 8, 1897; **"Infant Daughter of W.A. Todd,"** died at birth February 17, 1903.

Tuberculosis, aka "Consumption"

During the nineteenth and early twentieth centuries, TB—often called "consumption"—was the number one cause of death in the United States. "Consumption" was the term most commonly used by everyday people because it was relatively easy to see that an individual was "wasting away." Characterized by fatigue and night sweats, it usually attacked the lungs, which led to fits of coughing and exhaustion. TB is a disease caused by bacteria, and no one was immune or safe from infection. In fact, by 1900, one in seven individuals died from the disease. Victims of TB were encouraged to find a healthier, warmer climate, and to rest. Some patients checked into sanatoriums, hoping to find the cure there, but there was no reliable treatment for it. While TB did not always kill immediately, about 50 percent of patients died within five years. Some were fortunate enough to push past it, but remained ill for years. In 1900, besides TB, serious causes of death included pneumonia, cholera, typhus, diarrhea, and enteritis, which, when combined with diphtheria, caused one-third of all deaths around the world. Of this number, 40 percent were children less than five years old.

For a time, Guadalupe was the largest community in north-western Santa Barbara County. It was originally established around the Arellanes Ranch adobe, which was located on a 32,408-acre land grant deeded to **Teodoro Arellanes** (1782–1858) and **Diego Olivera** (1786–1868) in 1840. Supposedly, this location was used as a hideout by bandits during the 1850s, while Olivera and Arellanes grazed thousands of head of cattle on the acreage, until a flood, followed by a severe drought in the 1860s, caused many of their animals to die. By 1867, the ranch was owned by the Estudillo family, who had moved from San Francisco. John Ward, husband of one of the daughters, built a two-story adobe near the Arellanes home and began farming the land rather than raising livestock. The land continued to pass through other hands over the years until eventually these two adobes became the heart of the town of Guadalupe.

The **San Juan Bautista Post**, renamed **Camp Low** (in honor of California governor Frederick Low), located in San Benito County, was established in 1864 in response to attacks by the Mason Henry Gang during the Civil War. **George Gordon Belt** (1825–1869), a Southern sympathizer, had been using his ranch on the Merced River as a base for other Southern sympathizers known as "partisan rangers." Led by **John Mason** (unknown–1866) and **Jim Henry**—aka **Tom McCauley** (unknown–1865)—their goal was to recruit more partisans who would steal and take whatever they could from Union supporters.

The Mason Henry Gang

In the spring of 1864, the Mason Henry gang headed up to Santa Clara County, which was populated by a large group of Southern patriots; however, they were not able to recruit many partisans. After President Lincoln's re-election (Tuesday, November 8, 1864), the gang committed its first crime, as reported in the *Stockton Daily Independent*, on Monday, November 14:

On the evening after the election Mason and McHenry went over to Dutch Charley's, against whom they had a spite, and killed him. From his place they went to Mr. Hawthorne's, knocked at the stable, where 3 hired men were sleeping, and after cowing these men, obtained their pistols, went to the house and murdered Mr. Hawthorn [spelled two ways]. . . . They took Hawthorn's watch, double-barreled shot-gun, and 2 horses from the stable. From Hawthorn's they proceeded to the house of Mr. Robinson. After obtaining a drink of water they asked Mrs. Robinson where her husband was. She replied that he had not yet come home from the election, but that a wagon was coming up the road and she thought that was him. They set out for the wagon. Mason came up first. He accosted Robinson with—"I am told that you said there was not a decent woman in the South. Did you say so?" "No, I did not," replied Robinson. "You are a liar, and I am going to kill you," said Mason. Robinson then jumped for him. Mason snapped his gun, which missed fire, and then fired with the other barrel, breaking his victim's shoulder and arm. Robinson then ran, but was pursued by McHenry, who shot him twice, 1st in the hand and then in the back of the head, killing him. The murderers then told the man who was in the wagon with Robinson that he might go on to the house and tell who killed R. . . . Mason also told him that he was the man who had killed two soldiers at Fort Tejon and 1 at Camp Babbitt, and that MASON was not his real name; that he was after Republicans and intended to kill all he could.

The gang continued to terrorize people, not only in San Benito County but also in Santa Cruz and Monterey counties as well. In January 1865, Company B, First Battalion of Native Cavalry, California Volunteers—made up of Californios—traveled to Camp Low in San Benito County from San Francisco. In addition, a second detachment of Native cavalrymen was sent out to pursue the gang, but they failed to intercept them. Even after the Civil War ended, the gang continued to kill, rob, and assault civilians up and down the San Joaquin Valley, even into the eastern San Gabriel Mountains. In July 1865, Mason and another gang member, Hawkins, pulled their guns on **Philo Landon Jewett** (1806–1891), a rancher along the Kern River, who had just fed them dinner. Jewett got away, but Hawkins killed the ranch cook, John Johnson. Hawkins was later caught and hung. Finally, Henry was killed when San Bernardino sheriff **Benjamin Franklin Mathews** (1819–1888) and his posse arrived and trapped him. Mason, however, continued killing and robbing until April 1866 when he was killed by a miner, Ben Mayfield. Ironically, Mayfield was arrested, tried, and convicted of first-degree murder, but he was eventually exonerated.

George Balaam, Sr. (1805–1896) was born in England. He married **Sarah Swainon** (1805–1869) in 1826 in Leicester, England. After immigrating to the United States, George and his family settled in Kentucky, then Arkansas, and then Texas. In the spring of 1853, George, his wife, and their seven children (they lost two other children in early childhood), left Denton, Texas, to join a train of fifty ox-drawn wagons. They traveled across the southwestern plains to Tucson, then through Fort Yuma to Warner's Ranch in San Diego County. They reached the Los Angeles basin after six months, where George staked out a 160-acre cattle ranch. In late 1857, early 1858,

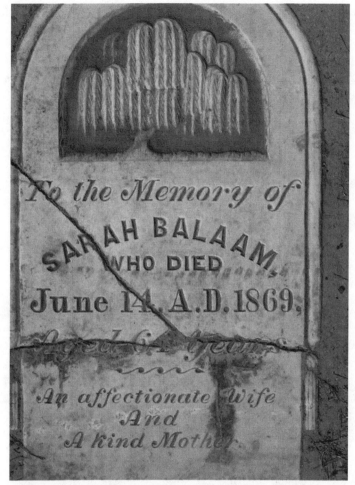

Sarah Balaam and her daughter Ann Elizabeth both died after being thrown from a runaway buggy in 1869.
COURTESY CAROL HIGHSMITH/LIBRARY OF CONGRESS

George and family moved further north to Tulare County, where they settled on 160 acres in the Four Creeks area of the San Joaquin Valley. It was here, in June 1869, that both his (first) wife Sarah and daughter **Ann Elizabeth** (1835–1869) died in a runaway buggy accident and were buried in the **Deep Creek Cemetery** in Farmersville, Tulare County. Sarah's headstone, though fallen now and broken, has an epitaph that reads "An Affectionate Wife and Kind Mother."

Six months later George married **Mary Ann Brown** (1851–1908), but the marriage lasted only six months. After a divorce in 1871, George moved to Cambria, in San Luis Obispo County. He lived there until his death in November 1896. George Balaam was buried in the **Cambria Cemetery,** located at 6005 Bridge Street in Cambria, Tulare County.

The Cambria Cemetery

The **Cambria Cemetery** was originally established in 1870, with its first burial on land donated by **George Leffingwell**. In 1877, the land was deeded over to the San Simeon Masonic Lodge. There are eighty unknown graves in the cemetery and over 300 veterans buried there. Sadly, dozens of headstones, made of wood, have deteriorated, and many of the unidentified graves belong to children and infants. Cambria Cemetery is unique, however, in that it is the only California cemetery located in the middle of the largest grove of Monterey Pines in the state. In 1940, the county established special districts for the eleven cemeteries in San Luis Obispo County. Today, the Cambria Cemetery District and the Cambria Community Cemetery are the same.

Ah Louis, also known as **Wong On** (1840–1936), was not only a well-known San Luis Obispo entrepreneur and shopkeeper, but he was also a successful Chinese American banker, farmer, and labor contractor, and his legacy has had a lasting impact on the entire county. Ah Louis emigrated from Guangdong Province, China, at twenty-one. While he did not do well in the gold fields, he went to work as a laborer in Oregon. Eventually he made his way south and settled in San Luis Obispo in 1870. An enterprising man, he told a reporter in the 1930s, "I worked in the French Hotel, then located across from the mission, as a cook. After that, I was the foreman and employment agent for Chinese working on the Pacific Coast Railroad. After that I had charge of the Chinese miners working the quicksilver mines near Cambria." Having recruited 160 Chinese laborers to sign on to the jobs, he became a labor contractor and assisted newly arriving immigrants who were looking for work.

Treatment of the Chinese

Despite the fact that **Ah Louis** became successful, there was continuous tension between the Chinese and the whites—not just in San Luis Obispo—but throughout California and the West. While many Chinese were permitted to live without harm as long as they remained in their own areas or cities, referred to as Chinatowns (*sic*), many communities resented their presence. From the 1850s on, that resentment grew. Fires frequently devastated the immigrant communities, and the people were often forced to move to new locations. In 1880, the San Luis Obispo City Council proposed that all Chinese laundries be closed as many residents were complaining about "clouds of steam" rising up from the laundries and the smell of opium on the streets.

On the other hand, a handful of communities at least tolerated the presence of the Chinese. **Happy Camp**, in Siskiyou County, supported the China Store, owned by Ah Ock, who also owned mines and employed his own laborers. By 1880, Happy Camp's Chinese population numbered 250—out of a total population of 597 miners. Supplies to the community were hauled in by the China Bow pack train, and the China Creek mine, owned by a Chinese mining company, successfully removed $200,000 worth of gold.

Ah Louis's youngest son **Howard Louis** also recalled later in life, "I don't remember being discriminated against in school. . . . In grammar school, I was a track star and won many awards and medals. When I went to San Luis Obispo High School, I was captain of the football team. Shortly after high school, I was admitted to the University of California (UC) at Berkeley, where I majored in Economics." When Howard entered the army during World War II, he said that he "was promptly assigned to intelligence school" where his mastery of foreign languages won him a specialist ranking. Later he served under the direct command of General George Patton.

In 1877, Ah Louis secured two road construction contracts: one was for a road from Paso Robles to Cambria and the other was for the first leg of a road from San Luis Obispo to Paso Robles—now known as Cuesta Grade, aka "Old Stagecoach Road." In 1884, Ah Louis also contracted with the Southern Pacific Railroad to build four Cuesta Grade tunnels on their coast route. To complete the job, which took ten years to finish, he hired nearly 2,000 workers. As a result, one in ten San Luis Obispo residents was Chinese.

Seeing a need for a store that served the growing Chinese community, Ah Louis opened a small mercantile on the corner of Chorro Street in downtown San Luis Obispo in 1874; it was the first commercial Chinese building in the county. Here he sold rice, rum, dry goods, tea, Chinese herbs, even opium—which was legal until 1915. His store also

The Ah Louis store still sits on the corner where it has stood since 1874.

served as a bank for his Chinese neighbors, even some Caucasians, and he loaned money on a handshake. His integrity led to his success, and in 1886, he replaced the simple wooden structure with a brick one, made from bricks manufactured in his own brickyard located near Bishop's Peak. His bricks were also used in the construction of the old court-house and even on a wing of the San Luis Obispo Mission.

Gon Ying's Death

When Ah Louis immigrated to the United States, he—like so many other Chinese men—left his first wife in China. She came to California in 1868 but returned to China six years later.

In 1886, Ah Louis met and married **Eng Gon Ying** on a trip to San Francisco. They then returned to San Luis Obispo where they raised eight children. In 1893, Gon Ying gave birth to a son, Young Louis, one of the first babies to be born in the Chinese community in San Luis Obispo. In addition, Ah Louis's son from his first wife, Willie Louis, age forty-one, arrived to live in the family home located above the mercantile.

It was in 1909 that Ah Louis's life turned inside out. Early in the morning of September 30, 1909, a gunshot rang out. As reported in the San Luis Obispo *Tribune*, "Some person stole up the stairway leading to the second floor where Ah Luis and his wife and eight children made their home. Placing a thirty-eight calibre pistol against the right temple of Louis's wife, the burglar sent a bullet crashing through the head of his victim and then fled taking with him a box containing gold coins and jewelry valued at about five thousand dollars. A bank book on a local bank was taken with several deeds, which are worthless to the burglar."

The San Quentin Cemetery overlooks the Bay, although few of the headstones are legible.

COURTESY BRET LAMA

Two of the Louis children had been asleep in bed with their mother—one only fifteen months old and the other three years old. Sadly, it did not take long to discover who the attacker was. Willie Louis, who some said was jealous of his stepmother and resentful of his father, confessed to the murder, declaring, "I am glad she is dead." He testified that he and Gon Ying had argued about his having to pay for anything he took out of the store. Infuriated, he burned with rage. In the end, he said he had no regrets. He was executed and buried in San Quentin in 1912.

In 1933, an aging, stooped Ah Louis returned to his homeland in Southern China with two of his sons, thinking to return to China to die, but he was dismayed, saying, "Nothing had changed." He returned to San Luis Obispo, content to sit with his long pipe and visit with his neighbors and friends. According to one report, "Ah Louis would sit in his armchair against the back wall, with an electric heater close by to warm his old legs." Surrounded by his children and their children, Ah Louis passed away in 1936, at the age of ninety-four. He was inurned in the mausoleum at the **San Luis Obispo Mission Cemetery**. Today, the Ah Louis store is listed on the National Register of Historic Places, a testament not just to the history of the Chinese in California, but, more importantly, to the resilience and entrepreneurial spirit of a man whose legacy lives on. And, in 2003, Howard Louis—then ninety-two and the only surviving son of Ah Louis—was present at the dedication ceremony at Railroad Square of a life-size bronze statue of two Chinese men working on the railroad. He passed away in 2008 at the age of 100. Howard and four of his siblings have been laid to rest in the family's San Luis Obispo Mission Cemetery Mausoleum.

Drury Woodson James (1826–1910) is considered one of the three founders of the town of Paso Robles. Drury was the eighth of nine children—all orphans. Born in Kentucky, he was raised by his sister Mary. After that, he worked for family members at various jobs. Finally, he enlisted and went off to fight in the Mexican War. He joined the Louisville Legion and fought in the battle of Monterey, Mexico. He was there to see the city surrender, but at some point, he burst a vein in his leg, which would plague him for the rest of his life. At the end of the war, Drury traveled to California and once there, realized that real money could be made in cattle. Everyone had to eat—and the hungry miners needed to eat most of all. He was also able to purchase an old Mexican land grant of 10,000 acres. Though he was successful, Drury had another dream—and as the uncle of Frank and Jesse James, he had the same kind of grit and tenacity. It is said that the brothers spent a year with their uncle in California.

In 1869, for $10,000, Drury purchased half interest in the El Paso de Robles Hotel owned by Daniel Blackburn and his brother James Blackburn. Drury and the Blackburns planned to develop a spa or health retreat, envisioning a city that would be served by a train. The hotel and the magnificent setting lasted for a while, but, ultimately, the dream—because of mismanagement and manipulation—collapsed. The partners sued each other and what money they had went missing.

The End of a Dream

Sadly, at the end of his life, **Drury Woodson James** ended up in San Francisco—sick and broken. One night a fire broke out and, though a young boy helped him to safety, the ordeal was too much. Drury passed away in the emergency hospital, and there remains controversy over where he was finally buried. Still, the city he envisioned is now known as Paso Robles. It had been called El Paso de Robles in honor of the large land grant of "six leagues" (or 25,933.18 acres) that the Blackburn brothers had originally bought in 1857. Meanwhile, Daniel D. Blackburn was interred in the **Paso Robles District Cemetery** in San Luis Obispo County (renamed in 1945)—once known as the **Catholic Cemetery**, the **Pioneer Cemetery, or the Heaton Cemetery**—while James Blackburn was interred in the San Luis Cemetery. His marker is a tall, obelisk-type monument made of pink granite and stands on three levels of stair-stepped cement pads. Above the carved name of Blackburn is the dedication, which reads: "James Hanson Blackburn/Native of Harper's Ferry VA/Born September 8 1828 / Died at Paso Robles/January 27th 1888/ Aged 67 YRS 4 MOS & 19 DAYS."

The San Luis Cemetery has large trees encircling it on two sides. It has an especially appealing area reserved for veterans near the edge of the grounds, the uniform white marble markers lined up neatly. In the center stands the American flag, raised and lowered each day, while in front of the first row of headstones, but just behind a large flat dedication plaque, stands "Big Bill" a large cannon.

William Lee Huston (1836–1911) was a pioneer who was laid to rest in Paso Robles. Born in Ohio, across the Ohio River from Kentucky, he was the oldest of five surviving siblings. By the time he was fourteen, he was farming full-time. He married a young schoolteacher,

Margaret Luticia Shuey (1837–1920) in 1858. Margaret's mother, **Sarah Stowe Shuey** (1809–1868), was the eighth cousin of General Ulysses S. Grant.

In 1860, Margaret and William Lee accompanied Margaret's parents to California. They then headed to Fruitvale (now Oakland, California) to connect with Margaret's grandparents who had already come west. William Lee and Margaret spent ten years working around Oakland and then purchased 130 acres in the San Ramon Valley, south of Walnut Creek, where their five children began school. William Lee hired out to do custom farming for others in the Salinas Valley, and in 1878, moved his family south to the Estrella Plain where he purchased farmland and built a house. Unfortunately, one night, a lantern caught the curtains on fire and burned the house to the ground.

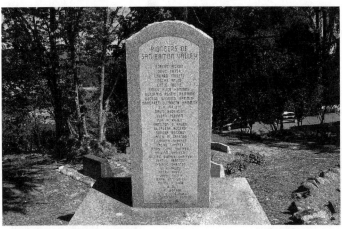

Along with others listed on this monument, William and Margaret Shuey migrated to California in an ox-drawn covered wagon to settle in the San Ramon Valley.
COURTESY JOHN D. CURTIS

Devastated, with all the work he'd done, William Lee decided he wouldn't be defeated. He built a second house on the plain plus a log cabin up in the hills. This proved to be a fateful decision; when diphtheria swept through the area, William moved his family to the cabin. Rather than returning to the second home down on the flat, he set to work on a fourth house—which became the Huston's family home for the ranch, which eventually grew to 4,000 acres.

William Lee and Margaret celebrated fifty years of marriage in 1908. In 1911, he passed away from pneumonia. He was buried in the **Pleasant Valley Cemetery,** located on Estrella Road, one mile east of Airport Road in Paso Robles. William Lee's wife, his parents, two of his brothers, and three of his five children were laid to rest there, too.

SAU-WEEP

Fall of
1825

Nov. 25,
1935

Old Man Joaquin

CHAPTER 7

NORTHERN SAN JOAQUIN VALLEY REGION

According to David R. Stuart in the *San Joaquin Historian*, Summer 2016, "Before Europeans arrived, what is now San Joaquin County was the most densely populated region in North America except Central Mexico, but it was divided into many small, sovereign nations. Even today, California has the largest number of Indian entities of any state—about 150 organized tribes, two-thirds of them recognized by the U.S. government."

Originally, the San Joaquin Valley was inhabited by the *Yokut* and *Miwok* nations, both large and well established. In 1772, the first European entered the valley, but it was Jedediah Smith who led the first Americans into the valley in 1827. Smith was able to make contact with the Yokut, whom he found a friendly peaceful people, numbering about 20,000. John Fremont also wrote about the valley and its people, as he passed through in 1844. Peaceful interaction, of course, changed as Europeans and Americans flooded the state when gold was discovered.

Bodie, in Mono County, is a ghost town today, as well as a California State Park. At one time, however, it was a major gold mining

This is the grave of Sau-Weep, the last headman of the **Wadatkuta Numu** (Paiute) and lone survivor of a massacre near Eagle Lake, Lassen County.

community. Located in the Bodie Hills, east of the Sierras, W. S. Bodey and a group of miners established a camp there in 1859, but Bodey died later in a blizzard. In 1876, a major vein of gold was discovered, and by 1879, its population numbered from 8,000 to 10,000 people. The **Bodie Cemetery** sits on the edge of town. While there are about 200 known burial sites around Bodie, there are about 150 markers in the Bodie Cemetery. For those individuals outside of Bodie's more proper population, the **Boot Hill Cemetery** was established as their final resting place.

One who was laid to rest in the Boot Hill Cemetery was the "soiled dove," **Rosa May May** (1855–1912), originally named Rosa Elizabeth White. Born in Pennsylvania to Irish immigrants, she ran away at sixteen. After falling into prostitution, she traveled from one mining camp to another, from Idaho to Virginia City to Carson City, and finally to Bodie, in Mono County, in the early 1890s. She moved in with her lover, who owned a saloon, and remained a prostitute until her death in 1912. It is said she contracted pneumonia while nursing miners who had fallen ill. After her death, however, the townspeople refused to have her buried in the town cemetery, so she was interred in Boot Hill, located outside the Bodie Cemetery fenceline. For years, there was confusion as to where her marker was located, but later it was found. Rosa May was fifty-seven when she died. **Ernest Marks** (unknown–unknown), Rosa's lover, was also buried in Boot Hill; his date of death is not known.

Life was hard in Bodie and those buried in Boot Hill reflect the frequent despair. **Harry Robbins** (unknown–1880) was shot on Election Day; **Shotgun Johnny Heilshorn** was found dead in an

Rosa May May's grave was not discovered for many years.
COURTESY DENISE BOOSE

opium den—after stealing a coffin during the night from the Bodie Cemetery. **Big Bill Monahan** was shot and killed by an unknown assailant; **Peekaboo Patton**, a prostitute, was laid to rest in the Boot Hill Cemetery, but no dates or details about her life are known; **Nellie Monroe**, also known as **Mollie Monroe**, committed suicide at the

Bodie Hotel at age forty-five—addicted to alcohol and opium, and whether her death was a suicide or overdose is not known; and **Jules "Joseph" Deroche** (unknown–1881) who murdered the husband of Mrs. Treloar after he accused Deroche of being too familiar with her at a town dance. Within twenty-four hours, the townspeople hanged Deroche.

A second woman of ill-repute buried in Bodie was **Eleanor Dumont**, better known as **Madame Moustache**. Details about her early life are fuzzy, at best, but it is believed that she was born in New Orleans to French Creole parents. She became a wildly famous and well-respected gambler who traveled all over the West and was respected as always dealing a "fair hand." Unfortunately, when she reached Bodie in May 1878, her luck began to change, and in September 1879, after losing and unable to pay her debt, she was found dead, a vial of poison beside her. As noted in the Bridgeport *Chronicle-Union*, regarding her burial: "It is said that of the hundreds of funerals held in the mining camp, that of 'Madame Moustache' was the largest. The gamblers of the place buried her with all honors, and carriages were brought from Carson City, a distance of 120 miles, especially to be used in the funeral cortege."

Hornitos, in Mariposa County, was one of the roughest of all southern mining towns. Named for the Spanish word, "little ovens," it was derived from the old Mexican tombs located nearby, which sat on top of the ground in mounds. According to the stories told of those early days, one old-timer related, "My brothers and I witnessed many shooting and stabbing affairs. . . . I well recall a morning when two

Mexican dance-hall girls fought it out, with daggers, in the Plaza. Each had a *mantillo*, or blanket scarf, which was generally worn around the neck, but, when fighting with daggers, was thrown over the left arm as a shield. No one interfered and both girls were mortally wounded."

The area was rich in gold and Hornitos was the first town to be incorporated in Mariposa County—in 1870. Hornitos was diverse, with many Chinese settling in and working creeks that others had abandoned. Their settlement was filled with two- and three-room cabins and many of these had basements dug under them—providing tunnels and walkways from one part of the community to another.

There was also a community of ex-slaves, many who had come from the South with their former masters. One former slave was **Moses Logan Rodgers** (1836–1900) who worked as superintendent of the Washington Mine. He married **Sarah Jane Quivers** (1845–1910) in 1873, and they had four daughters. When Moses passed away, he was interred in **Cherokee Memorial Park** in Lodi, San Joaquin County. He was sixty-four years old.

One very important Hornitos pioneer was **Dona Candelaria de Saphien** (1817–1903), who was responsible for keeping alive Mexican traditions and festivals. When she passed away at age eighty-five, she was interred in **St. Catherine's Catholic Church Cemetery.** According to one historian, "She would skimp and save, to buy candles so that in the evening of 'All Soul's Day,' she could place two candles, one at the head and one at the foot, on each grave, many of which were unmarked and the occupant known only to herself. These lighted

St. Catherine's Catholic Church is an important part of life in Hornitos.
COURTESY GARY GRAGNANI

candles, on the graves, were to her emblems of faith." The *All Souls* tradition has been restored by members of the Hornitos community and continues to this day.

Copperopolis, in Calaveras County, had its origin during the gold rush, but its claim to fame was its deposits of copper ore, first discovered by Hiram Hughes in 1860. With the advent of the Civil War, copper was needed for munitions, and the area soon became the second most important copper site in the nation. As often noted, "Copper was King" in Calaveras County. With such strong ties to the Civil War, it is no wonder that several businesses and streets reflected the Northern sentiment; there was the Union Hotel, Union Mine, Union Street, and Union Bridge. Although copper production waned as time went on, Copperopolis remained a supplier of copper until 1930.

Copperopolis Cemetery is the resting place of some of the earliest residents of Calaveras County. It was originally partitioned off by stone walls, creating four separate sections: one for the IOOF; one for Masons; one for Catholics; and one for Protestants. Presumably, there are more than 650 individuals interred in this cemetery. **Charles A. Smith** (1829–1878) was laid to rest here at age forty-nine. The epitaph on his headstone reads: "A native of Hamburg Germany/Dear wife, farewell/ I go to dwell with _____." The writing is "lost" at the bottom of Smith's tombstone, making it hard to discern. One wonders if Charles was referring to a mother, a brother, a child, or God?

The name of **Private George William Bowie** (1893–1918), who died and was buried in France after the Battle of the Ardenne in World War I, was added to the gravestone of his parents, **Henry Bowie** (1862–1939) and **Jane Hoar Bowie** (1855–1937) in the Copperopolis Cemetery. In a letter to his family, it was written, "Private

Charles Smith's headstone rests against one of the rock walls that outlined various sections of the cemetery.
COURTESY LINDA RHOADARMER

George W. Bowie, 115th Trench Mortar Battery . . . died of bron-cho-pneumonia, date undetermined, while serving as a member of the American Expeditionary Force." Sadly, George was one of three Bowie cousins to die in the war. All three were buried in France.

Mokelumne Hill, in Calaveras County, was by far one of the most important gold mining towns established in the San Joaquin Valley in the 1850s. By 1850, the population topped 15,000, includ-ing 6,000 to 8,000 French immigrants. The French Benevolent Soci-ety even established a hospital that took in the indigent and/or those with no outside resources. They also created a cemetery. The **French Hospital County Cemetery** was located in Pleasant Springs—about six miles from Mokelumne Hill. Today this cemetery is located on private land and there is no sign of the cemetery.

Solon Greenleaf Blaisdell (1834–1897), a Civil War veteran, was interred at **Mokelumne Hill Cemetery** (Protestant Section). Born in Vermont, he served as a sergeant in Company F, Twelfth New Hampshire Infantry, also known as "The Mountaineers," from August 1862 to November 1863. In November, he was wounded at Cold Harbor, Virginia. In 1865, Blaisdell re-entered as a second lieutenant during the months of May and June 1865. When he died in 1897, he was laid to rest in the Protestant section of Mokelumne Hill Cemetery.

Isaac Lurch (1831–1859) was buried in the **Pioneer Jewish Cemetery**, located within the Protestant Mokelumne Hill Cemetery. Originally from Upper Rhenish, Bavaria, Isaac arrived in Lancha Plana, located south of Mokelumne Hill, sometime after 1855. Details about his death were not available, but he was an active member of the Masons and Odd Fellows' Lodges as well as the fraternity of local firemen. Isaac's funeral procession was led by a band and accompanied by 500 people from the community and was one of the largest funerals to take place in Mokelumne Hill. It was also the first burial to take place in the Jewish Cemetery. Isaac was only twenty-eight years old.

The **Altaville Serbian Cemetery** is located west of the Altaville Catholic and Protestant Cemeteries on the Old Stockton Road. The cemetery contains graves of Serbian pioneers, miners, and their families from the mid-1800s on. **Elizabeth Allison Kapor** (1852–1916) was one of those interred here. Born in California, she married John Synilerd Wright in 1876, at age fifteen. Together they had one child, but by 1880, Elizabeth was married to her second husband, George William Stacey. By 1885, she was married to her third husband whose last name was Pusich and together they had a son. In 1893, she was married to her fourth husband, Lazar Tusup. They ran a boarding house, and she and Lazar had a son, plus there were older Tusup children as well. Finally, in 1908, Elizabeth married Kris Kapor, her fifth husband. According to the 1910 census, she was married to Kapor and had four children (three living) plus fifteen boarders. She led a strange but fascinating life and leaves many questions! Elizabeth passed away at age fifty-four, in 1916, in Stockton, but was laid to rest in the Altaville Serbian Cemetery.

Petar Bojanich (1870–1905), a native of Austria, age thirty-five, was also buried here. There are no details except that he was from Austria, but his headstone is unique and not a small or insignificant

This headstone in the Altaville Cemetery belongs to Manuello Airolla, a native of Genoa, Italy, and his son Luigi who passed away at a year old.

one. A large cross of white marble, with a long ribbon or vine of ivy leaves running down the main "timber" of the cross. Ivy is generally symbolic of fidelity or immortality; it is strong and represents the strength incorporated into everlasting life.

San Andreas, Calaveras County, was first settled by Mexican miners in 1848. A thriving tent city, by 1852, even a "tent church" had been built. It was named in honor of Saint Andrew (San Andreas). One interesting note regarding gold mining here: in August of 1852, a single nugget was found and sold to Wells Fargo & Co. for $12,000.

Fourth Crossing is located along Highway 49 in San Andreas, Calaveras County. The date of its founding is not clear, but likely around 1848. The community had, at one time, a hotel, store, saloon, ferry, stage stop, and one of the earliest organized schools in the county. A post office was established in 1855. The **Fourth Crossing Cemetery** reportedly has forty-plus individuals interred there, although there is only one gravestone still standing. The cemetery is much like other small pioneer cemeteries in California—hidden or out of the way. It is now on private property between Angels Camp and San Andreas, at the site of the former town and stage stop.

Horace Cottle (1852–1865) was reportedly the first white child born in Calaveras County on March 4, 1852. Though he was buried in the small cemetery of Fourth Crossing, details regarding his death are sketchy. What is known is that in some kind of freak accident, Horace's father unintentionally shot him. This, after the Cottle family had lost their two-year-old daughter, **Cornelia Cottle** (1863–1864), the year before.

Petar's cross, found in the Serbian Cemetery, with its carved garland of leaves, speaks of someone's great emotion and loss.

Child Death

Sadly enough, child death was not infrequent and tragedy struck unexpectedly. In the **Altaville Protestant Cemetery**, located on Stockton Road at Monte Vista Street in Angels Camp, Calaveras County, **George W. Osborn, Jr.** (unknown–1865), son of Rebecca and George W. Osborn, passed away at the age of five years, nine months, and nineteen days. **Leslie Alfred** (1889–1890) was thirteen months old when he was buried in the Altaville

In searching for family members, there were no records that correlated with the dates of this child's birth or death.
COURTESY PJH/ANGELBIRD

Cemetery. There is no mention of parents, but his gravestone is precious and unusual; there is a cement "crib," and the head of the bed is the marble marker with Leslie's name and dates carved into the stone. Above the flat marble block rests a large open "clam," which holds a sleeping baby curled up on a blanket that drapes over the edge of the clamshell. The baby's countenance is peaceful and at rest. No doubt, a monument of this size and complexity reflects the devotion and love this child must have felt in life.

Emilio Ayala was only two years old when he passed away.
Courtesy M. Simonelli

Child deaths occurred so frequently, it was hard to escape: Little **Victor Bongard** (1896–1896) was twenty-one days old when he passed away. He was the son of **John Peter Bongard** (1865–1896) and **Felicite Hansemme Conte** (1859–1935). John Peter, aged thirty-one, died the same year in the Utica Mine, leaving a pregnant Felicite grieving for both her infant son and husband. She then gave birth to a daughter five months later. Eight years later, in 1904, Felicite married **John Conte** (1866–1916), who—ironically—died at the same mine as did her first husband, "when a cable broke, sending a skip loaded with water onto Conte and Frank Merlot, killing both." Another child, **Emilio Ariel Ayala** (1892–1894), the son of **Jacob Angel "Jake" Ayala** (1858–1921) and **Kittie Teague** (unknown) lived only two years.

One last heartbreaking tragedy is the story of **Amanda Henrietta Bechait** (1891–1906). She was the fourteen-year-old daughter of **Wilhelmina Ketzerberg** (1891–1906) and **Joseph Alfred Bechait** (1867–1906) who emigrated from Belgium. On the evening of July 5, 1906, Amanda's father was thrown from his horse and died. On the day of his funeral, Amanda blew out the oil lamp at the Marble Springs Hotel in Albany Flat when, unexpectedly, it exploded and covered her in burning oil. Amanda died three days after the death of her father, on July 9, 1906. The hotel also burned to the ground. Their shared headstone is one of the loveliest in the Altaville Protestant Cemetery.

Sonora City Cemetery, also known as the **Sonora Cemetery**, is located at the corner of Jackson and Solinsky Streets near Highway 49, in Sonora, Tuolumne County. It sits on a sloping hillside overlooking homes below. There is no grass, but trees give the entire cemetery a very woodsy feel. As you glance out over the terraced levels, most of the plots are separated by cement or wooden barriers. It is quite interesting that there are a number of Chinese also interred in the Sonora Cemetery. It seems likely that most of the Chinese here were laborers or miners, although a few have more than a line regarding their lives or history. **Bun Ah** (1836–1873), age thirty-six, was a miner from Chinese Camp and arrested and convicted of the murder of Ah Mow. In 1872, Bun Ah committed suicide by hanging himself in the county jail. Another individual, **Bung Ah** (1832–1922) lived to be ninety years old. A native of China, he had apparently gone missing. Though I could not find any details, his bones were found in Big Creek at least one year later. His bones were then buried in the Sonora City Cemetery in March of 1923.

Amador County and the city of Amador were named after soldier, rancher, and miner **Jose Maria Amador y Noriega** (1794–1883), although he died in Watsonville, in Santa Cruz County, and was buried in Santa Clara County. Jose married three times and reportedly fathered twenty-one children. His life story was recorded by Thomas Savage in *Memorias sobre la Historia de California*, which is housed at the Bancroft Library.

The **Amador City Cemetery**, however, in Amador City, Amador County, is the resting place for forty-one pioneer memorials. One individual, **Frank Carveth** (1863–1903), wandered into the mountains, possibly en route to a new mining location, and was found dead near a pond of water. According to the July 17, 1903 *Amador Ledger*, "The remains were conveyed to Wiley's Station and buried in the vicinity. . . . A brother arrived from Nevada on Tuesday, who had the remains dug up and re-buried in the Amador cemetery."

Another pioneer, **Daniel W. Moon** (1837–1875), only thirty-eight years old and a native of Ohio, died on July 19, 1875. He, too, was buried in the Amador City Cemetery after being killed while blasting logs near Amador City. A third pioneer buried in the Amador City Cemetery, **Samuel G. Mugford** (1835–1876), was originally from England. He married **Johanna Thomas Pryor** (1845–1882) in Mormon Island in 1860 (a mining community in El Dorado County). By 1870, they were running a boarding house in Amador City. While working at the Keystone Mine, however, Samuel fell to his death. His expectant wife and five young children were left behind, although they had lost two other children prior to Samuel's death.

CARIE·DEMARTIN
DID·JUNE·10·1900
AGE·24·IEARS

CHAPTER 8

SAN FRANCISCO BAY AREA REGION

While Juan Rodriguez Cabrillo was the first explorer to touch California's shores in 1542, it was Sir Francis Drake who landed at Bodega Bay in July 1579, Juan Vizcaino who entered Monterey Bay in 1603, and Captain George Vancouver who reached the northern coastline in 1792. The Russians established only minor settlements at Fort Ross and Bodega, beginning in 1805, but their focus was on the fur trade. The Spanish missionaries brought real change to the region surrounding **Mission Dolores** and the San Francisco Bay Area beginning in 1776.

Located at 3321 Sixteenth Street, San Francisco, Mission Dolores, also known as **Mission San Francisco de Asis**, was at first just a log and thatch structure. The formal construction began around 1782. It took more than 36,000 adobe bricks—manufactured by Indian converts—to build the church and mission, which was completed in 1791. Still today, the church's roof is supported by its original redwood beams and is the oldest building in San Francisco, having even survived the 1906 earthquake.

The **Mission Dolores Cemetery**, in San Francisco, San Francisco County, was originally larger than what it is now. As the city

Interesting tombstone of Carie DeMartin who died in Altaville, Calaveras County, at age twenty-four, on June 10, 1900; the interior of her stone is filled with coral.

COURTESY PJH/ANGELBIRD

moved in, the cemetery's boundaries were reduced. It's been estimated there were at least 10,000 burials over time—half of which were for Native American converts or their families. The first graves had wooden markers, so as they were lost or thrown away, and the graves were used again. Some remains were reinterred on site in a mass grave. In addition, a number of burials took place inside the church, under the floor, including those of some of the founding friars or some of San Francisco's early arrivals, including: the first Mexican governor of Alta, California, **Captain Luis Antonio Arguello,** who was also the first recorded burial in 1830; **Francisco De Haro** (1792–1849), the first alcalde (mayor) of San Francisco; **Lieutenant Jose Joaquin Moraga** (1745–1785), the leader of the 1776 California expedition; and **William Alexander Leidesdorf** (1810–1848), America's first African American millionaire and one of the founders of San Francisco.

A West Indian immigrant, Leidesdorf's father managed a Danish plantation and his mother was of African and Spanish descent. As soon as he was naturalized in San Francisco, he received 35,000 acres along banks of the American River. He was only thirty-eight years old when he passed away and was interred in the Mission Dolores Cemetery. His estate at the time totaled about $1.5 million.

The Mission Cemetery and Reinterment

Regarding the exhumation of those in the cemetery, when it was clear the church and mission authorities were going to have to sell much of the property to the city, it was decided the bodies would have to be reinterred in other cemeteries. The *San Francisco Morning Call* on June 8, 1889, wrote: "Ten of the bodies have been interred in Mount Calvary Cemetery; 40 at the cemetery of the Holy Cross in San Mateo County; one, that of Senor Peralta, has been sent to Oakland; one, named Murphy, sent to Vallejo; two children sent to Odd Fellows' Cemetery, and the remainder, in number 446 have been reinterred in another part of the Mission Cemetery. One of these is Thomas Ford, a former stockbroker and society leader, and Senor Diaz, an old Spaniard Don. The three bodies disinterred yesterday were found beneath the roots of cypress trees that had been planted upward of thirty years ago."

Unfortunately, thousands of remains belonging to Native Americans (most from the Ohlone and Miwok tribes) were never identified. In fact, as recorded, "In every instance, except two or three recent interments, there was nothing to be found except a few bones, or badly corroded coffin plates. These, as a rule, were placed in new boxes. There was no mixing of bodies."

There were more than 5,500 additional Native American graves on Chula Lane. These were removed and placed in a mass grave "in accordance with the Indians' wishes." Others, however, still remain interred under roads and building sites around the mission and the city. Unfortunately, "Mission Dolores had one of the highest death rates of Spain's 21 missions in California. . . . Nearly all [of them] died of European diseases, or overwork, or of the destruction of their culture." It's hard not to walk around the grounds of this or any mission and not feel a complex range of emotions. In the center of the graveyard stands a large statue of Father Serra. Surrounding him are fragrant roses.

The *Ohlone* were the first people to inhabit the area in and around San Francisco's mission and the location of what would become Mission Dolores Park. During the gold rush, it quickly became a rowdy settlement, populated by wild saloons and bars. Then, as Jewish settlers moved into San Francisco, they wanted to build a specific graveyard for their community, and two Jewish congregations decided the would-be Mission Dolores Park was the best location. In 1861, Congregation Sherith Israel purchased the location for a Jewish cemetery, and for thirty years, it functioned as such. In fact, two Jewish cemeteries were developed. In 1894, however, the sites became inactive when the city decided to create a park close to the mission.

Cemeteries as Parkland

All over the nation, the trend was spreading; where there were no parks, cemeteries were being reimagined, and people were claiming them as "public spaces" where they could stroll or picnic. The movement was triggering a reformation of sorts, and even cemeteries were being reimagined. Many cemeteries were becoming less crowded and dreary and more than just rows of gray headstones and forgotten graves. While only four parks existed in Yerba Buena in 1849, the Mission Park Association, organized in 1897, wanted to bring about improvements to the Mission neighborhood. The district was the most populated but overlooked neighborhood in the city. The association's primary goal quickly took shape: to establish a park of international quality.

In 1903, the Mission Park Association started a campaign to purchase the former Jewish cemeteries and transform them into a park. More than 1,000 property owners authored a bond measure that would secure funds to purchase the cemeteries. It passed overwhelmingly, a result of the City Beautiful Movement that had taken hold of San Franciscans. According to one member of the association, "The garden effect will be semi-tropical and the entire park stocked with broadleaf plants. A row of palms will border the entire square and an avenue of trees will be planted along the inner edges."

And then, without warning, the great earthquake of 1906 and its aftermath transformed the park—not into an exotic green space—but into a crowded refugee camp for more than 1,600 families.

With the rising incidence of disease and mortality among the hundreds of mission Indian converts, the priests at Mission Dolores decided on establishing an *assistencia*, or medical facility, somewhere north of the bay where the weather would be more temperate, and so **Assistencia of San Rafael Arcangel** was dedicated on December 14, 1817." Of all the missions, **Mission San Rafael**, in Marin County, was the first to be "secularized" and partitioned off after the Mexican Revolution, although the church remained the local church for the area's families. The Mission Cemetery also remained active—though not officially—and continued as the final resting place for local Native American Indians and others, including **Chief Marin** and **Fr. Juan Amoros**.

Chief "Marino" Marin (1781–1839), whose given name was *Huicmuse*, was born circa 1781 in the area of Mill Valley, Marin County. Along with others of his nation, he spoke the Miwok language, but he was also well known for his skills as a sailor. General Mariano Vallejo reported to the California's first State Legislature gathering in 1850 that Marin was the "great chief of the tribe *Licatiut*" (or branch of the Coastal Miwok).

Mission San Rafael, known as Assistencia of San Rafael Arcangel, was dedicated in 1817 and in 1839 became the resting place for Chief "Marino" Marin.

Author Betty Goerke in her book, *Chief Marin*, gathered a number of interesting details about his life. According to her, Marino was not a chief, but a leader of the Southern Marin band to which he belonged, the Huimen. Marin remained with the mission for over thirty years. He died from a possible ulcer in 1839 and was buried in the Mission Cemetery, though there is no recognizable burial site or recorded information. However, his legacy has been preserved in the naming of Marin County.

Maria Loreta Altamirano Garcia (1810–1873) was buried in the San Rafael Mission Cemetery in 1873. Her husband, **Rafael Garcia** (1791–1866), an officer in the Mexican Army, was buried in the same cemetery in 1866. Married in 1827, at **Mission San Juan**

Bautista, in San Benito County, Rafael Garcia and his wife received the Mexican land grant Rancho Tamales y Baulines—today's present-day Bolinas, in Marin County—as a gift from the governor. Widowed in 1866, Maria Loreta inherited the Garcia adobe and "the property on which it was situated, and a third part of the lands." The remaining land was divided among Garcia's heirs, including **Maria Dolores** (Hurtado); **Maria Hilaria** (Noriel); **Jose; Juan; Felipe; Feliz;** and **Ava Thomas** (a minor). Unfortunately, in 1868, an earthquake destroyed her home, and many of the lands inherited by her children had already been sold or lost. Then, on April 17, 1873, Maria Loreta was shot and killed in her home. Her six-year-old adopted daughter witnessed the murder and was able to testify that a man had entered the house and after an argument—something about marriage—he drew his pistol and shot her mother. When Maria Loreta fell to the floor, the man shot her again. Then he tried to burn down the house. The child, screaming for help, fled, and the assailant fled, too. At the end of the road, he turned the gun on himself and fired.

Mount Tamalpais Cemetery in San Rafael, Marin County, is also known as the **Kol Shalom Cemetery** and **Sha'arei Shalom Cemetery**. Located at 2500 Fifth Avenue, it contains more than 22,000 graves. A number of intriguing individuals have been laid to rest here. One enterprising man was **Robert Dollar** (1844–1932), born in Stirling, Scotland. At eleven years old, he and his family immigrated to Canada, and soon he was earning his living as a "shore boy" in a lumber camp. In 1874, he married **Margaret Snedden Proudfoot**

(1852–1941). By 1893, Robert was flourishing as a lumberman on the Pacific coast. Two years later he purchased his first vessel—a schooner called *Newsboy*—and was shipping his own lumber down the Pacific coastline. Eventually he established the Dollar Line, in 1900, and began traveling to the Orient with his lumber business. He became known as the "Grand Old Man of the Pacific." Robert Dollar passed away in 1932 and was buried in the Mount Tamalpais Cemetery.

Another interesting individual interred at Mount Tamalpais was **John Worthington Ames** (1833–1878). Born in Massachusetts, Ames was appointed a captain in the Eleventh U.S. Infantry in May 1861. For "gallantry in action at Gaines Mill," in June 1862, he was promoted to major. He then commanded Company C of the Eleventh Infantry during the Maryland Campaign, and after serving at Gettysburg, he was promoted to lieutenant colonel. In September 1863, he accepted a commission as colonel of the Sixth U.S. Colored Volunteers Infantry regiment. He led his troops through action in Virginia, near Richmond, and was slightly wounded in September 1864. He was brevetted out of the army in September 1865 as brigadier general of Volunteers. Ames was forty-four when he was buried in San Rafael's Mount Tamalpais Cemetery.

The **Mountain View Cemetery** in Oakland, Alameda County, is located on Piedmont Avenue. It was designed in 1863 by Frederick Law Olmsted who also designed Central Park in New York, part of Stanford University, and much of UC at Berkeley. One section of the cemetery has a lane that is known as "Millionaires' Row." This is where the large and extravagant tombs and crypts have been built for and by the families of great wealth or prestige from around San Francisco and the East Bay.

One of these family crypts belongs to **Charles "Chas" Crocker** (1822–1888) and family. Charles Crocker became one of California's famous "Big Four," that is, one of the four tycoons who built the Central Pacific Railroad (CPRR) in the 1860s. Crocker also founded Crocker Bank as well as the larger Southern Pacific Railroad in 1883. He married **Mary Ann Deming** (1827–1887) in 1852. Their first child, **Emily Crocker** (1853–1853), only lived a month and was buried in the **Sacramento City Cemetery** in October 1853. Another daughter, **Fannie Ella** (1858–1862), contracted diphtheria and died at age four. Meanwhile Crocker's financial success soared, and in 1860, he was elected to the State Legislature. At this point Crocker joined with three other successful entrepreneurs, and the dream of a railroad took shape. The other members of the Big Four included: **Leland Stanford** (1824–1893), president of the CPRR and later, founder of Stanford University; **Collis P. Huntington** (1821–1900), vice president of CPRR; and **Mark Hopkins** (1813–1878), treasurer of CPRR. As part of the Big Four, Crocker was the partner who managed the actual construction of the railroad. One of his strategies was to hire Chinese immigrants, driving them hard to finish construction. In 1886, however, Crocker was seriously injured in New York while riding in a carriage. He suffered for a time before passing away in 1888, in Monterey.

Located at the top of Millionaire's Row, along with the Merritt Mausoleum, sits the large and impressive, circular Crocker Mausoleum, designed by architect Arthur Page Brown, who also designed

San Francisco's famous "Ferry Building." Constructed in 1888, the design was inspired by classic Greco-Roman styled temples and tombs. One interesting side note: because the monument is actually solid granite, none of the Crockers is entombed inside. According to Douglas Keister, photographer and author who has studied cemetery art all over the world, Oakland's cemetery records indicate that the remains of four Crockers lay around the monument, including Charles; his wife Mary; their son George; and Emma, George's wife.

A notable Western figure that rests in Mountain View Cemetery is former Texas Ranger **John Coffee Hays** (1817–1883), also known as "Captain Jack" Hays. Born in Tennessee, he moved to Texas when he was nineteen. With a letter of recommendation from his great uncle, President Andrew Jackson, Hays approached Sam Houston—who also knew the Hays family from Tennessee—and Houston responded by appointing Hays to a company of Rangers. A captain at only twenty-three, Hays successfully led his men against the Comanche, even riding with Flacco, an Apache chief, who often co-led the attacks. In 1840, Hays also rode with Tonkawa Chief Placido in tracking down a large war party.

Texas Ranger John Coffee Hays

When war with Mexico broke out in 1846, Colonel John Coffee Hays commanded the First Regiment of Texas Mounted Riflemen. While many might have thought of him as rough and rugged, Nelson Lee wrote of his first encounter with Captain Hays: "He was a slim, smooth faced boy not over twenty years of age [actually twenty-four], and looking younger than he was in fact. In his manner he was unassuming in the extreme, a stripling of

---

few words, whose quiet demeanor stretched quite to the verge of modesty . . . young as he was, he had already exhibited abundant evidence that, though a lamb in peace, he was a lion in war."

It was also recorded that, "While he [Hays] could outride them [his men], he could also use his fists, Bowie, or Colt better than any in his command."

In 1847, Hays married **Susan Sophia Calvert** (1827–1913) in Seguin, Texas. Because the Comanche had a great admiration for Hays, when Susan gave birth to their first child—a son, in California—Chief Buffalo Hump sent them a gift, a gold spoon engraved with "Buffalo Hump Jr."

In 1849, Hays was appointed to serve as the U.S. Indian agent for the Gila River country in Arizona and New Mexico. He also led a group of Forty-Niners to California. Then, in 1850, he was elected the first sheriff of San Francisco County. Hays and his wife Susan were some of the first residents of Oakland, now the city seat of Alameda County. Hayes invested in real estate and accumulated a small fortune. Perhaps the saddest aspect of John and Susan's life in California was that out of six children, only two sons grew to adulthood. Four of their children died either as infants or in childhood. John Coffee Hays passed away at age sixty-six, in 1883; Susan passed away at age eighty-six, in 1913. Interestingly, while John, Susan, and five of their six children are listed as being interred at Mountain View Cemetery in Oakland, the Hays plot—composed of six layers of stone blocks pressed against a grassy slope, more like a wall than a monument—has no headstones for any of the family members. There's only a plaque set in the wall that summarizes the life of John Coffee Hays.

William Thomas Shorey (1859–1919) was also interred in Mountain View Cemetery. Born in Barbados, his mother was of African and European descent, and his father was a Scottish sugar planter in the British

West Indies. Living on an island, his whole life revolved around the sea, and in 1875, he joined the crew of a ship headed to Boston. After ten years of sailing, Shorey was ready to captain his own whaling bark. His men often called him the "Black Ahab." In 1886, he married **Julia Ann Shelton** (1865–1944), the daughter of one of San Francisco's leading African American families. They had three children, although one daughter, **Zenobia Pearl**, died in 1908. When Shorey retired in 1908, he settled permanently in Oakland. There he became a strong civic leader and worked as a special policeman for the Pacific Coast Steamship Company, until he contracted the Spanish flu during the 1919 pandemic. He died on April 15, 1919, and was buried at Mountain View. He was fifty-nine years old.

A woman who is also interred in Oakland's Mountain View Cemetery and is considered one of California's most important poets was **Josephine "Ina" Donna Coolbrith** (1841–1928). She was the third daughter of **Agnes Moulton Coolbrith** (1811–1876) and **Don Carlos Smith** (1816–1841), who was the brother of **Joseph Smith**, aka the founder of **The Church of Latter-Day Saints of Jesus Christ**. Don Carlos died when Ina was just four months old, from malaria. Ina's mother, Agnes, then married Joseph Smith as his sixth or seventh wife in 1842. When Smith was killed by anti-Mormon zealots, however, Agnes took her daughters and moved to St. Louis. There she met and married **William Pickett** (1816–1891). The couple had twins (Don Carlos and William), and in 1851, they headed west. On the trail, ten-year-old Ina read aloud to the family, and as they entered California, she rode with the famous mountain man, **James "Jim" Beckwourth**, the wagon train's master and guide. Beckwourth, son of a slave and her slave master, was not only articulate and spoke several languages, but he was also an avid storyteller himself. No doubt, Ina would have thoroughly enjoyed the time spent with him.

A California Poet

Titled the "Sweet Singer of California," Ina **Coolbrith** was named the *first* Californian poet laureate as well as the *first* poet laureate of any state in the nation. She became part of the "Golden Gate Trinity," along with Mark Twain and Charles Warren Stoddard, and they all worked with the literary journal *Overland Monthly*. She befriended many writers and when she worked as a librarian in Oakland, Alameda County, she mentored two up-and-coming artists, author Jack London and dancer Isadora Duncan. Sadly, when the 1906 San Francisco earthquake hit, Ina—living in Oakland—was lucky to escape with her cat and some of her writings and books, but her house burned to the ground and she lost everything else. Her friends and associates helped her fund a new home, and, resettled, she continued to write and publish. In 1919, she was named California's Poet Laureate.

When Ina passed away in 1928, she was buried in the Mountain View Cemetery in Oakland; however, it wasn't until 1986 that a literary group raised money to fund a headstone for her grave. Her poem "Beside the Dead" is appropriate for this volume on historic graves and cemeteries. The following is only a brief excerpt:

> It must be sweet to slumber and forget;
> To have the poor tired heart so still at last;
> Done with all yearning, done with all regret,
> Doubt, fear, hope, sorrow, all forever past;
> Past all the hours, or slow of wing or fleet—
> It must be sweet, it must be very sweet!

Reverend Henry Durant (1802–1875), a Congregational minister, was also buried at Mountain View Cemetery in Oakland. After graduating from Yale University in 1827, he married **Mary E. Buffett** (*c*. 1807–1884), of Connecticut in 1883. He remained in ministry for sixteen years then resigned in order to head the Dummer Academy. He remained at the academy until 1852, but Durant had his eye on California, spurred by the desire to develop opportunities for higher education in the new state. He arrived in San Francisco on May 1, 1853. Renting a house in Oakland, he proceeded to open the Contra Costa Academy, a private school for boys. By 1855, the school had become the College of California, and in 1867, the state entered a contract with the college so that it could become a true university, thus the UC was born on March 23, 1868. This campus later became UC at Berkeley, and Durant served as its first president from 1870 to 1872, retiring at age seventy. He was elected the mayor of Oakland but died unexpectedly in 1875 and was interred at Mountain View Cemetery. His tombstone reads: "Henry Durant/ Founding President of the University of California/He brought light to the Golden State."

In addition to others along Millionaire's Row, Mountain View Cemetery is home to several impressive mausoleums. One belongs to chocolate officianado **Domenico "Domingo" Ghirardelli** (1817–1894). Born in Italy, in 1837, he married **Carmen Alvarado Martin** (1829–1887), from Lima, Peru. With the 1849 gold rush, Domenico decided to go to California and try his hand at mining. Failing to do well, he opened a tent store in Stockton and became successful. He also established a store in Hornitos, in Mariposa County, in 1852, and

The massive Ghirardelli family mausoleum resembles a small fortress.
COURTESY CHRIS NELSON

then opened a store and hotel in San Francisco. The company was first called Ghiradely & Girard (Girard was his partner), because Americans could not pronounce Ghiradelli. To make it easier, Domenico featured a parrot on the packaging, squawking, "Say Gear-ar-delly!"

Even the earthquake of 1906 did not destroy Ghirardelli's business, and Domenico was able to incorporate three of his five sons into the operation. Sadly, his fourth son died while in boarding school in Italy, and his youngest son disappeared in 1909 (declared dead in 1921). The Ghirardellis also lost a daughter in 1867. Then, in 1879, when a granddaughter, Aurelia, fell quite ill and the family priest refused to give her last rites—supposedly because Domenico had not paid his tithe to the church—Domenico declared that no member of his family would ever step foot into a Catholic Church again, and Aurelia died without being given the sacraments. The family, however, had already constructed a tomb at **Saint Mary's (Catholic) Cemetery** where family members had been entombed. According to Douglas Keister, "In 1890, Domingo Ghirardelli had [a new] mausoleum constructed at Mountain View. Then, one night, he and his sons took a wagon to St. Mary's Cemetery, removed the four bodies from the Ghirardelli tomb, transported and reinterred them at Mountain View." The mausoleum is a grand classic structure—certainly one of the largest in the cemetery—and reflects Domenico's strong character. After Domenico Ghirardelli passed away on a trip to Italy in 1894, he was laid to rest in his mausoleum at Mountain View Cemetery in Oakland.

Joe Shoong (1879–1961), whose Chinese name was originally **Zhou Song**, was one of the first Chinese American millionaires to eventually be laid to rest in the Mountain View Cemetery. As a boy in China, Shoong sold eggs in order to save money, and at nineteen, he was able to immigrate to the United States. He settled in Vallejo, Solano County, where he worked in a factory, but by 1901, he entered into a partnership with three other men and opened a store in Vallejo. A year later, he bought them out and moved the store to San Francisco and then changed the name to China Toggery. His goal: to sell quality goods at low prices. In 1924, Shoong and his wife **Rose Elizabeth Soohoo** (1890–1951) moved to Oakland into a house designed by Julia Morgan, the architect who designed homes for William Randolph Hearst. In 1928, Shoong changed his store's name to National

Dollar Store—and by this time, there were sixteen stores in the West. The stores did well, even with a labor dispute in the 1930s. By 1959, there were fifty-four stores with 700 employees, worth $12 million. However, when Shoong passed away in 1961, his son took over the leadership, but business declined. In 1996, ninety-five years after Shoong opened the doors to his first store, National Dollar Stores closed their doors.

African American historian and author, **Delilah Leontium Beasley** (1867–1934), spent her last years in Oakland, California, and was interred at Saint Mary's Cemetery. Located at 4529 Howe Street, Oakland, Alameda County, Saint Mary's Cemetery was consecrated in December 1863. Delilah was born in Ohio where she attended one of the state's segregated public schools. By the time she was twelve years old, she was already having articles published in local African American newspapers. Unfortunately, her parents passed away unexpectedly in the 1880s, and Delilah and her siblings were separated and raised by different families. In order to make her way in the world, Delilah went to work as a domestic but sought training as a hairdresser and nurse. Around 1910, she moved to Oakland and began working as a nurse. At the same time, she became interested in researching and preserving black history. She visited public and private libraries and collected oral histories from elderly black residents. She also began speaking to groups about the history of slavery and of African Americans who had overcome life's tragedies and obstacles. Several of her articles were published in the *Oakland Tribune*. In 1918–1919, she published her groundbreaking book, *Slavery in*

California, and her years-in-the-making book, *The Negro Trail Blazers of California*. Delilah passed away in 1934 after suffering poor health, but she is recognized as the *first* to present the history of African Americans in California, from slavery to triumph. Delilah was laid to rest in Saint Mary's Cemetery, where her simple headstone belies her impressive life of perseverance; it is just a small, dark gray granite block with her name and the dates of her birth and death.

Another historic Californian interred at Saint Mary's Cemetery in Oakland is **Juan Bautista Alvarado y Vallejo** (1809–1882), a Mexican colonial governor of Alta California. Born in Monterey, Monterey County, to **Juan Francisco Alvarado** (1775–1809) and **Josefa Maria Vallejo Madariaga** (1794–1836), he served as governor twice, from December 1836 to July 1837, and again from August 1839 to December 1842. A self-taught man in many ways, he was eager to learn about science and history and even "modeled" himself after George Washington. As with many Mexican and Spanish Dons, he had *hila natural* (illegitimate) children with **María Raimunda Castillo y Sinoba** (1813–1880), but he married **Maria Martina Castro Alvarado** (1814–1875) who descended from one of the oldest families of early California. Out of their many offspring, they lost two children, **Maria Alvarado** (1840–1840) and **Valentin Alvarado** (1854–1861). Then, at age twenty-two, their daughter **Maria Celinda Gabriela Alavarado** (1852–1875) passed away—just three short months before Maria Martina died. Juan Bautista passed away in 1882 and, along with his wife and children, was laid to rest at Saint Mary's Cemetery.

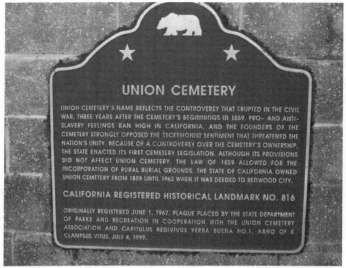

Redwood City's Union Cemetery, located in San Mateo County, was established in 1859, before the outbreak of the Civil War, but the name reflects the strong anti-secessionist point of view of the cemetery's founders.

COURTESY KIM S. HURST

Redwood City's **Union Cemetery** was the first and oldest official cemetery in San Mateo County, established in 1859. Located on Woodside Road near El Camino Real in Redwood City, San Mateo County, the land was provided by **Horace M. Hawes** (1813–1871) who owned large tracts of land in the area. Horace Hawes—teacher, lawyer, diplomat, landowner, and politician—was also the man responsible for writing the charter for San Francisco and for creating the boundaries of the City and County of San Francisco, which led to the creation of San Mateo County itself. For that, he is known as the "Father of San Mateo County."

Horace M. Hawes

Born in New York, Horace M. Hawes had a difficult childhood, being shuffled from place to place and having to buy his way out of indentured servitude at age sixteen. In spite of that, he managed to study and practice law even as he taught school. As early as 1835, Horace was an outspoken abolitionist, though not a member of the party. He married in 1846, but his wife died within a few months.

He was selected by President James K. Polk to act as the U.S. Consul to the South Sea Islands. He then chose to settle in San Francisco, where he served as district attorney and prosecuted the infamous San Francisco gang, the "Hounds." Meanwhile, he began to purchase property in and around Redwood City. The small community was going to become an important location. Redwood City at this time was overlooking the bay and it was a convenient place for shipbuilding. Hawes was as eager as anyone to invest in the area. However, when he discovered that people were burying their dead on his land, he eventually decided to donate a piece of it for a proper cemetery—which became Redwood City's historic **Union Cemetery**. Even Redwood City's Sequoia High School campus sits on what was once Horace's property. After he married **Caroline "Dolly" Combs** (1828–1895) in 1858, his health began to fail, and some suggested that perhaps he was suffering from dementia or was going insane. Reportedly, Horace grew eccentric and almost paranoid, even thinking he was being poisoned. In 1871, he died. Rather than being buried in the Union Cemetery, however—which he basically created by his earlier donations—he left instructions to be buried at **Cypress Lawn Cemetery**, in Colma, San Mateo County. In his honor, his wife also ordered a seven-foot-tall red granite memorial be built for him.

Ludwig Christian Peterson (1849–1925) was born in Denmark and left Copenhagen in the early 1870s to immigrate to America. He was a cobbler and his first stop was Philadelphia. He then moved to Chicago, where he met **Mathilda Ericson** (1847–1930). She had recently immigrated from Sweden because of the terrible famine that had persisted for two years. Mathilda and Christian were married in 1875 and then they moved to Iowa. In 1886, when Christian was thirty-seven, he moved his family to Redwood City where opportunities seemed to be everywhere. Christian opened his "boot and shoe" business and he became the leading shoe merchant in the area; readymade shoes were not available in those days, of course, so cobblers were important.

Christian and Mathilda had at least seven children. Three of their four sons, namely, **Martin Charles Peterson**, born in 1878; **Frank Emmet Peterson**, born in 1887; and **Stanley T. Peterson**, born in 1893, all died young. Martin died at age twenty-five, in 1903, of "asthenia" (a muscle weakness condition); Stanley died of TB in 1912, at age nineteen; and Frank died in 1919, at age twenty-eight. All three sons were buried in the Union Cemetery. Their daughter, **Aurora Mathilda Peterson (Grainger),** born in 1885, attended high school at Sequoia High School, which was established in in Redwood City in 1895. She then attended Stanford University, where she graduated in 1905 with a bachelor's degree in Latin. Aurora went on to teach high school, but she died in 1922, at thirty-seven, from TB. She, too, was buried in the Union Cemetery with the Peterson clan.

One memory shared by the Petersons was about the annual Redwood City parade—down Broadway from Arguello to Main Street thence down Main Street to Five Points and the Union Cemetery. The honored gentleman for the day was usually a Civil War veteran and later a Spanish American War veteran. Before the annual Memorial Day parade, everyone in the community came and cleaned up the graves and plots.

The Unknown

Although Redwood City's **Union Cemetery** was closed to new burials in 1918, administrators continued to use it as a Pauper's Field, especially during the Great Depression when people could not afford a plot. Since many of the original grave markers were made of wood, they have been lost over time. A few old-timers, though, recalled that there had been one old wooden cross with "Unknown Man Found Hanged" scratched into it, but the cross and the story have been lost or buried as well.

There are also thirty-eight graves of Yankee veterans buried in the east corner of the Union Cemetery. One of those buried here is **Jasper Peace** (unknown–1890), although he did not serve in the Civil War or in any branch of the armed services. He was given an honorary military headstone and a place in the G. A. R. section of the Union Cemetery because he was "the first man to raise our flag in San Mateo Co."

Another soldier, **Joseph Henry "Joel" Mansfield** (1850–1916), served in the U.S. Navy as a messenger boy until he was old enough to serve as a soldier. Then he enlisted as a private in Company F of the Second Massachusetts Cavalry. Although wounded three times, after the Civil War, Mansfield ended up in California, where he was appointed sheriff of San Mateo County from 1897 to 1906 and then again from 1910 to 1914. Each of Union Cemetery's

Oak Hill Memorial Park Cemetery was established in 1846, predating the California Gold Rush, and is the oldest secular cemetery still operating in California.

veterans' tombstones is "overseen" by a statue of a Northern soldier standing atop an eight-foot granite pedestal.

Oak Hill Memorial Park, located at 300 Curtner Avenue in San Jose, Santa Clara County, actually predates the California Gold Rush by one year. Established in 1847, it is the oldest secular cemetery still operating in California. A number of notable men and women have been interred here, including **Bernice C. Downing** (1878–1940) and her twin sister **Bertha C. Downing** (1878–1925). These two were the first women in California to edit and publish a newspaper, the *Santa Clara Journal*, which they inherited from the father when they were only seventeen. In addition, President Warren G. Harding appointed Bernice postmaster of Santa Clara in 1922, a position she held for more than a decade. Bernice also held several offices in associations, won a number of journalism awards and was a frequent speaker. While Bertha passed away in 1925, Bernice lived until 1940.

Paul Masson (1859–1940) was interred in his mausoleum at Oak Hill Memorial Park Cemetery in 1940. Born into a winemaking family in the Burgundy region of France, he immigrated to the United States in 1878. After settling in California, he met **Charles Lefranc** (1825–1887), another French immigrant involved in the viticulture of Santa Clara Valley. In 1892, Masson introduced his sparkling wine as "champagne" and was soon dubbed the "Champagne King of California." His Mountain Winery, located in Saratoga, Santa Clara County, is now a historic landmark. After Charles Lefranc passed away, Masson married **Louise Lefranc** (1861–1932), one of Lefranc's daughters. He also took over the Lefranc business. Louise Lefranc Masson passed away in 1932; Paul Masson passed away in 1940.

Dr. John Townsend (1783–1850) and his wife were both buried in the pioneer section of Oak Hill Memorial Park, located at 300 Curtner Avenue, San Jose, Santa Clara County. Dr. Townsend was the first fully licensed doctor in California and arrived as a member of the 1844 Stephens-Townsend-Murphy Party, the first wagon train to cross the Sierra Nevada Mountains successfully. While selecting a shortcut, their decision, unlike the decision that doomed the **Donner Party**—where forty-one people perished— might have saved lives. The route they chose would later become known as Sublette's Cutoff.

At first, Dr. Townsend served under John Sutter at Sutter's Fort in Sacramento, but he then moved to San Francisco where he became the fourth mayor of the city. Finally, in 1850, Dr. Townsend was called on to battle a cholera epidemic. Both he and his wife, **Elizabeth Louise Schallenberger Townsend** (1810–1850), tried to help as many victims as best they could— until they both fell victim to the disease and died only two days apart.

Epidemics and Pandemics in the Nineteenth Century

Epidemics and pandemics in the nineteenth century included a range of diseases such as smallpox, typhus, and yellow fever. Cholera emerged suddenly, as well, and spread worldwide in six separate pandemics. Unfortunately, medical advances did not include a thorough understanding of germs or causes of disease, and antibiotics did not appear until the mid-twentieth century. The first cholera pandemic started in 1816, lasting until 1826. It touched Southeast Asia and Central Europe. A second pandemic began in 1829, reaching Russia, Germany, Hungary, and Egypt. It hit New York and then the Pacific coast in 1834. In New York, it was noted, "On a Sunday in July 1832, a fearful and somber crowd of New Yorkers gathered in City Hall Park for more bad news. The epidemic of cholera, cause unknown and prognosis dire, had reached its peak." Former president James K. Polk died of it, as did more than 4,000 people in St. Louis and 3,000 in New Orleans.

A third pandemic broke loose in 1846 and lasted until 1860. In 1849, Ireland—having already gone through the infamous potato famine—lost almost as many lives from cholera as from the famine. It then spread to immigrants traveling to America and in particular, New York City. Cholera also traveled along the California, Oregon, and Mormon Trails in the years from 1849 to 1855, claiming somewhere between 6,000 to 12,000 lives. In Chicago, an outbreak in 1854 claimed about 3,500 people—or 5.5 percent of the population. Another wave from 1866 to 1873 killed about 50,000 Americans, and again, in the 1870s, it spread from New Orleans up the Mississippi River. In a fifth cholera epidemic, from 1881 to 1896, more than 250,000 people died in Europe and 50,000 died in the Americas. Meanwhile, thousands of California's indigenous people died from cholera. They were helpless in fighting it.

Smallpox killed more than 400,000 Europeans annually during the nineteenth century, and over 300–500 million in the twentieth century. In fact, one-third of all blindness was caused by smallpox during the Victorian Era. Most terrible, 80 percent of all children infected with smallpox died, while smallpox decimated many Native American tribes. In fact, it is difficult to even calculate the millions of individuals across the nation who died from smallpox.

Typhus, which comes from the lice from the fleas on rats, was also a terrible plague. In fact, during Napoleon's retreat from Moscow, in 1812, more French soldiers died of typhus than were killed by the Russians. In the United States, typhus spread through Baltimore, Memphis, and Washington, DC, and following the Civil War, from 1865 to 1873.

Another pioneer who was laid to rest at Oak Hill Memorial Park was **William Henry Eddy** (1817–1859) who was one of the forty-five individuals who survived the horrific tragedy of the **Donner Party**, but was also one of its heroes. As the most experienced hunter, he was able to secure what meat there was and build a cabin up against the rocks for a few of the families, including his own. Like several individuals, he joined the "hopeful" rescue party, leaving behind a chunk of bear meat for his wife and children. On the trek, however, he discovered that his wife had hidden half a pound of the meat in *his* pack. Later he declared it saved his life. Sadly, however, his wife, **Eleanor Priscilla Eddy** (1821–1847) and their two children—**James** (1843–1847) and **Margaret** (1845–1847)—perished before her husband and help returned. Eleanor was twenty-five; James was three; and Margaret was a year old. As recorded in Patrick Breen's diary from Donner Lake, "February 5, 1847, Eddy's child died last night; on the 6th, Mrs. Eddy very weak; on the 8th, Mrs. Eddy died on the night of the 7th; and on February 9, John went down today to bury Mrs. Eddy and child."

Twelve years later, inscribed on William Henry Eddy's grave-stone was this tribute: "He led the forlorn HOPE/of the **Donner Party** / Dedicated Memorial Day / 1949 / By the Ancient & Honor-able/Order of the E Clampus Vitus."

One extremely intriguing Santa Cruz pioneer was the former slave, **Dave Boffman** (*c.* 1808–1893). He was born on the Baughman Plantation in Kentucky—his parentage never revealed. In 1837, he was "married" to a sixteen-year-old slave girl, Mathilda. They had six children in the next ten years—three boys and three girls. When Dave's old master Baughman passed away, his son **Newt Baughman** became the new master. Young and restless, when news of California's

William Henry Eddy's grave marker is an oblong stone with a unique medallion; its inscription pays tribute to Eddy's heroism in rescuing members of the **Donner Party**.

gold rush reached them, Newt decided he and his family would move west. He took Dave and his family along. They made it to Clinton County, Missouri, where Newt purchased a farm.

Still restless, however, Baughman decided to leave his wife and child behind, and in order to fund his trip to California, he sold three of Dave's children to a slave buyer from the South. Newt then asked Dave to go with him, promising to give him an opportunity to buy his freedom. Dave said yes; no doubt, he hoped he could afford to eventually purchase his family's freedom.

But the trip for any slave or former slave was dangerous. Slave hunters were everywhere, and—as it happened—Dave had to escape into the river to outmaneuver slavers and their hounds twice on the journey. The two men were also attacked by the Pawnee, and Dave was captured in the melee. Taken into the Indian camp, the people found him quite appealing, touching his skin as if for good luck. Unafraid of him, they allowed him substantial freedom, so it was not hard for him to escape. Newt and Dave somehow met up again at Fort Laramie where they joined a wagon train headed west.

Uncle Dave's Story Continues

Once in California, Newt and Dave began panning for gold, and Dave collected enough to finally buy his freedom—$1,000. A free man at last, he was determined to earn enough money to purchase his family's freedom so he set out on his own. Soon he met a man headed to Santa Cruz County to log redwoods. They partnered up, and spent the rest of the year milling enough timber to fill a schooner. Unfortunately, the entire load was lost in a storm, leaving both

---

men broke, but Dave was not about to give up. He went to work at a lumber mill and earned enough to set up a little farm. He also took on a partner, a German immigrant named Seigmann. One day, Seigmann found an unbranded colt that he decided to catch and trade off. Dave cautioned against it, but Seigmann traded the colt to stock trader Martin Kinsley for a mare and her foal. As luck would have it, the sheriff and trader Kinsley showed up days later. The colt belonged to the sheriff, and, suddenly, he reminded them that since the two men had committed a crime they could go to prison, unless they paid up.

Dave, knowing he would not be allowed to testify in court, and though he had nothing to do with the trade, agreed to pay up. When all was said and done, however, he was swindled out of much more. In fact, to satisfy the demands and a court's order, Dave had to sell his property, including his stock. Still, Dave Boffman pressed on. He went to work as a day laborer and met **Elihu Anthony** (1818–1905), considered to be a founding father of Santa Cruz, also a merchant and Methodist minister who settled in Santa Cruz in 1848. The two men became good friends. Elihu even helped Dave obtain eighty acres. But here, in the small cabin he built, is where Dave Boffman lived for the next thirty years. Though he still hoped desperately to free his family, he could never earn more than just enough to live on. He walked everywhere, never riding the old mare he had bought and never wearing a pair of shoes. He became friends with many of the outcasts who became outlaws, even providing them shelter when they were on the run. His hair and beard turned white, and the children in town came to know him as Uncle Dave, and they loved his stories.

Meanwhile Elihu continued to search for Dave's family, so when he located a granddaughter—**Annie E. Drisdom** (1863–1926)—in northern California's Colusa County, Elihu purchased her a train ticket. From Annie, Dave learned that Mathilda had moved to Kansas and remarried, thinking Dave had died, and only one of his children still lived, a son, George, who had been an infant when Dave left home. Annie stayed with Dave for six months, but she finally had to leave. He was alone, except for an old dog, "Watch." Then, one night, Dave's cabin burned down after a fire escaped the fireplace, so he moved in with Elihu and his wife. He lived with them until he was senile and had to be admitted to Agnew Hospital. In September 1893, Dave Boffman died in his sleep. He was buried in Elihu Anthony's family plot at the **Santa Cruz Memorial Cemetery**, located at 1927 Ocean St. Ext. Santa Cruz, Santa Cruz County.

After his passing, the *Santa Cruz Sentinel* wrote about **Uncle Dave** Boffman, recalling a day "thirty years earlier when we saw Uncle Dave carrying on his back a heavy plow from a Santa Cruz blacksmith shop to his farm, a distance of fully eight miles, performing this task to save the strain on his old horse." And for many months, Dave's old dog—having run away from Elihu's place—lay in the "burnt out shell of a cabin, waiting for his master."

A land grant that included Soquel and much of today's Capitola plus a portion of Monterey Bay Heights and all of New Brighton Beach State Park, and more, was awarded to **Maria Martina Castro Lodge** (1807–1890), who came from a long line of elites, beginning with her grandfather, Joaquin Isidro Castro, who had accompanied the de Anza expedition in 1776. However, Martina became trapped between two worlds. Her first marriage ended when her husband died, leaving her with four children. She married a second time in 1831 to Michael Lodge, and it was he who actually pressed Martina to apply for the initial grant, and as time passed, he pressed her to petition the Mexican government for more. Lodge also pressed for a sawmill to be built along Soquel Creek because of the amount of timber available, so he hired two immigrants to build the mill: John Hames and John Daubenbiss.

Maria Martina Castro Lodge

As with so many men, the gold rush immediately drew **Michael Lodge** to seek a new opportunity. Taking **Maria Martina** and his family with him, he headed to Mokelumne Hill. The dream soon turned to despair when the three youngest Lodge children died from typhoid fever. Michael sent Maria Martina and the remaining children home, and either Michael died, as well—from fever or by accident or foul play—but he never returned to his home in Soquel. Totally at a loss, Maria Martina—who could neither read nor write English or Spanish—was vulnerable in matters of finance and managing the ranch, so she married a third time, a French-Canadian Louis Depreaux. Only it wasn't long before her new husband and her sons-in-law began to manipulate her and press for a division of her ranch. She was coerced into signing, or accepting, the breaking apart of her estate and the disposal of other property as well. In the end, Maria Martina became so emotionally unstable and defeated that she was forced to turn to her daughters, a son, and her granddaughters for her care. She died in 1890 and was interred in the **Old Holy Cross Cemetery**, at 2271 Seventh Avenue, Santa Cruz, Santa Cruz County.

John Daubenbiss (1816–1896) was an important Soquel pioneer who immigrated to America from Bavaria, Germany, at age nineteen. In 1841, he journeyed west to Oregon then traveled south to Sacramento, and finally ended up at Mission Santa Cruz. Daubenbiss partnered with John Hames (and, for a time, they hired out to Maria Martina's husband). The pair then managed to purchase Rancho del Rodeo, a 1,668-acre Mexican land grant, which stretched from the mountains to Monterey Bay.

John Daubenbiss Establishes Himself

Early in 1846, Daubenbiss married **Sarah Catherine Lard** (1829–1891), whose family had traveled with the ill-fated **Donner Party**, but thankfully parted company before reaching the

Sarah Catherine Lard Daubenbiss passed away only a few years before her husband John. Sadly she outlived six of her eleven children.

snow-packed Sierras. Daubenbiss and his wife eventually had eleven children, but six of them tragically passed away before reaching adulthood. He also served in John Fremont's battalion during the **Mexican American War**, and he was with Commodore Sloat when the Americans raised the flag at Monterey in 1846. On September 9, 1850, it was Daubenbiss who was selected to raise the flag and read California's new state constitution in Santa Cruz.

As an entrepreneur, Daubenbiss built a flourmill in Santa Clara, actually the first one to be built in California. He built a second one at Soquel and then constructed California's first sawmill. The wharf at San Francisco was built from the lumber milled at his sawmill in Soquel. He also raised 100 head of cattle he purchased from General Vallejo. At John Daubenbiss's funeral, in 1895, it was written, "At the cemetery, Naval Battalion Fourth Gun Division and Veterans of the Mexican War fired a farewell salute and sounded taps over the grave of him who will ever be fresh in the hearts of the people of Santa Cruz county. Thus was laid to rest one of the noblest of his kind, one who left a grand impression upon the state and the Pacific coast."

Charles Henry McKiernan (1825–1892), also known as **"Mountain Charlie,"** was the first white settler in the Santa Cruz Mountains and was laid to rest in the **Oak Hill Memorial Park** at 300 Curtner Avenue, San Jose, Santa Clara County. After sailing into the San Francisco Bay in 1849, he immediately headed to the northern mines of California, but he soon decided to put his money to work by purchasing a pack train. He hauled freight between Trinidad on the coast and the Trinity mines around Weaverville, and though his first trip was profitable, which allowed him to purchase more mules, his second trip was not. Charles's animals were stampeded by a band of Indians, and later he claimed he was lucky to escape.

With a partner named Page, McKiernan set out for the Santa Cruz Mountains, following the myriad Indian trails through the rugged country. Here he finally found a place to settle. Here he established his camp—at the highest peak where a plaque now marks the site of his first cabin. After building his cabin and corrals, all from redwood, he purchased sheep. Unfortunately, the "Grizzy" (*sic*), as well as mountain lions, coyote, and eagles, found the sheep easy prey. Disgusted, he purchased some cattle and also hunted deer since they were easy to track and easy to trade and sell.

Mountain Man McKiernan

McKiernan's mountain adventures soon spawned his reputation as a mountain man—including one event when he faced a she-grizzly in 1851. Along with a man known as Taylor, McKiernan spotted a grizzly with two cubs. Trying to get into position to take a shot, he suddenly turned and came face to face with another enormous bear standing six feet away, her immense paws reaching for him. He fired and Taylor fired, too, but the grizzly was able to knock McKiernan's gun away and grab him, crushing his skull and tossing him aside. It was Taylor's dog that distracted the she-bear and saved McKiernan's life.

When Taylor got McKiernan home, a doctor from San Jose was able to create "a silver plate out of two Mexican half dollars to fit in the broken portion of his skull, where the bear had bitten through the frontal bone and the top of his skull over his left eye." Unfortunately, after three weeks, the plate corroded and had to be replaced. For two years afterward, McKiernan suffered from headaches and pain. Then a Dr. Spencer, from Redwood City, reopened the wound and removed a lock of hair! After this, though McKiernan was disfigured, the headaches and discomfort disappeared. To hide his appearance, he wore a hat pulled down over his left eye for the rest of his life.

McKiernan lived in his mountains undisturbed for a couple of years, accumulating more than 3,000 acres of redwood forest. He established a lumber mill and lumberyards in San Jose where he sold his redwood lumber. In 1862, he married **Barbara Berricke Kelly**, the woman who served as his nurse after his ill-fated run in with the grizzly. Together they had seven children, although they lost a son at age nine in a shooting accident. Their six remaining children grew to become prominent citizens of the area.

In the 1870s, McKiernan and Barbara opened a stage stop, known as the Halfway House or Station Ranch. They were successful until the railroad put them out of business.

In 1884, the couple retired to San Jose, and by 1890, McKiernan had become ill with some kind of stomach ailment. He died on January 18, 1892, and was interred at Oak Hill Memorial Park.

Stephen Hobson III (1800–1885) was also buried in Oak Hill Memorial Park, but he was not the first Hobson to migrate to California. **David Hobson** (1822–1916), the second of the six children born to Stephen and his first wife **Mary E. Langensee** (1847–1912), was among the first Quakers to settle in the Santa Clara Valley. David and his brother **Jesse Hobson** (1826–1879) are also credited with building the first Friends church in San Jose. Later Jesse Hobson became the first Quaker politician in San Jose.

Hobson Family

David Hobson crossed the plains with a younger brother, **Stephen IV** (1826–1896), and an uncle, arriving in Sacramento in October 1850. Stephen IV then returned home to North Carolina to guide the next wagon train west. **Alfred David Hobson** (1825–1898) also crossed the plains, while **George Hobson** (1823–1889) and his wife had made the trek in 1846. George struck gold along the Feather and American Rivers, and "from one pocket alone, (he) washed out $1,000 in three days."

David used his gold to purchase acreage and plant fruit trees. While some suggested it might be a losing effort, David wrote, "In Feb. 1860, I planted the first fruit trees on this place . . . and after eighteen years rolled by, in 1875, my apricots sold in San Francisco at nine cents a pound per box, and after paying the expenses for picking, shipping and selling, I had thirty dollars per tree net cash for six of these trees."

Stephen Hobson III outlived three of his wives. In 1872, he left North Carolina with his fourth wife, Mary Calloway, and moved to California—just as his sons and nephews had done twenty years earlier. Sadly Stephen passed away almost immediately after arriving in California and was interred at Oak Hill, leaving his wife Mary and their many children without a father. It was David Hobson and his wife who stepped in to help Mary raise the youngest of his half-siblings, although they had five children themselves. Tragically, in 1888, they lost three of them in seven days to one of the epidemics that came too frequently— most likely diphtheria or cholera. They were: **Charles Stephen Hobson** (1879–1888), age nine years; **Jesse Valentine Hobson** (1881–1888), age seven years; and **Ruth Hobson** (1888–1888), age nine months old.

What made the older Stephen Hobson III's "headstone" truly unique, however, is that years after his death, circa 1926, the youngest of his eighteen children, **Evan Hobson** (unknown), shipped out the *1,500-pound* millstone Stephen had used for fifty years in his occupation as a miller in Yadkin County, North Carolina. It stands upright, looking much like a giant cement tractor tire, with Stephen's name written across one side. It's a tribute not only to the years of milling that Stephen worked at so hard, but it also speaks to the respect his son felt for him in sending such a monstrous item across country. Oak Hill Memorial Park has no fewer than fifty-two Hobsons interred there.

Mission City Memorial Park, also known as the **Santa Clara Cemetery** and/or the **Santa Clara City Cemetery**, is located on 420 N. Winchester Blvd. in Santa Clara, Santa Clara County. Its records go back to 1864 and today it has over 22,000 memorials interred within its thirty acres. It is important to note that this cemetery is not the same as the **Santa Clara Mission Cemetery**, which is only a block or two away.

Buried in Santa Clara County's Mission City Memorial Park was **Harry Love** (1810–1868) who is considered a folk hero to many. He was head of the first California Rangers, a law enforcement agency. Born in Vermont, he ended up in Texas where he joined the Texas Rangers then went on to fight in the **Mexican American War** of 1846–1848. He reportedly worked as an army scout and express rider and even led an expedition up the Rio Grande River. He eventually moved to California during the gold rush but took a job as deputy sheriff in Santa Barbara instead of mining for gold. As it turned out,

Harry became a bounty hunter and went after three men who had possibly robbed and killed young **Allen B. Ruddle** (1852–1869), an unarmed young man, perhaps sixteen or seventeen, traveling to Stockton. After tracking the three men, Love and a partner captured one of the three outlaws—Pedro Gonzalez, a member of **Joaquin Murrieta's** (1829–1853) gang. The gang, also known as the "**Five Joaquins Gang**," supposedly stole more than $100,000 in gold in the Mother Lode of the Sierra Nevada Mountains. Some reports suggest the gang killed up to twenty-eight Chinese and thirteen whites in the course of their years on the run, while others felt that Murrieta had reason to seek revenge after his wife was ravaged and his livelihood destroyed. Nevertheless, in July 1853, a group of California State Rangers, led by Captain Love, cornered a gang of men, and a showdown took place. Two gang members were killed, including "Three-Fingered Jack" and supposedly Joaquin Murrieta. To this day, however, Murrieta's death has been disputed. A plaque marks the spot where Murrieta was possibly killed.

Harry Love married **Mary Amanda McSwain Bennett** (1803–1868) of Santa Clara in 1854. She was six years older than Harry and had been widowed, circa 1849. When Harry Love, the "Black Knight of Zayante," passed away, he was buried in Mission City Memorial Park, a large, sleek black granite dedication stone marking his grave.

Sunrise Memorial Cemetery is located at 2201 Sacramento S, in Vallejo, Solano County. One man interred there is **William S. Bond** (1839–1892) who served in the Union Navy during the Civil War. He received the Congressional **Medal of Honor** for his bravery when the sloop-of-war on which he was serving, the USS *Kearsarge,* destroyed the Confederate Navy's CSS *Alabama* off the coast of Cherbourg, France, in June 1864. Bond's citation reads, "Bond exhibited marked coolness and good conduct and was highly recommended for his gallantry under fire by his divisional officer." He was one of seventeen on the USS *Kearsarge* to be awarded the Medal of Honor. Bond passed away in 1892 and was interred in the Sunrise Memorial Cemetery in Solano County.

Another veteran deserving recognition who was laid to rest in the Sunrise Memorial Cemetery in 1923 was **Samuel Brown** (1833–1923). Born in Georgia, Samuel was a freed slave who joined the Union Army the day before General Lee surrendered, serving briefly with the 137th Colored Infantry Regiment. In 1913, he went to California where several of his children already lived. He lived to age ninety and passed away in December 1923. At his funeral, he was recognized as both a Civil War Veteran and as a member of the G. A. R. Unfortunately, Samuel's headstone indicated that he had served in the Confederate Army, and the error was not realized until 2009 when a cemetery employee brought it to the attention of the Sons of Union Veterans of the Civil War. The Department of Veteran Affairs provided a corrected headstone and organized a dedication ceremony provided by members of the Sons of Union Veterans of the Civil War and the Auxiliary to the Sons of Union Veterans of the Civil War.

Hills of Eternity Memorial Park at 1301 El Camino Real, in Colma, San Mateo County, is probably best known for the fact that

Wyatt Earp (1848–1929) is interred here. Born in Illinois, he was the third of five sons born to Nicholas and his second wife, Virginia Ann Cooksey Earp. While Wyatt Berry Stapp Earp grew up working on the family farm in Iowa, he wanted very much to follow after his brothers, James and Virgil, as well as his half-brother Newton, who had enlisted in the Union Army. Near the end of the war, the family moved to San Bernardino, California. In 1868, they moved to Lamar, Missouri. There, in Missouri, Wyatt accepted the job as constable after his father resigned. In 1870, he married **Urilla Sutherland** (1849–1870), but she died of typhoid fever within the year, as did their unborn child.

Devastated and bitter, Wyatt roamed the West, working as a buffalo hunter and stagecoach driver—but spending most of his time in saloons, brothels, and gambling houses, even stealing horses (or some suggest)—until he ended up on the police force in Wichita, Kansas (it's been noted that many lawmen started out as outlaws or renegades). That led to his becoming the marshal of Dodge City, the frontier city known as the "Wickedest little city in the West." It was here, too, that Wyatt met Doc Holiday. He also married again in 1878, to a former prostitute, **Celia Ann "Mattie" Blaylock** (1850–1888), but that marriage soon failed.

Wyatt moved to Tombstone along with most of the Earp family and where brother Virgil was working as town marshal. Soon a feud developed between Wyatt and Ike Clanton, and it eventually led to the famous, but controversial shootout at the OK Corral. Though Doc Holliday, Morgan, and Virgil Earp were injured, Billy Clanton and the McLaurys were killed, and the Earps were arrested for murder, but later acquitted. The killings fueled the feud, however, and Virgil lost the use of his arm in an ambush, and brother Morgan was murdered.

After Wyatt married **Josephine Sarah Marcus** (1861–1944) in 1882, the pair moved first to San Diego then to Nome, Alaska, and finally to Tonopah, Nevada. Returning to California, Wyatt died in 1929 in Los Angeles at age eighty-one. He was cremated and taken to Colma and interred in the Jewish Hills of Eternity Cemetery. Josie passed away in 1944, and today she and Wyatt share a large upright black headstone, elegantly etched in white. At the bottom of the stone

General Mariano Guadalupe Vallejo served as commander of the Presidio of San Francisco, and also laid out the town of Sonoma and participated in the Bear Flag Revolt. He was interred in a tomb in the Mountain Cemetery in Sonoma in 1890.

under their names, it is written: "That nothing's so sacred as honor, and nothing so loyal as love!"

Edward Frisbee (1826–1908), son of Eleazer Frisbee and Cynthia Cornell of New York, died of a heart condition in 1908 and was buried in the **Carquinez Cemetery** in Vallejo, Solano County. He arrived in California in 1855 and purchased the Bella Vista Ranch near Napa, where he soon became an important breeder of cattle. He even contracted to bring a shipload of purebred stock via the Horn in order to raise the quality of his herd. After ranching in Napa for twenty years, Edward purchased 26,000 acres from James Ben Haggin in Shasta County. The property was so vast it included much of what is today's Redding and Anderson. Edward was married twice. From these unions, there were thirteen children, although only eleven survived their father's death. More famous than Edward Frisbee was his brother, **General John Baptist "Juan Baptista" Frisbie** (1823–1909). Although not buried in California, John Baptist traveled to California in 1847 while serving in the First Regiment of New York Volunteers. Though he was a lawyer, he became a merchant, opening the first store in Napa. He married **Epifania "Fanny" Vallejo** in 1850, and in 1851, founded the city of Vallejo in Solano County—naming it after his father-in-law, **General Mariano Guadalupe Vallejo** (1807–1890).

A Union soldier overlooks the veteran graves in San Mateo County's Redwood City Union Cemetery.

CHAPTER 9

NORTH COAST REGION

Until the mid-1800s, ten major tribes lived along the northern California coast, including major tribes like the *Yurok, Tolowa, Hupa, Karuk*, and *Chilula*. The coastal villages of the Yurok were generally built at the mouth of a stream or on a lagoon; the Chilulas lived inland where their lands started near the Tall Trees of Redwood Creek and included parts of the Bald Hills; and the Hupa (aka Hoopa) lived on the big "Y"—the Trinity River and above, where it flows into the Klamath River. Though they spoke different languages, these tribes all shared a number of similar cultural traits. The area came under assault as miners and settlers, and then lumbermen, moved into the region. The redwoods became a rich source of timber that, of course, changed the traditional lives of these people. Ships traveled the coastline as the timber industry and towns were established up and down the northern California coast.

With the challenging, rocky coastline, however, shipwrecks occasionally occurred, many of them disastrous. One tragic wreck occurred off Point St. George, near Crescent City, Del Norte County,

The James B. and Ellen Murphy McDonald Mausoleum at the Marysville Cemetery, Yuba County, stands out with its bright red door.

Situated along the shoreline of Crescent City, the memorial to the *Brother Jonathan* includes a monument and a flag around which the graves of some of those who were recovered from the shipwreck are interred.

in 1865. The wreck of the paddle mail steamer *Brother Jonathan* was the deadliest Pacific shipwreck up to that time. It became memorialized with the construction of the **Brother Jonathan Cemetery** in Crescent City.

A dedication plaque was erected for the 225 who lost their lives when the steamer went down in a violent storm on July 30, 1865.

As it struggled to reach the harbor, it struck an uncharted reef. Only nineteen people survived. In addition to the plaque, the graves of a number of recovered victims and their families encircle a flagpole; the park-like setting makes it an attractive place to linger. The ocean is in sight, just across a circular roadway. Those who were never recovered were "buried" by the sea. The bronze memorial plaque reads: "Brother Jonathan Cemetery—This memorial is dedicated to those who lost their lives in the wreck of the Pacific Mail steamer Brother Jonathan at point St. George's Reef, July 30, 1865. California Registered Historical Landmark No. 541. Plaque placed by the California State Park Commission in cooperation with the Del Norte Historical Society, October 20, 1960."

Lost at Sea

The following list of individuals includes some of those whose bodies *were* recovered and interred at the Brother Jonathan Cemetery in Crescent City: **George Church** (unknown–1865) was an African American male who perished in the wreck. **Private Oscar F. Leach** (unknown–1865) who had enlisted as a private at Sacramento and was mustered into Company D, Second California Cavalry in the Civil War. At the time of the wreck, he was working as an orderly to Brigadier General George Wright, who also perished in the wreck along with Mrs. (Margaret) Wright, Major Ellery W. Eddy, Lieutenant Edward D. Waite, and Captain Samuel De Wolfe, captain of the steamer.

Mary Berry (unknown–1865) was a single woman whose body eventually washed up to shore at Eureka, south of Crescent City. **Dwight Crandall** (1827–1865) was a hotel proprietor and stageline operator who also served as a state senator from Amador County and as a deputy naval officer in San Francisco. **A. Drawlson** (unknown–1865) was, according to the coroner's report:

> [Body No. 26] a white man, supposed from a diary found on his person to be A. Drawlson, and left Springfield, June 19, 1865, and sailed New York on steamer Ocean Queen, July 1st, landed in San Francisco July 25th, had on his person a gold watch, No.14,755, hunting case, etc.; he was about five feet ten inches in height, medium stature, dark brown hair, mustache and whiskers, no hair under his chin, from thirty to forty years old, plain gold ring on his finger, gold pen in a silver case.

Albert Dyer (unknown–1865) was a freight clerk and crew member of the steamer. **Daniel C. Rowell** (1827–1865) was a miller, originally from England, whose entire family, including his wife **Polina (Buell) Rowell** (1843–1865), and four children, including Elias, age eight, Henry, age seven, and Charles, age two, all perished. The children's bodies were never recovered. **Rosanna "Rose" Hughes Keenan** (1831–1865), married to John C. Keenan, was returning to Victoria, Vancouver's Island, where her husband was working at their saloon and restaurant. She had gone to Sacramento to hire seven women to work as serving staff. When the steamer crashed, she had been seasick so she was in her cabin, and she did "make it into the water with two life preservers when she was hit on the head by a plank or lifeboat and drowned. . . . Two of the women accompanying her made it to safety in a lifeboat. One, a mother named Mrs. Stott, had her little son with her. The other, Elizabeth Wild, was a young woman who had been hired as a nurse by Mrs. Keenan, and was also going to Victoria to work as a serving girl. The other five women accompanying Mrs. Keenan drowned." Mrs. Keenan was about thirty-three years old. **Charles Law** (unknown–1865) was a crew member (cook). **Izza L. Chrisman Logan** (1827–1865), daughter of Joel D. and Mary (Sprowl) Chrisman, with her husband, **William Logan** (1825–1865), also perished. They had been in San Francisco, seeking medical attention for Mrs. Logan. William's body was never recovered. **Mrs. Alzina (Comstock) Stone** (1841–1865), only twenty-three years old, along with her husband **Albert A. Stone** (1837–1865) and their twenty-one-month-old son **Charles Stone** (1863–1865) all perished. Her body was later recovered. Albert's brother **Bowen H. Stone** (1835–1865) and his second wife **Martha A. (Daniels) Stone** (1842–1865), and a child by Bowen's first marriage, **Lillian A. Stone** (1858–1865), aged six or seven, also drowned. Bowen and Martha's bodies were later recovered.

Horace Gasquet (1828?–1896) traveled to Crescent City in Del Norte County in 1855 to mine for gold. He purchased 320 acres and established a settlement he called Gasquet, with a hotel, bar, barn, blacksmith's shop and store. In 1860, he finished a mule trail into the interior between California and Oregon, and he built a second road to Happy Camp on the Klamath River. The "Gasquet Toll Road" was built by Chinese American workers and was completed in 1886. Gasquet also established a second store at Waldo, Oregon.

"Madame (Pesnel) Gasquet," (1812–1889) came from France with her husband, Mr. Fournier, to open a restaurant in Crescent City. When she returned to Gasquet alone sometime later, she and Gasquet became companions. She was well known as a wonderful cook and became quite popular with the community. After her health failed, Madame Gasquet was buried in a private cemetery called French Hill Cemetery, in Gasquet. The lane leading to the woodsy cemetery site curves through the trees and suddenly opens up to a small clearing.

Three separate graves, each one surrounded by white picket fences make up the French Hill Cemetery. Madame Gasquet's gravesite is the largest and her headstone leans against the back of the fence. It reads: "Here rests Madame Madeleine Gasquet, nee Pesnel, born at Brie,

Madame Gasquet requested that she be buried under French "soil," so Horace Gasquet ordered soil to be delivered from France, which he then sprinkled over her grave.

Depr'r of Manche, France/ Died at Gasquet, Nov. 27, 1889/Aged 77 years." A simple white cross sits above the gate. A second gravesite belongs to **Michael O'Meara** (1833–1874), "Born in Ireland/Murdered in Happy Camp, Cal/ May 18, 1874/ Age 40 years." The third gravesite belongs to **Paul Moller** (1817–1896), from Missouri, but his tombstone is missing.

Horace Gasquet was laid to rest in **Saint Joseph's Catholic Cemetery**, located on Cemetery Road in Crescent City, Del Norte County, in the 'Whisper Pine Green' plot—after being moved from the **Holy Cross Cemetery** located at 1500 Old Mission Road, in Colma, San Mateo County. Many have wondered why he was not buried with Madame Gasquet.

In Hoopa, **Ada Strothers Nelson** (1889–1946), daughter of Michael Strothers and Jessie Hostler, and the wife of **George William Nelson** (1884–1986), passed away in the hospital and was laid to rest in the **Nelson Family Cemetery** in Hoopa, Humboldt County. Born and raised in Hoopa, she and George and their family lived near the village of *Takimildin*. Ada had been a member of the Hoopa Presbyterian Church, and she'd helped her husband on their Nelson Dairy Farm and Ranch in Hostler Field. According to her daughter **Muriel Adale "Diddie" Nelson Jackson** (1920–2017), "All six of the Nelson children participated in helping supply milk to the Old Indian Hospital and the Boarding School." **George William Nelson**, the son of Daniel Nelson and Annie Kane and the grandson of *E-Ne-Nuck*, had attended the boarding school in Hoopa and then was transferred to the Chemawa Indian School in

Salem, Oregon. When he returned to his homeland, he married Ada Strothers in 1912.

George was enterprising and industrious, from driving wild horses into California and breaking them for fifty cents each, to hauling freight by wagon and working in the woods, to blacksmithing and carrying mail on horseback, to farming and developing the first dairy. He continued to fall trees until he was eighty-plus years old. He even built three houses for his family. He passed away at the age of 102 and was laid to rest in **Willow Creek Cemetery** in Willow Creek, Humboldt County.

In 1858, Hydesville, in Humboldt County, sprang up along the Van Duzen Fork of the Eel River, named after Mr. Hyde who had owned the land where the town now stands. **Hydesville Cemetery** is located off of the Redwood Highway, a small cemetery with fewer than 400 graves. Unfortunately, the graveyard has deteriorated over the decades. One who was laid to rest here was **Private Jacob Alfred Baird** (1840–1908) who was born in Lawrence County, Illinois. He married **Ellen Roselthia Geitner** in 1861 and joined the Union Army in 1863. After mustering out, he and his wife moved west to California where he worked at a number of jobs—as farmer, carpenter, and water agent. He passed away at age sixty-seven in Rohnerville, Humboldt County, and was buried in the Hydesville Cemetery.

Fannie Ellen Nelson Baxter (1866–1944), who was also buried in the lonely Hydesville Cemetery, was an industrious woman who took on more than most people in one lifetime. She was born in Pennsylvania and came west with her brother, sisters, and mother after her father perished in a snowstorm in Kansas. At sixteen, she married **James Franklin "Frank" Baxter** (1858–1927) and gave birth to six sons, including **Frank Alonzo "Little Nibsey"** (1891–1893), who died after choking on a piece of food. On his headstone it was written, "He shall not return to me but I shall go to him." While James ran a general store, pool and card hall in Carlotta, Fannie raised not only her five sons but also her husband's younger siblings after his father's death, and her son Lyle's three children. In addition, she cooked for local loggers as a side job. James passed away in 1927; Fannie passed in 1944, one year after her son **Arlington Levi Baxter** (1885–1943) died on Christmas Day 1943. Except for one son, Delwin Arthur, who was buried in **Sunset Memorial Park** in Eureka, Fannie and her family were all buried in the Baxter family plot at the Hydesville Cemetery.

An interesting pioneer cemetery in Mendocino County is **Evergreen Cemetery.** Located along Highway 1 at Mt. View Road, it is sheltered by the familiar coastal eucalyptus trees—an overgrown, forgotten lane runs through the middle of it and it's clearly a cemetery rarely visited except, perhaps, by family or tourists who stumble across it. It has a forgotten air, although with the heavy coastal climate, it feels almost other worldly. One intriguing spire monument belongs to the Allen family. On each side of the four-sided tombstone is a family member's name: **Vesta P. Allen** (1839–1901), **Reuben M. Allen** (1835–1901), **George W. Allen** (1859–1883), and **Margie G. Allen** (1870–1888). Under Vesta's name is the statement, "Wife to Reuben Allen" and the epitaph, "In death they were not divided."

El Dorado County has at least 100 pioneer cemeteries. As the heart of the gold country, it is hard to calculate how many miners and early settlers—let alone Native Americans of the region—lay beneath the soil here without recognition. It's been suggested that 10,000 individuals died here in the fifty years following the initial rush to gold. Located in Coloma, at the site of James Marshall's gold discovery, the **Pioneer Cemetery** is one of those step-back-in-time cemeteries. It fascinates with its random collection of terraced levels and headstones, some fallen, some falling, many indecipherable. The first known interments took place in 1849, and roughly 600 individuals have been interred here, although 200 or 300 graves lack any kind of marker. Over time this cemetery has been called by various names—**Sutter Mill Cemetery**, **Coloma Protestant Cemetery**, and **Vineyard Cemetery**. Today it is part of the **Marshall Gold Discovery State Park**.

Rufus Morgan Burgess (1827–1900) is buried in Coloma's Pioneer Cemetery. He and his parents were slaves in Tennessee. They crossed the plains with their owners in 1850, but when they arrived in California, they were granted their freedom. Although Rufus tried mining, he gave it up to purchase some farmland where he planted a variety of fruit trees. He also worked as a blacksmith, morning to night, or as long as a job required. His shop was located where today's Grange Hall sits in Coloma. He passed away unexpectedly at seventy-two and was survived by his wife, **Josephine P. Burris Monroe** (1862–1921), and three young children. According to one account, "The oldsters can still hear the music of that anvil, busy all day and every day, except Sundays."

One of the most fascinating individuals interred in Coloma's Pioneer Cemetery is **Ellen "Texas Ellen" Wilson** (1822–1855). Her headstone is small, almost inconsequential, until you read the epitaph: "Shot and died on March 14, 1855 in Coloma. Proprietor of the 'Lone Star of Texas' (a house of ill-fame)." Pennies, nickels, and dimes line the small metal plaque that's been riveted to a flat stone, indicating, no doubt, the people who have stopped to pay respects. But the story of Texas Ellen's last day is equally as tantalizing. According to the March 24, 1855, issue of *Empire County Argus*:

On Friday night, 16th inst., a row occurred among three or four vagabonds, in this place, when knives and pistols were drawn and several shots fired; one of which took effect in the breast of Ellen Wilson. . . . A coroner's inquest was held, and the jury returned a verdict that "deceased was killed, by a host from a pistol in the hands of some person to the jury unknown." The funeral of Ellen took place on Sabbath last. A sermon was preached on the occasion, and a number of persons followed her remains to the grave.

Other details give her story even more allure. Apparently, the man who fired the gun was, in fact, infatuated with her and grew jealous when he saw her dancing with another man. Furious, he pulled out his gun and fired through the window, killing Ellen by mistake. He fled, never to be found. Another interesting note is that while normally prostitutes were forbidden to be buried in consecrated ground,

Texas Ellen's gravestone is simple but frequented regularly as noted by the coins and trinkets that are left in tribute to her pioneering spirit.

the people of Coloma were beholden to Ellen because of "her many generosities and kindnesses during the cholera and smallpox epidemics of 1852 and 1853, in which she nursed and comforted the many sick and dying."

A sad but intriguing bit of Coloma history revolves around the Allhoff family. **Martin Joseph Allhoff, Sr.** (1827–1867) was born in Germany. He immigrated to the United States and became a naturalized citizen in 1856. A farmer by trade, Martin established the Coloma Vineyard and Winery in the 1850s and worked hard to expand his markets. He married **Louisa S. Weaver** (1838–1913) in 1858, and they had three sons, born in 1857, 1858, and 1863. In the mid-1860s, Martin's winery agent was arrested for tax evasion in Virginia City, Nevada.

Martin, hoping to clear things up, traveled to Nevada; however, he was immediately arrested on a minor charge. Whether Martin understood fully what was happening, or would happen, the arrest was devastating. In addition to the arrest, in April 1866, Louisa and Martin lost their youngest son, Charles. He was three years old. No doubt, between facing the loss of his son and the fear that he might go to prison and bring nothing but shame to his family, in October 1867, Martin Allhoff committed suicide by cutting his own throat.

John Barclay (unknown–1851) met his end at Somerset, eight miles from Coloma, and now rests in **Indian Creek Cemetery** in Coloma, El Dorado County. Mr. Barclay, having emigrated from New York to California, was stabbed by Alexander Hall while the two played cards in the Missouri House. Words were exchanged and when Barclay attempted to leave, Hall stabbed him just below the heart. He lived for three days. At the inquest, it was ruled that Barclay had been murdered, but Hall had already escaped. Barclay was interred at Indian Creek Cemetery.

Hunter, trapper, pioneer, Indian fighter, craftsman, saloon and hotel proprietor, **Seth Kinman** (1815–1888) was larger than life. Born in Pennsylvania, he married **Anna Maria Sharpless** (1820–1853) in 1840, but she and two of their children died during the winter of 1853 and were buried in Illinois. Sadly, Kinman had already headed west where he'd become a successful trapper and hunter, and Indian fighter. He did not learn of their deaths for several years. At six feet tall, 200 pounds, with a beard that hung down to his chest, Kinman was famous for having killed 800 grizzly bears in his lifetime and for constructing a grizzly bear chair for President Andrew Johnson and elk-horn chairs for Presidents James Buchanan, Abraham Lincoln, and Rutherford B. Hayes. He also made a violin out of an elk skull. In 1888, he accidentally shot himself in the leg, below the knee. His leg was amputated but he died from complications. Seth Kinman was buried in his frontier buckskin clothes at **Table Bluff Cemetery** located in Loleta, Humboldt County.

Charles Moon, Sr. (1860–1943) was born in China and immigrated to the United States as a young man. He married an Indian woman, **Minnie Tom**, and they had three daughters and five sons. He was one of only a handful of Chinese immigrants allowed to remain in Humboldt County after the infamous Tong uprising in April 1885, which forced a mass exodus of Chinese immigrants. For more than seventy years, he worked as a cook at the Redwood Creek Ranch with Thomas Bair and Fred S. Bair. When he passed away, he was buried in the **Moon Family Cemetery** in Hoopa. Several of his offspring were buried in other local cemeteries, including the **Hoopa Tribal Cemetery**, just off Highway 96; the **Blue Lake Cemetery**; and the **Ocean View Cemetery** in Eureka. One son and his wife were buried in the **Masons and IOOF Cemetery**, located in Rohnerville, Humboldt County.

Chinese Tongs

The Chinese arrived in California as early as 1849 as part of the gold rush. In San Francisco's Chinatown, groups called tongs, competing over territory, engaged in minor or major conflicts—whether for control over opium or for payment for a slave girl or for any number of conflicts. Much like gangs today, these tongs had paid "soldiers" called **boo how doy** who did the fighting. In San Francisco, the Tong Wars lasted into the twentieth century although the earthquake of 1906 demolished many of the rival opium dens, brothels, and gambling houses.

As reported by the **Crescent City Herald** of July 29, 1854: "On July 15, the Chinamen (*sic*) who have been so long preparing for battle met and had an engagement one-half mile east of Weaverville, but within full view of the town. Some six or eight were killed, also one white man. A large number were wounded. . . . One party is about 150 strong, the other three times as numerous."

The Carr family was an early pioneer family in Trinity County and several members are buried in the **Weaverville Cemetery**, located in Weaverville, where more than 2,500 individuals have been interred. In addition, the Carr family established the Carrville Inn in 1854, located on the old California-to-Oregon Stage Road. James E. Carr, who had helped in the construction of the stage road, brought his wife Sarah to the area and she immediately fell in love with the luscious forests and rugged countryside. Today the large and impressive inn is still in operation. Up behind the inn, wending its way into the trees is the very small and private **Carr Family Cemetery**.

One of the older members of the community to be laid to rest in the Weaverville Cemetery is **Spencer Lowden** (1806–1870), whose tall marble memorial is enclosed by an elaborately designed iron fence. Along the bottom of the tombstone is written, "Rest in Peace." The Lowden family is well represented in the cemetery, with the graves of two infants and a dozen or more family members interred here.

Two more out-of-the-way cemeteries in Trinity County include the **Big Bar Cemetery**, located on 44 Lakewood Drive, in Big Bar, and the **Price Creek Cemetery**, also found in Big Bar. Only fifteen graves have been identified as memorials in the Big Bar Cemetery, but many dates do not appear on the small metal markers. The cemetery was only "discovered" in 1970 by a survey plat "of the cemetery prepared and filed for record by Harley Lowden." Family names include Griffith and Pattison.

The Price Creek Cemetery notes eighteen graves, more than half identified by headstones. Gold miner **Thomas B. Price** (1824–1911), from Tennessee, along with **Pierce Trimble** (1830–1910), from Kentucky, and **Thomas Treloar** (1831–1919), from England, appear to be the three oldest individuals interred here. Trimble's headstone is interestingly handwritten in large, black, bold print.

Joseph Martin (1829–1862) drowned while trying to cross the Trinity River, in June 1862. A native of Darbyshire, England, he was only thirty-three years old at the time of his death. His gravesite is located on Grave Creek Road, off Highway 3, near Coffee Creek, Trinity County. An upright, slab-type monument is located alongside the roadway.

August Riecke (1841–1916), who was laid to rest in the **Trinidad Cemetery**, located on Stagecoach Road in Trinidad, Humboldt County, was born in Bremen, Germany. A sailor, he worked on masted ships of the 1800s, as well as steam-powered ships. He married **Mary Helena Fabel** (1844–1918) and together they immigrated to America where August worked on cargo ships traveling between San

The lone headstone of thirty-three-year-old Joseph Martin,
who drowned in the Trinity River in 1862, stands along
Graves Road off of State Highway 3.
COURTESY DEE CRAMER

Francisco and Trinidad. In 1871, they settled in Trinidad where they
raised ten children. In 1906, August became a city councilman. He
died in 1916 after suffering a stroke. Two sons died young, reasons not
known: **Joseph Warren Riecke,** who married in 1902, died in 1903,
only a few days before his own son was born. He was twenty-six when

he was interred in the **Greenwood Cemetery,** located in Arcata, Humboldt County. August's second son, **Charles Alfred Riecke,** died at age thirty-one.

Corporal James David Barnes (1822–1864), who mustered into Company B, First Battalion of Mountaineers, California Volunteers, at Arcata, Humboldt County, in 1863, was also interred at Greenwood Cemetery. At various times, Corporal Barnes was called upon to serve as escort for government pack trains and protection against Indian raids. In 1864, while stationed at Camp Curtis, Barnes died from gunshot wounds he received in a skirmish against Indians at Boynton's Prairie, east of Eureka.

Lawrence Ford (1839–1908) was born in Ireland. In 1868, he and his wife founded the Ford Ranch on Liscom Hill near Blue Lake. Daughter **Abbigail "Abbie" Ford** (1874–1971) was born on the ranch in 1874; her brother **Lawrence A. Ford** (1880–1957) was born six years later. When Abbie passed away in 1971, she was the last of a generation of one of Humboldt County's pioneer families. While her brother Lawrence was interred in the Greenwood Cemetery, Abbie was laid to rest near her father Lawrence Ford in **Saint Mary's Cemetery,** in Arcata. Her father's memorial is a large, elaborate red granite stone that is trimmed and wonderfully etched, with a cross at the top and the large letters "FORD" etched across the bottom.

Sunset Memorial Park is located in Eureka, Humboldt County. One pioneer interred here was **Joseph Porter "J. P." Albee** (1815–1862). In 1850, he came overland to California with three partners and two four-horse teams. Near "Hangtown" (Placerville)

Lawrence Ford emigrated from Ireland to establish the Ford Ranch near Blue Lake.

they engaged in mining with modest success. In 1852, J. P. journeyed to Humboldt County with a herd of cattle. In 1853, he brought his family to Humboldt and settled on Table Bluff where he opened a hotel. He also invested in a pack train that ran from Arcata to Klamath, and then in 1855, he moved his family to Redwood Creek where he built a large hotel and planted an orchard. He and his wife, **Caltha Putnam** (1816–1905), had eight children, four boys and four girls. Described as a man of integrity and quiet manner, J. P. was often seen on his big gray horse and was considered to be a friend to local Indians, too. However, when he did not return home one evening, his neighbors went in search of him. Suddenly they encountered a handful of Indians torching J. P.'s barns and buildings. After an exchange of gunfire, the men rescued Joseph, but he was already dead. They buried him where he lay, and later, they laid him to rest in Sunset Memorial Park. He was only forty-six years old.

Lake County was the home of the Pomo people, and along the northern edge of Clear Lake lived two bands, the *Kulanapo* and *Habenapo*. Clear Lake was one of the principal fishing spots for the people living here, and a small island on the north shore was a favorite fishing sits. Today this location is known for the Bloody Island Massacre, also known as *Bo-no-po-i*, the tragic attack that occurred on May 15, 1850. Captain Nathaniel Lyon led soldiers and volunteers onto the island where they murdered 60 of the 400 Pomo who had taken refuge there. Another seventy-five Indians were killed on Russian River.

Lower Lake Cemetery District is also known as **Lower Lake Catholic Cemetery**. Located at 9040 Lake St, Lower Lake, it contains 5,800 graves. Lower Lake was first known as Grantsville; Lower Lake was founded in 1858, but what is called Lower Lake Cemetery opened in 1850 and is one of California's oldest cemeteries. Unfortunately, the original records were destroyed in a fire at the Lakeport courthouse. Supposedly the earliest burial was for **John Bainbridge**, but there is no headstone or marker and no record of his burial. The earliest confirmed burial was for **Sophia Bower**, a young girl who died in May 1857. Sophia's father, **Jacob Bower**, had come to California in 1849 and mined throughout the region until 1853. In 1855, he married **Clarinda Thomas**, and in 1857, they came to Napa County and settled where the Lower Lake wharf landing originally stood.

One of the oldest individuals buried in the Lower Lake Cemetery was **Charles Colbert Copsey** (1798–1881). Originally from Maryland, he served with the U.S. Army Cavalry during the **Mexican American War** and was one of the first settlers in Lake County, California, in a settlement called the Copsey Settlement. His second wife, buried alongside him, was **Sarah Rice Copsey** (1810–1887). Charles was her fourth husband, having been widowed three times. Though they each had children from their previous marriages, they had no children of their own.

Charles's second son, **Charles Noble Copsey** (1827–1868), was murdered after he sold an Indian girl to J. Marvin a storekeeper in Pope Valley—for $100—and then, accompanied by his niece, persuaded the girl to run away with them. Marvin and a second man, Juan Burton, gave chase and in the melee that followed, Copsey was killed by Burton and buried in the Lower Lake Cemetery. At his trial, Burton was found not guilty. Sadly, and ironically, the older son of Charles Noble Copsey, **Wirt Copsey** (1865–1879), was accidentally shot and killed by a friend when he was fourteen. He was also laid to rest in the Lower Lake Cemetery. Finally, **Sophronia Tabathy Copsey Coffman** (1837–1924), the only sister of Charles Noble Copsey (and daughter of Charles Colbert Copsey), died tragically in her home in Middletown, Lake County, at age eighty-seven, from a fire most likely caused by an oil lamp. Her body was "much consumed when it was recovered." She was laid to rest in the **Middletown Cemetery**, located at 16357 Butts Canyon Road, Middletown, Lake County, although the location of her grave is unknown since she was not provided a headstone.

William Lawton Allen (1835–1900), originally from Missouri, was buried in **Upper Lake Cemetery**, located in Upper Lake, Lake County. In 1856, he married **Catherine Boyd Boyes** (1832–1864) and together with her parents and siblings they crossed the plains to settle near Millville, Shasta County. The family then went back to Missouri for three years and, with William as captain, they returned by wagon train to California. They resettled on a farm on Old Cow Creek where tragedy soon struck; in September 1864, William was haying two miles from the house. Without warning, two Indians attacked Catherine and the four children. Catherine was killed outright, but Dr. Guptill of Millville was able to save the children. He "covered a hole in baby Robert's head with a silver fifty-cent piece and put a silver plate in Lillian's head. . . . All four [children] survived." Catherine was buried near the house where she was killed.

But tragedy struck again. After William married a second time, his new wife, **Julia Ann Kilgore Allen**, and their young son both died, likely from disease. He laid them to rest beside Catherine. William then moved to Upper Lake with his mother and his daughter Lillian. He did marry a third time to **Nancy Celia Moore Hust** (1851–1914) and they had two children. William passed away on May 2, 1900, and was buried in the Upper Lake Cemetery.

The **Tulocay Cemetery** is the largest cemetery in the Napa area. Located at 411 Coombsville Road in Napa, Napa County, over 200 veterans of the Civil War are interred here. **Mary Ellen Pleasant** (1817–1904) was also laid to rest in the Tulocay Cemetery. Often called the "Harriett Tubman of California," much of M. E. Pleasant's life has never been revealed and remains somewhat mysterious.

A Pioneer Who Achieved Much

According to Lerone Bennett, Jr., in *Ebony,* Mary Ellen (M. E.) Pleasant was "a bold Black pioneer who was one of the most enigmatic and mysterious women in American history." Some say she was born to a free black woman, while others say she was the daughter of a slave. Either way, she often passed as white, which helped her in her efforts to free slaves as well as gave her opportunity to pursue her business interests. She ended up in California in 1851, where she amassed a substantial fortune. M. E. was also a friend of John Brown and others in the abolitionist movement. Very importantly, in 1863, she participated in a case that "earned Blacks the right to have their testimonies heard in California court." Second, her 1866 lawsuit in San Francisco actually ended segregation on local public transportation.

Mary Ellen Pleasant has been titled the "Mother of Civil Rights in California" for her actions to end segregation and promote abolition.

Courtesy Janice Janek

M. E. lived to be eighty-six and was interred in the Tulocay Cemetery where her original cemetery marker was made of wood. It was replaced once, but then, in 2011 it was replaced again. Her epitaph reads: "Mary Ellen Pleasant/ Mother of Civil Rights in California/1817–1904/ She was a friend of John Brown." In addition, a metal sculpture by R. Alan Williams, a prize-winning African American artist was commissioned, which depicts "a forceful stand, holding a body of purpose." While modernistic, the sculpture appears to be a "world" held up by a crossed stand.

Calistoga, California's **Pioneer Cemetery**—also known as the **White Church Cemetery**—is located within the Bothe-Napa Valley State Park. It is hidden by redwood trees and is not visible from the road, but it is accessible from 3801 St. Helena Highway North. There is a plaque that marks the site of the first church (White Church) and a white picket fence that encloses the cemetery. Here lie at least fifty-one graves. Although there is a second cemetery also known as the **Calistoga Pioneer Cemetery** only fifteen minutes away on Foothill Blvd., and is visible from the road, these are not the same cemeteries.

The first of three brothers to be buried in Calistoga's **Pioneer Cemetery** was **Stephen F. Tucker** (1834–1896). Along with his father **"Captain" Reason Penelope Tucker** (1806–1888) and four brothers, Stephen left Ohio to cross the plains in 1846, by oxen, as part of the original **Donner Party.** As one of those in command, however, Reason pushed on—one day earlier than the remaining Donner Party—thus escaping the horror that followed. Reason did lead the first rescue attempt and participated in the successive attempts to rescue the Donner Party survivors. Ultimately, Reason married three times and fathered ten children. He died in 1888, at age eighty-two, after moving south to Santa Barbara County, and was interred there, in the **Goleta Cemetery**, located at 44 S. San Antonio Rd. in Goleta, Santa Barbara County.

However, Stephen Tucker, the fourth of Reason's ten children, settled near Kelseyville in Lake County. He accumulated a fair amount of wealth, which he bequeathed to his nieces and nephews since he never married or had children. He moved into his brother's home in Lakeport after suffering heart problems. There he remained until he died in March 1896. He was buried in the Pioneer Cemetery, aka the White Church Cemetery. Two other Tucker brothers were also laid to rest in the Pioneer Cemetery. Strangely, **George Washington Tucker** (1831–1907), the eldest son of Reason P. Tucker's children, and **Burd Tucker** (1844–1907) both passed away in August of 1907—only thirteen days apart. Burd had served as the postmaster at Kellogg in Knights Valley. George, at sixteen when crossing the plains with their father Reason, had participated in the Donner rescue attempts. In 1848, he helped construct the area's first schoolhouse as well as the first timber house in Napa in 1855. He outlived four wives and died at age seventy-five after a long illness. George and Burd and three more of Reason's children were also buried in Calistoga's Pioneer Cemetery.

One of the first graves recorded in the Pioneer Cemetery is for **Ora Leona Pratt** (1875–1902), daughter of Washington Burdette Pratt, a local farmer. Ora married farmer **Mitchell Orland**

Bartholomew (1871–1937) in 1898. In 1900, they were living in Hot Springs, Napa, and then moved to St. Helena. A victim of TB, however, Ora died at age twenty-six, leaving behind her husband and two young children (ages three and one). She was laid to rest in the Pioneer Cemetery. Her epitaph reads, "A Christian wife & mother."

Mitchell Bartholomew then married **Mary Alice Patrick** and the couple moved to Vallejo, in Solano County. Together they had four more children. Unfortunately, in 1937, working as a winter caretaker for the Fresno County Trimmer Civilian Conservation Corps Camp, he was found dead in his bunk at Oak Flat CCC Camp, probably from a heart attack. He was buried in **Belmont Memorial Park**, located at 201 N. Tielman Avenue, Fresno, Fresno County. He was sixty-five years old.

John B. Barham (1800–1864) was interred in the **Santa Rosa Rural Cemetery**, located on Franklin Avenue in Santa Rosa, Sonoma County. Though born in North Carolina, his family moved to Illinois where he assisted his father, the Reverend Daniel Barham, in building log cabins. An interesting side note: the Reverend was buried next to Abraham Lincoln's father in the **Thomas-Lincoln Cemetery** in Pleasant Grove Township, Illinois. Barham married **Jemima "Minnie" Moore** (1806–1881) in 1826, and together they raised eight children, four boys and four girls. Settling in California, Barham's sons became leaders in the new state: **John All Barham** (1843–1926) became a three-term U.S. Congressman; **Richard M. Barham** (1837–1911) became a sheriff in Anaheim; **Henley W. Barham** (1835–1915) became a rancher; and **James F. Barham** (1827–1906), along with

The Barham family plot is located in the Santa Rosa Rural Cemetery; however there is little to identify any but two of the family headstones.

his son, John Henry, founded the community of Barham, in northern San Diego County. John B. Barham passed away in 1864, but Minnie lived until 1881. She was interred in the Santa Rosa Rural Cemetery alongside her husband.

Interestingly, there were twenty-three African Americans who made their home in nineteenth century Santa Rosa, Sonoma County. It is believed that up to seven had been slaves prior to moving to California, including former slave-turned education and civil rights activist, **John Richards** (1824–1879), who managed to hire teachers and provide educational opportunities to many of the town's African American children. What is ironic, however, is that Santa Rosa was avidly pro-Confederacy at this time, and racism was deeply embedded in the community. **Thomas Larkin Thompson** (1838–1898), publisher of the *Sonoma Democrat*, commonly fueled the racism in his newspaper. For instance, when it was learned that a boy nearly beat a Chinese man to death in the street, Thompson dismissed it as a youthful prank, and when some boys were discovered pelting rotten eggs and rocks at the home of African American **Henry W. "Shiner" Davison** (1819–1900), Thompson wrote, "They do it to hear the old gentleman complain." Thompson was elected as a Democrat to the U.S. Congress in 1887 and also served as commissioner from California to the Chicago World's Fair. He died in 1898 and was interred in the Santa Rosa Rural Cemetery, as were both John Richards and Henry Davison.

Ag Gow (1846–1916), from China, was living in Honcut, Butte County, when his life was cut short. He was interred in the **Oroville Chinese Cemetery**, located at 2780 Feather River Blvd. and near the intersection of Gold Dredger Drive, in Oroville, Butte County. The cemetery was established in 1850 and the last burial took place in 1944. According to the *Chico Record* of August 22, 1916, Ag Gow was "murdered by parties unknown, by a knife wound in the neck." His body was "found in the ruins of his burned hut, with his own butcher knife still sticking in the gaping wound." A vegetable peddler, Ag Gow had lived for thirty years in Oroville and was well known to everyone in the area. At least two theories were discussed: had Ag Gow been a victim of a tong conflict? Or had it been a robbery? A number of people knew Gow to have money stashed away in his cabin, and Sheriff Riddle learned from community members that there had been two

Chinese men spotted near Gow's cabin earlier in the day—two men that no one seemed to recognize. In an effort to catch them, the sheriff sent out notices all around northern California. Unfortunately the murder was never solved.

Thousands of Chinese worked and lived in northern California during the gold rush. One Chinese temple was built in Oroville in 1853, when there were roughly 10,000 Chinese residing in the area. It continued to be used well into the 1920s and 1930s. Today it serves as a museum. The Weaverville Joss House is the oldest continuously operating Chinese temple in California. It was built in 1874 to replace earlier structures destroyed by fire. In 1938, a descendant of one of Weaverville's Chinese settlers, **Moon Lee**, became the trustee for the Temple, but in 1956, he and his wife, Dorothy, donated "The Temple of the Forest Beneath the Clouds," to the California State Parks. The interior has been preserved as it was 100 years ago. Today the Weaverville Joss House Association assists the California State Parks in preserving the temple. As stated on the Trinity County website, "The true historical significance of the Joss House is that during China's Cultural Revolution, many of the old rural-style temples were dismantled or destroyed. The Weaverville Joss House is an intact and complete temple of that era, which no longer exists in many parts of China."

CHAPTER 10

SUPERIOR CALIFORNIA REGION

This northern region, labeled as "Superior" California, is made up of seventeen counties, or almost 30 percent of the physical landscape of California. In addition, its relevant history would fill volumes when it comes to relating its early, middle, and later histories, in addition to the number of historic cemeteries located here. For that reason, this chapter will skim the surface in presenting the region's history and focus more on a sampling of the area's cemeteries, which could still fill volumes.

Sacramento, of course, is not only the state capital, but it also provides the starting point for a look at Superior California's historic cemeteries. Of the thirty-five cemeteries in the city, **Sacramento City Cemetery**, also known as the **Sacramento Historic City Cemetery**, located at 1000 Broadway, is the oldest existing cemetery. It was created in 1849 when John A. Sutter, Jr., donated ten acres. As was the trend across the country, the cemetery was landscaped to resemble a luscious Victorian garden, with roses and terraces of flowers and plants and walkways, something of a park rather than a gloomy haunted graveyard.

This headstone is one of few remaining in Yreka's Chinese Cemetery, Siskiyou County; note the fruit offerings.

Yet the first major burials came from the 1850 cholera epidemic that killed almost 2,000 people in the area. The first 600 victims were buried in a mass grave at Sacramento City Cemetery. Another 800 or more were buried in a mass grave at the **New Helvetia Cemetery** at Sutter's Fort; however, because the New Helvetia Cemetery often flooded, bodies were frequently exhumed and reburied in a mass grave at Sacramento City Cemetery. A monument was erected to honor those who died and were interred there. The New Helvetia Cemetery is now defunct, but it was the first official cemetery established in Sacramento, created by Captain John Sutter, Sr. The first recorded interments in Sutter's "Burying Ground" occurred in 1845. The graves were shallow and markers were made from simple, flat boards.

By 1850, Sacramento City Cemetery had grown to twenty acres. One burial that took place that year was for Mayor **Hardin Bigelow** (1809–1850), who was elected the first mayor of "Sacramento City" after he promised to help build levees and dams following the mighty January 1850 floods. Then, in May, squatters who had been fighting against John Sutter and other landowners for a right to settle on what they considered open land marched to free two squatters who had been jailed for unlawful occupation. In the melee, Bigelow was wounded and taken to San Francisco to recover, but in October, cholera struck the region, killing seventeen of Sacramento's doctors. Bigelow succumbed as well. He was buried in the Sacramento City Cemetery.

In the 1950s, the New Helvetia Cemetery site was marked as the new location for the Sutter Middle School, meaning that well over 4,000 "pioneers" had to be moved. Most were resettled in the

East Lawn Memorial Park—but these were the "unknowns," without identification. The memorial park was once a country farm, so it has a park-like character. It is located at 4300 Folsom Blvd. in Sacramento. It was not until the 1980s that a monument was erected memorializing these "lost" pioneers resettled at East Lawn. Another 400+ "known" pioneers were moved to the Sacramento City Cemetery. Today the Sacramento City Cemetery has recorded nearly 30,000 individuals, while East Lawn has over 55,000.

On December 1, 1856, **Barton Lee** (1813–1856), "one of the State's oldest and boldest" pioneers who helped build the largest hospital in California for the times, was laid to rest in the Sacramento City Cemetery. Lee, who arrived in California in 1848, turned his hand at whatever opportunity came along; he had been a salesman, builder, banker, merchant, and investor. He also served on a committee at the Constitutional Convention for California statehood. When his position and fortune were suddenly reversed, however, he closed the doors to his bank and retreated to a quiet life. He died in 1856, at the age of forty-three and was laid to rest in the Sacramento City Cemetery.

Mark Hopkins (1813–1878) was born in New York. In August 1849, he and his fellow passengers aboard the *Pacific* arrived in San Francisco. His first enterprise was a grocery business. Other early entrepreneurs he met at this time included Collis P. Huntington, Leland Stanford, and E. B. Crocker. Even as the Civil War loomed, this enterprising group of men met with Theodore Dehone Judah, a railroad and civil engineer, who proposed they become involved in the construction of a railroad that would open California up to the rest of the nation. He outlined a route from Dutch Flat, across Donner Summit Pass and along the Truckee River. While no one else could envision such a project, these four men—who soon became known as "The Big Four"—immediately joined in, even though their combined capital at the time only amounted to $159,000.

When Leland Stanford won the governorship of California in 1861, he sent Judah east to Washington, D.C., to petition for financing for the railroad. President Lincoln signed the bill in July 1862, which gave the CPRR Company a right-of-way "two hundred feet wide on each side of the railroad across all government lands, including lands for stations, machine shops." The Big Four soon became four of the richest and most influential men in the West.

Mark Hopkins had always lived a modest lifestyle, but at forty-one, he went east to marry his cousin, **Mary Frances Sherwood** (1818–1891). Returning to San Francisco, Mary Frances convinced him to build a home in a fashionable neighborhood, so he bought half the block on Nob Hill from Leland Stanford. Sadly, Hopkins passed away unexpectedly on a business trip. His body was returned to San Francisco for a funeral, and he was temporarily buried in San Francisco until his tomb at the Sacramento City Cemetery was completed. According to Oscar Lewis in his book *The Big Four*, Hopkin's mausoleum boasted "massive bronzed doors flanked by urns, and within was a frieze of acanthus leaves."

John A. Sutter, Jr. (1826–1897) was the son of Captain John Sutter, Sr., who built Sutter's Fort and established his "empire" of New Helvetia. John Sutter, Jr., however, was responsible for laying out plans

Mark Hopkins's mausoleum reportedly cost $150,000 and was made of "rose-colored" marble.

CAROL HIGHSMITH/LIBRARY OF CONGRESS

for the city of Sacramento. When an argument with his father led to his leaving California, John Jr. moved to Mexico, where he lived the last fourteen years of his life. He was buried in Guadalajara and was not returned to Sacramento until 1964, when his children "brought him home." He was reinterred in the Sacramento City Cemetery.

William Gordon, or "Uncle Billy Gordon," who arrived in the neighboring region of Yolo County from New Mexico around 1841, is considered the area's first "official" white settler. However, there are tales of a Scottish sailor who arrived earlier, circa the 1820s, and married a Native American woman with whom he raised a number of children. After him came the explorers Jedediah Smith and Alexander R. McLeod.

This area is often called the "Sonoma District" because the **Sonoma Mission** was the last and most northerly mission built by the Spanish, and included what are now Yolo, Solano, Napa, Sonoma, and parts of Mendocino and Lake Counties. Tragically, during the early 1840s, smallpox decimated much of the region, killing at least 75,000 Native American people.

In company with William Gordon was **Dr. William Knight**, a physician from Maryland who had become a mountain man and fur trader, who traveled through Los Angeles then made his way north. He married a native woman and received a Spanish land grant along the Sacramento River at what is now called Knight's Landing in 1843. The site became an important landing and shipping point. Knight, along with his wife Carmel and their children, then moved to the Stanislaus River and founded a second town, Knights Ferry. Here he established a ferry crossing. Sadly, in November 1849, Dr. Knight was murdered, gunned down in the streets of his new community. He was buried at **Knights Ferry**, Stanislaus County, "near the southeast corner of the Masonic Hall on Main Street." A plaque was also placed in his honor at Knight's Landing by E Clampus Vitus in March 1974.

The **Woodland Cemetery**, located at 800 West Street, Woodland, Yolo County, was established in 1869; it lay adjacent to the
old cemetery beside Union Church. More than 18,000 burials have
taken place in the cemetery, and one of the oldest individuals interred
here was **Catherine Reynolds** (1782–1876). Her tomb is a tall, and
likely expensive, granite monument placed on a three-tiered base of
granite. Catherine's daughter, **Cornelia D. Reynolds Byrns** (1829–
1911), along with her husband **John Byrns** (1825–1883), and their
two infant daughters—**Sarah Bell Byrns** (1862–1864) and **Dasie
Byrns** (1867–1867)—are also buried in the Woodland Cemetery.
The shared family monument is tall and elaborately decorated, with
sculpted edges. Topped by a draped urn, the tombstone is etched with
the names of Cornelia and John's family.

Stephen Meek, Trapper and Mountain Man

While Russian fur trappers entered Northern or "superior" California as early as 1825, and Jedediah Smith crossed the Trinity
Mountains above the mouth of the Klamath River in 1828, it was
the Hudson Bay trappers—including Alexander McLeod—who
traversed the area looking for beaver. Apart from Jedediah Smith,
the most famous trapper to spend time in this region was **Stephen
Hall Meek** (1807–1889), brother to the well-known mountain man
Joseph "Joe" Meek. Harvey E. Tobie, however, wrote in his biography of Stephen Meek:

Stephen Meek is more aptly describable as a Mountain Man
than his more famous younger brother Joseph. Although
the latter devoted eleven years to mountain operations, he
should be remembered essentially as a politician. Steve, on

---

the other hand, never achieved lasting prominence in any public or private career. Though his activity was tremendous, his struggles brought him full circle into the mountains again; and there he died.

Stephen Hall Meek was buried in the **Etna Cemetery**, Siskiyou County, only a few miles from where he spent his last days. As he aged, his storytelling became so entertaining that one woman, "hearing of his daring escapes, declared, 'Law Sakes! Mr. Meek, didn't you never get killed by none of them Indians and bears?' To which Meek replied, 'Oh, yes, madam, I was frequently killed.'"

In 1848, the first pioneer settler in the Shasta region, **Major Pearson Barton Reading** (1816–1868), successfully mined the Trinity River near Douglas City. He established his Reading Homestead near the junction of Cottonwood Creek and Sacramento River—where he would eventually be buried—but there was no other settlement in Shasta County until the arrival of emigrants crossing the plains. Reading also blazed the trail that would become the Shasta-to-Weaverville Road. He married **Euphan "Fannie" Wallace Washington** (1831–1918) in 1856, and they had six children (including a set of twins), although Major Reading did have another daughter, **Jeanette "Janet" Reading Simson** (1842–1909), with his first wife (unknown). While the Fannnie and Pearson's firstborn, **Anna Washington Reading** (1857–1906), was born in Washington, D.C., their second daughter, **Alice Matilda Reading** (1859–1939), was born in Shasta County, making her the first white child born there. The Readings also lost a son at a young age. In Alice's obituary, posted in 1939, it was written:

> She [Alice] was the first white child born in Shasta County, her birth occurring at the old Reading adobe near Cottonwood on August 15, 1859. . . . Major Reading came here in 1844 and is credited with being the second man to discover gold in California. After James Marshall's strike, Major Reading found gold in 1849 on Clear Creek, Shasta County. He was the first white settler in the county.

Alice was buried alongside her father at the family's homestead, as was her infant brother. A large stone sits at the head of the small, enclosed graveyard as a memorial to Reading's life and achievements. Rocks piled onto each grave eerily point out the differences in size and age.

The first cemetery in Redding, Shasta County, was actually located at 2146 Pine Street—between Market and Pine Street. Today that site is a parking lot. The cemetery was established in 1867, but abandoned, to be rediscovered in 1906. It is now known as the **Redding Abandoned Cemetery.** The first interment was for **Samuel Dinsmore** (1841–1867), the eldest of four children born to **John W. Dinsmore** (1809–1891) and **Arabella (MacGlashon) Woodrum-Dinsmore** (1808–1904). The Dinsmores came to Shingletown in Shasta County in 1852. John Dinsmore was a millwright, and he and his partner Merriman Ferrel built the Dry Mill in Shingletown.

In 1857, he purchased a section of land from Pierson B. Reading's Rancho Buena Ventura land grant. The Dinsmore home, called the Four Mile House, was located four and a half miles from Shasta, where Highway 299 meets Ridge Drive. Samuel was twenty-five when he died in April 1867 from consumption. Later that same year, Samuel's eleven-year-old niece, **Arabella Ferrel** (1856–1867), became the second interment after succumbing to congestive chills. Both Samuel and Arabella's bodies were reinterred at **Redding Memorial Park**, which was established in the 1890s.

In 1857, several Jewish merchants living around the town of Shasta established the Hebrew Benevolent Society. One of their goals was to insure that Jewish burials took place with all the traditions of Jewish customs. The site represented one of the earliest such sites consecrated for Jewish people in the state. So, when in 1864, **George and Helena Cohn Brownstein** from Red Bluff lost their eight-month-old son **Charles**, they loaded him into a wagon and headed north. It was a two-day drive before they were able to place their son in sacred ground. Unfortunately, Charles's grave was threatened when a highway crew in 1923 stumbled over the grave, which had gotten "lost" or forgotten. Fortunately, the state redesigned the throughway, and in 1933, the Shasta Historical Society was able to mark the grave as an historical site. Today Highway 299 West wends past the brick monument entitled "Pioneer Baby's Grave." The large brass plaque framed in brick gives the history of Charles's death and burial. There is also a narrow walkway down to the actual gravesite, protected by metal fencing.

Many pioneer gravesites have been lost over time, requiring great effort to locate them. One of them is the **Tuttle Gulch Cemetery** in Shasta County, where fifty-seven identified gravesites are barely visible from a road in the Bald Hills. The earliest grave marker is dated July 20, 1864, for the infant **Anna E. Thompson** (unknown–1864), believed to be the daughter of **Ann Thompson** (unknown–1866), buried nearby, who died at age nineteen in February 1866. Also buried in this small cemetery are **Henry Jefferson** (1828–1913) and **Martha Frances (Duggins) James** (1864–1923), although Martha's grave does not have a tombstone.

Born in Millville, Shasta County, **Herman Frederick Ross** (1823–1901) was born in Sweden. His father was involved in iron manufacture, but Herman joined up as a sailor at fifteen, although his first voyage ended in a near sinking in the English Channel. His next trip was on an English vessel headed to Africa to capture or take down "slaving ships" in the hopes of freeing slaves packed tight in the bottom of the ships. Once overtaken, the rescued men and women were returned to the shores of Sierra Leone.

Herman finally ended up in the United States, working for the government during the war with Mexico; however, he caught yellow fever and returned home to recuperate. Then, learning of the gold rush, he sailed to California and engaged in mining on the American River. He also mined on the Salmon, Scott, Klamath, and Trinity rivers. In 1852, he found himself in Shasta (city). It was a rapidly growing area, so he bought 160 acres at Oak Run and went to farming. In 1859, he married **Margaret Elizabeth Hunt**

Baby Charles is known as the "Pioneer Baby" whose grave altered California's state road construction outside of Redding, Shasta County.

(1840–1864). They had two sons, **Albert F.** (1861–1919) and **Harold M.** (1863–1910). In 1864, however, Margaret died and was buried in the **Hunt Cemetery** in Shasta County. Three years later Herman married **Clarissa Powers** (1845–1887). A strong Republican, Herman opposed slavery and supported the North in the "great war of the Rebellion." He also served as a justice of the peace, was a charter member of the Legion of Honor, and belonged to a number of lodges. He passed away in 1901 at age seventy-seven and was buried in the **Millville Masonic Cemetery** located at 23799 Old Highway 44 Drive, Millville, Shasta County. This cemetery is small, grassy, and peaceful, encircled by trees. Herman's grave marker is a rectangular pink granite slab etched in a simple, straightforward font. Clarissa's marker, next to Herman's, is also pink granite but is larger and has the following epitaph etched below her name: "She has crossed the river to the silent shore, where billows never break or tempests roar."

Olonzo "Alonzo" Engle (1824–1910) died on March 30, 1910, and was buried in the **Igo Cemetery**, Shasta County. Considered one of the earliest pioneers of the area, he was born in Ohio in 1824. In the 1850 census, Alonzo, age twenty-five, was married to **Margaret Williamson Engle** (1831–1853), age eighteen, in Michigan. He traveled to California in the 1850s, and by 1860, he was settled in Horsetown, Shasta County, along with a younger brother, **Austin Engle** (1827–1881). He took up mining, tried his hand at raising livestock and butchering, worked as a steward in the county hospital at Shasta, and served as Igo's postmaster for many years. According to Alonzo's obituary, he left behind his widow, **Mary O'Dell Engle** (his second wife), along with five of his six children: **Mercelia Agnes "Celia" Adkins** (1851–1929), Igo; **Mary Adeline Peterson** (1881–1955), Redding; **Rosa Margaret Maupin**, Benicia; and **William Engle**, location unknown. Sadly, **Louis Engle**—Mary Adeline's twin—burned to death when he was eight years old while trying to light a fire in the stove with coal oil. Alonzo's daughter, Mercelia Agnes "Celia" Adkins, married **John Thomas Adkins** (1845–1917), who was also from Igo. A strong-minded young woman, Celia registered her own livestock brand and earmark for her cattle in 1902. According to one story, Celia once invited a stranger into the house and prepared breakfast for him since he seemed gentlemanly and polite. Later she learned that the sheriff and his deputies were after a stage bandit, and Celia realized it was the same man she'd invited in, none other than **Black Bart (aka Charles Bowles)**, the "gentleman bandit" who had held up many stages in Northern California (and whose last years and final resting spot are still controversial). Celia and John remained in Igo their entire lives—ranching, farming, and raising six children. John died in 1917; Celia died in 1929. Both were buried in the Igo Cemetery, Shasta County.

The **Anderson Pioneer Cemetery** is located eight miles south of Redding, in Anderson. Visible from Interstate 5, most drivers rarely look over the roadway into the abandoned, triangular-shaped area tucked under a few trees, just over the old railroad tracks. It is the older Anderson cemetery, and the assortment of tombstones are half-hidden by knee-high grass. Two important individuals are interred here:

Elias and Elizabeth Anderson, the town's founders and namesake. **Elias Anderson** (1817–1907) was a rancher, farmer, hotel owner, and postmaster. He married **Elizabeth Summers** (1820–1895) in 1839. In 1856, he purchased the American Ranch and built the American Ranch Hotel. He also purchased 230 acres from Pierson B. Redding in 1865. Hoping to encourage business, he offered a right-of-way to Central Pacific so the town and his business would grow. In return for the right-of-way, the railroad agreed to name the town in his honor. Sadly enough, the railroad bypassed the pioneer community, merely skimming the area. In 1880, Elias Anderson sold the hotel to his son George. Elizabeth Summers Anderson passed away in 1895, at the age of seventy-four. When Elias passed away, he had been living with his daughter. He was ninety years old and was interred beside Elizabeth. Their headstones are the two tallest ones, and as you enter through the wide, but broken down gate, the line of Anderson "family" markers are the first to greet you.

August Schuckman (1827–1907), born in Prussia, immigrated to California before marrying **Augusta A. Feidler** (1835–1887), also from Prussia, in 1865. Initially they settled in Stony Creek, Colusa County, where August was employed as a farmer. Their seven children—four sons and three daughters—were all born in California, although **Minnie Schuckman** (1873–1892) died at age eighteen, in 1892; **Will Schuckman** (1872–1901) died at twenty-nine; and **Samuel Schuckman** (1870–1904) died of consumption at age thirty-three. They were each buried in the **Williams Cemetery**, located at 2438 Zumwalt Road in Williams, Colusa County.

Elias Anderson, for whom the city of Anderson was named, is interred in Anderson's out-of-the-way Pioneer Cemetery.

One of August and Augusta's initial achievements was establishing the Mountain House in the foothills of Colusa County as a popular rest stop and bar. August also founded a telephone company as well as helped build Williams's City Hall. Daughter **Ida Schuckman** (1878–1974) married **Edmund Joseph Brown** (1870–1942), who then became the parents of California governor **Edmund G. Brown** (1905–1996) and grandparents of California governor **Edmund G. "Jerry" Brown, Jr.** Son **Frank Schuckman** (1868–1959) and his wife **Margaret Henneke Schuckman** (1875–1958) continued to operate the Mountain House. One interesting side note: Margaret's father, **William Henneke**—a Civil War veteran—was one of the guards that accompanied President Lincoln's casket from Washington to Gettysburg by train after his assassination. August's extended family have all been interred in the Williams Cemetery.

Also interred in the Williams Cemetery are members of the Williams family. **William Henry Williams** (1828–1909) was born in Maryland as the sixth of nine children. In March 1850, he and three companions crossed the plains in a wagon pulled by oxen. Once in California, he went to mining but soon moved to Sacramento where he worked as a clerk. He purchased a team of horses and began hauling freight. After a year, he bought twenty-two hogs. He married **Sarah W. Cary** (1832–1908), with whom he had four children, and they settled in Colusa County where Williams hoped to sell lots for a new town—appropriately named Williams. He married his second wife, **Mary Eugenia McEvoy** (1859–1937), in 1880. Together they had six children; however, four died before reaching a year old, including a set

William H. Williams settled the city of Williams and helped to establish Colusa County.

of twins. Williams built their home out of brick, hauled in by wagons from Marysville. In fact, the town's founding fathers were able to build a number of buildings with brick. The town became a stop along the railroad and helped secure it as a permanent settlement. William H. Williams passed away at age eighty-one, in 1909. He was interred in the Williams Cemetery.

LaPorte, located in the mountains of Plumas County, sixty-five miles northeast of Marysville, California, became an important settlement during the gold rush. Originally known as Rabbit Creek, the citizens voted in 1857 to change the name to La Porte—in honor of the birthplace of one of their early pioneers. Another early pioneer was **Jesus Maria Bustillos** (1837–1913) was born in Mazatlan, Mexico, and immigrated to California in 1851. In March 1866, he became a naturalized citizen and by the 1870 census, he was listed as a mule packer, which is one of the occupations the Bustillos family became known for. In fact, in 1851, when Jesus arrived in La Porte, he came with 125 mules. It wasn't long before Jesus and **John Rosseter** (who ran seventy-five-mule pack trains) became partners, but Jesus bought Rosseter's seventy-five mules in 1855 and ran the pack train as sole owner. By 1860, Jesus was running a string of 140 mules with forty hired drivers. The route he drove was from Marysville to LaPorte, which took five days, and then to Jamison and Quincy. Mules were favored because of their hardiness and sure-footedness, often dubbed "the clipper ships of the mountains."

Jesus married **Maria Jesus Yrigoya** (1850–1891), and they had nine children, although they lost **Gonsalo Bustillos** (1873–1879) at age six and **Maria Rosa Bustillos** (1884–1900) at age fifteen. As time went on, Jesus and his sons advertised as teamsters and packers and were able to pack just about anything at any time of year, including sixty to ninety packs of first class mail on snowshoes. Jesus was quoted as saying they occasionally had to "hole-up under snow-covered trees during blizzards." Maria Jesus passed away in 1891 at age forty-one and was laid to rest in the **LaPorte Cemetery** in LaPorte, Plumas County. Jesus passed away in 1913, at age seventy-five. He, too, was interred in the LaPorte Cemetery.

Tucked away in Weed, Siskiyou County, is the **Lincoln Heights Cemetery**. Now an historic landmark, it ranks number three in California on the list of black cemeteries. Originally it was the **Mt. Shasta**

Baptist Church Cemetery. Unfortunately, a lot of the graves lack markers—although for years a wooden stake was inserted wherever a body was interred. Today the surface of the cemetery seems to roll, and grass covers the sites where there are no headstones or markers. **Ella Dawson Berryhill** (1885–1949) was one of those laid to rest here. Born in Lincoln Parish, Louisiana, she married **Dan Berryhill** (1877–1949) in 1911, before moving to Weed. Together, Ella and her husband ran the Berryhill Hotel and "The Club," for twenty-four years. The Club was known for its great bands and musicians. Ella also served on Franklin Delano Roosevelt's National Recovery Administration Blue Eagle Committee during the years following the Depression of the 1930s. Dan, also born in Louisiana, was one of thirteen children. As a trimmer, he first worked for Longville Lumber Company in Louisiana and was then transferred to Weed. He was also interred in the Lincoln Heights Cemetery.

Mary Long Banks (1840–1946) was laid to rest in the Lincoln Heights Cemetery on April 7, 1946. According to her son Thomas who worked as an edgerman for Long-Bell Lumber Company, she was born in Fort Bend County, Texas, around 1840—as a slave. In the 1930 Weed census, she was reportedly ninety years old. Her marker has crumbled and is no longer legible. Thomas' wife, **Mary Liza Tillman Banks** (1890–1944), however, is buried alongside Mary Long Banks.

As in all parts of California, the clashes with Native American tribes in the north came with the crush of miners and settlers. Tragedy played out many times over: in 1851, miners killed 300 *Wintu* near Old Shasta (aka Shasta City); in Trinity County, the sheriff led a party of seventy men against the Wintu living in Hayfork Valley, killing more than 150. In 1859, whites attacked a *Mechoopda* (Maidu) camp near Chico Creek, killing forty men, women, and children. **Chief Kimolly**, of the Shasta tribe, was incarcerated at Alcatraz Island for many years, though he eventually returned home and was buried in an unmarked grave in the **Hamburg Cemetery**. This cemetery is definitely an out-of-the-way, rarely visited pioneer cemetery. Located east of the community of Hamburg, it is ten miles north of Yreka, on Highway 96 near the Klamath River. The sign is a quaint, hand-painted wooden plaque, and the cemetery is a little more than a walk among trees and brush (and poison oak).

Clara H. Wicks (1879–1978), daughter of Charley and Margaret Wicks, who lived to be ninety-nine, was another important member of the Shasta. Undaunted by bear or mountain lions, with her .22 rifle at her side, she traversed the hills and forests to gather wild plums, *pipsissewa*, and *icknish*—all the while telling important Shasta stories to the children she took along. She was buried in the **Fort Jones Cemetery**, just off Eastside Road past Fort Jones, in Siskiyou County. The epitaph attached to her large rock headstone, reads: "Aunt Clara Wicks/ Loved and Respected by All."

"Indian Peggy" (1800–1902) was another significant woman in Siskiyou County history. While relations between the Shasta and the miners in the area were strained, at best, sometime in 1852, Peggy warned the people of Yreka and Humbug of an impending attack by members of her tribe. The tiny mining town was abandoned, and when the attackers arrived, they found it empty. Whether her warning was a way to protect the miners or her tribe from retaliation will never be fully known, but it saved many from bloodshed. For the rest of her life—and she lived to be 100+ years old—she was a welcome visitor to local communities. In 1951, the Siskiyou County Historical Society dedicated a plaque that was added to the boulder at a **private gravesite**, which is located along a narrow lane off of Fairlane Road, just down from Siskiyou County's Fairgrounds. It reads: "Indian Peggy, born about 1800. Died October 26, 1902. Beloved member of the Shasta tribe. A friend of Indians and Whites. Saved Yreka by warning them of an Indian attack."

In Chico, Butte County, the **Mechoopda Cemetery** is located between West Sacramento Avenue and Rancheria Drive. It is a narrow strip of land, but neatly fenced, set between two buildings.

Indian Peggy, a Shasta, established herself as a friend of the whites of Siskiyou County while protecting her own people.

Plants and grass keep the grounds cool, especially when Chico's summer temperatures spike at 110 degrees. One tribal member interred in the Mechoopda Cemetery was **John "Captain John" Tonoka** (1803–1899), who lived to be ninety-six years old. He died at his home at Rancho Chico and was buried in the Indian village. General John Bidwell, Chico's renowned founder, reported that Tonoka had been around when the first white settlement began on Butte Creek in 1844.

Henry Azbill (1899–1973), also a member of the Mechoopda Maidu, was an important historian and provided detailed narratives about life on the Chico Rancheria and in Butte County. He worked with Dorothy Hill and Robert Rathbun, who spent "35 years . . . documenting what they called 'California Native oral traditions' throughout parts of Mendocino, Lake, Yolo, Sonoma, El Dorado, Placer, Amador, Mariposa, Nevada, Sierra, Yuba, Plumas, Butte, Sutter, Colusa, Glenn, Trinity, Tehama, Humboldt, Shasta, Lassen, Siskiyou, and Modoc counties." Henry was actually both Mechoopda and *Kanaka* (Hawaiian), and he taught how the Kanaka came to California and Chico to work on John Bidwell's ranch. All over Northern California, the Kanaka and various tribes intermarried.

As a side note: there is a **Kanaka Cemetery** located not far from a mining settlement known as Gottsville, along State Highway 96 and the Klamath River, in Siskiyou County. While findagrave.com lists thirty-five graves, designated only by small metal markers, many of Kanaka and/or Kanaka/Shasta or Karuk shared heritage are buried in other locations. Several of the markers do indicate individuals born in

Henry Azbill, from Chico, in Butte County, spent years teaching about the life and culture of the Mechoopda Maidu and other regional tribes; here he appears with Dr. Teresa Davis of CSU Chico, in the 1970s.
COURTESY DR. TERESA DAVIS

Hawaii, including **William Makakoa "Bill" Butler** and **James "Jim" Alpia**, both born in 1832.

It's impossible to talk about Chico or Butte County without talking about **General John Bidwell** (1819–1900) and his wife **Annie Ellicott Kennedy Bidwell** (1839–1918). John Bidwell was a pioneer, farmer, soldier, statesman, prohibitionist, and philanthropist. Anxious to head west, he joined a wagon train in 1841. This became the *first* wagon train to arrive in California. Initially Bidwell worked for John A. Sutter and then received a Mexican land grant, known as Rancho Chico, totaling 22,000 acres. An agriculturalist, Bidwell cultivated new crops on his ranch in Chico. In 1864, he was elected to Congress as a Republican and served one term. He died in 1900 and was laid to rest in the **Chico Cemetery.**

Annie Bidwell was born in Pennsylvania, but her father worked in Washington, D.C. At age twenty-nine, she married John Bidwell. Attending their wedding were such elites as President Andrew Johnson, Elizabeth Cady Stanton, and Ulysses S. Grant. After the wedding, they traveled to Chico where Annie immediately became involved with the Mechoopda who worked for her husband, as well as those living in the Rancheria village. According to Thelma Wilson, a Mechoopda member, "Mrs. Bidwell came down off her pedestal [as an eastern socialite] to minister as an angel. . . . When everyone else was seeing us as the lowest form of animal, she was able to see us as human beings, and when a baby died, she became as morose as if she had lost a child of her own."

In her elegant Victorian home, Annie entertained individuals such as John Muir, Susan B. Anthony, and others who were the thinkers and doers of the time. After John Bidwell passed away, Annie donated 2,200 acres to Chico for a natural park, appropriately called Bidwell Park. Annie died in 1918, at seventy-eight, and was interred alongside her husband in Chico Cemetery. Their "headstone" is unique: a large boulder at the end of a lane in the cemetery. As you approach it, you realize it represents the natural world in which they lived their lives.

Daniel N. Friesleben (1832–1897) was raised on a farm in New York. When he was old enough to learn a trade, his parents apprenticed him to a cigar maker, after which he went west to California. He arrived in San Francisco, on January 1, 1854, with only $10 in his pocket. From San Francisco, Friesleben traveled to Marysville, in Yuba County, but with no jobs available, he set off for the mines. His first stop was Camptonville, also in Yuba County, and this time he had "five bits" in his pocket. He did not fare well there, however, and so he returned to Marysville, where he sold his blankets and where he found work on a ranch. In 1857, Friesleben moved to Oroville, Butte County, and opened a mercantile business. In 1864, he invested in the stock company that built the Union Hotel; three years later, he bought the stock and became the proprietor. Still interested in farming, however, he helped found the Oroville Citrus Association, which planted the first forty-acre commercial orange orchard in Northern California. In time, the Friesleben Ranch totaled 1,800 acres near the junction of the Feather River and Honcut Creek. Friesleben's last years were spent between his ranch in Oroville and his home in San Francisco. He died in San Francisco on January 25, 1897, but was interred in the **Oroville Jewish Cemetery**, located on Feather River Blvd. in Oroville, Butte County. Originally established in 1859, the first recorded burials occurred in 1862. In total, seven members of the Friesleben family are interred in the Jewish cemetery, including children **Nelson Friesleben** (1861–1862), **Eda Friesleben** (1867–1867), and **Louis Friesleben** (1863–1869).

The Millsaps family was a pioneer family that settled in Glenn County. **George Washington Millsaps** (1822–1905), originally from Kentucky, arrived in 1854 and began homesteading in 1858. For half a century he made his home in the settlement named after him; the post office operated at Millsaps from 1894 until 1927, and then it moved to Orland, Glenn County. George married **Elizabeth Dunn** (1826–1884) and he also established the Glenn County Mining Company in the Dog Creek mining district. When his wife passed away, Millsaps opened the **Chrome Cemetery**, along County Road 306, for both his family and his neighbors' families. There are a number of Millsaps also interred in the **Willows Cemetery**, the **Grindstone Cemetery**, and the **Newville Cemetery**—all located within Glenn County.

Glenn County has six public cemetery districts, including Newville, Elk Creek, German, Marvin-Chapel, Orland, and Willows. Other cemeteries include **Stonyford-Indian Valley Cemetery**, which has land in Glenn as well as Colusa counties, and **Monroeville Cemetery**, located five miles south of Hamilton City. The most famous individual laid to rest at Monroeville (although there is some controversy over where his grave is located) was **William B. Ide** (1796–1852), governor of California and leader of the Bear Flag Revolt in 1846, which helped lead to the **Mexican American War** and statehood.

Oak Hill Cemetery in Red Bluff, Tehama County, is home to many early settlers. Founded in 1859 by members of the IOOF and Masonic Lodges, it is located at 600 Cemetery Lane, off Walnut Street, three-quarter of a mile from Main Street in Red Bluff. Two brothers, **John B. Graves** (1867–1925) and **Richard Benjamin**

Graves (1857–1918), came to the area to ranch. They moved to Trinity County for good grazing ground, but lost their entire herd during that harsh first winter. They switched to farming, but with little success, they decided to try prospecting. One day on Coffee Creek, the miraculous thing happened, and the brothers struck it big, even taking out a single $42,000 nugget ($1.3 million in today's dollars). Around 1912, Richard built a store in Ono, on land purchased from Frances McCormick. After Richard Graves passed away in 1918, the store was sold but remained in operation until 1955. He was laid to rest in the Oak Hill Cemetery in Red Bluff. His headstone resembles a log rolled onto its side with a "piece" of fabric draped over the top. John B. Graves is not recorded as being interred in any Tehama County cemetery.

John D. Flournoy (1847–1935) was a pioneer of Modoc County, one of the earliest. Originally from Missouri, he crossed the plains to California driving a herd of 200 cows when he was seventeen. He settled in Modoc County, near Likely, and soon established a livestock business that became the J. D. Flournoy Cattle Company. Flournoy was a reasonable man who was able to work with the Indians, and it's said that at one time, he mediated issues between the Pitt River tribe and the settlers. He married **Frances H. Jackson** (1857–1937), and they had four sons. John Flournoy died at eighty-seven and was buried in the **Likely Cemetery** in Modoc County. Frances passed away two years later and was laid to rest beside him.

In 1938, **Minerva C. Ivory** (1848–1938) passed away in Modoc County and was interred in the **Alturas Cemetery**, located in Alturas.

She was born in Council Bluffs, Iowa, and crossed the plains with her parents when she was three years old. After moving to California, she met and married Peter Ivory, with whom she had fourteen children, but only five of her children outlived her. She is considered one of Modoc County's earliest pioneers, and it was said that even as she aged, she could walk or "outfish" anyone. She was eighty-nine when she died, having outlived nine of children in addition to her husband. Minerva's headstone is a small one, nestled into the grass, but it lacks any epitaph or indication of the kind of rugged life she obviously lived.

Rosannah Josephine Brown (1885–1971) was the youngest of seven children, born in October 1885. Her parents owned a ranch near Dana, California, along Fall River, where her father also worked as a house painter. When Josephine was twenty-one, her mother, **Rosannah Stuart Brown** (1840–1906)—a guest at a hotel in Santa Rosa—was crushed to death when the San Francisco earthquake of 1906 sent waves of destruction in every direction. She was buried in the **Santa Rosa Rural Cemetery**, located on Franklin Avenue in Santa Rosa, Sonoma County. Though Josephine was an amateur photographer, her photos became popular with area residents. She married **Albert H. "Bert" Bosworth** (1869–1951) of Fall River Mills. Albert was a jeweler and watchmaker, so the couple established Bosworth's Jewelry Store and Gift Shop. Even the death of Albert in 1951 did not deter Josephine from keeping the business going. He was interred in the **Fall River Cemetery**, in Fall River Mills, Shasta County. In addition to maintaining the Bosworth business, Josephine advocated for the Fort Crook Historical Society and museum. She donated land and as curator, she approved all exhibits before being displayed. Josephine Bosworth passed away in 1971 and was laid to rest beside her husband in the Fall River Cemetery, Shasta County.

Yreka, Siskiyou County, is one of the few cities with an independent **Chinese Cemetery**. Situated on Highway 3 east, on the road to Montague, it is easily spotted. Originally, fifty-two individuals were buried in the cemetery, but most of those buried were exhumed and returned to China. Still, there remains a handful of graves. A bronze plaque lists the names, birth dates (where known), and death dates (where known) of those originally interred there, including **Ah Guey** (1857–1945), who had been a miner and storekeeper in Yreka for seventy-five years and was well known up and down Miner Street. Believed to be eighty-eight, he began to fail and was taken to the Yreka General Hospital where he passed away.

Manuel Mencibo Quadros (1834–1899) was born on the Azorean island of Sao Jorge. In order to avoid army service, he headed out to sea. When his ship finally anchored in the San Francisco Bay, gold had just been discovered in the Sierras. Manuel and a shipmate, Joe Lewis, disembarked and headed to the northern mines. They traveled through Redding and Shasta, in Shasta County, crossed the Trinity River, in Trinity County, and journeyed through Callahan and over to Yreka, in Siskiyou County. Manuel considered returning to the Azores to get a wife, but when he met **Mary Constant Deas**, his trip to the Azores became unnecessary. They were married in November 1866. As he grew more successful, Manuel bought a ranch from "Indian Tom" near the mouth of Bogus Creek. In 1891, he purchased another ranch. Manuel died in October 1899, at age sixty-nine. Mary passed away eleven years later, in 1910. Both were interred in the **Saint Joseph's Catholic Cemetery**, originally established in 1854 and located on E. Center Street (just off Interstate 5), in Yreka, Siskiyou County.

Manuel Sylva (1836–1916) likewise emigrated from the Azores and ended up in Siskiyou County. He arrived in the United States in 1862, and then traveled to California and Trinity County to try his hand at mining. In 1869, he homesteaded 160 acres on Willow Creek in Siskiyou County. He married **Maria Coelho** (1850–1918), also from the Azores. They had thirteen children and eventually five of their children homesteaded adjoining properties. Manuel and Maria were also buried in Saint Joseph's Catholic Cemetery in Yreka. They share a unique headstone, a single upright gray granite stone with a carved cross extending from the left side of the slab.

Significant members of the region's Portuguese population emigrated from the Azores, families like those of the Solus, Costa, Serpa, Scala, Mello, and other clans.

Frederick "Fred" Charles Burton (1879–1968) was born on the Burton family's Scott Valley, Siskiyou County homestead, one of twelve children born to **Stephen Taylor Burton** (1847–1925) and **Sarah Jane Shelley** (1854–1887). Fred married **Gertrude Claire Bryan** (1880–1961) in 1907, after which they purchased the stage stop known as Forest House, outside of Yreka. In its heyday, the Forest House boasted the largest apple and fruit orchards in California, produced its own wine, and became a popular stopping place for travelers. It also served as a local hostelry and location for dances and celebrations. Married for fifty-four years, Gertrude Burton passed away in 1961 and Fred passed away in 1968. They were both interred at **Evergreen Cemetery**, located on Evergreen Lane in Yreka, Siskiyou County.

The Red Rock area of Butte Valley, Siskiyou County, was a barren landscape in the early days of settlement. With few homesteads and poor roads, it was difficult for children to attend school regularly and just as difficult to attract teachers. In 1911, young **Earnestina Catherine Walter** (1893–1921), who had just graduated from Yreka High School the year before, traveled to Red Rock for her first year of teaching. She was the daughter of two pioneer families; her grandfather Walter had emigrated from Germany and her mother's family, the Spannaus clan, had settled along the Klamath River.

Earnestina's year at Red Rock was difficult. Some of her students were nearly as old as she. After returning to Yreka, Earnestina married **Charles Henry Ruggles** (1874–1941) of Fort Jones in 1914. She taught at a local school until her death in 1921. Only twenty-eight years old, she was laid to rest in Evergreen Cemetery in Yreka, Siskiyou County. Charles, however, was buried in Yolo County, at **Woodland Cemetery** in November 1941 after marrying **Mollie A. Russell Coonrod** (1882–1976). Mollie lived to be ninety-three and was interred at **Evergreen Cemetery** in Yreka in September 1976.

Stephen H. Soulé (1836–1917) was the son of Ebenezer and Cornelia Soulé. Born in Yates County, New York, he was only three weeks old when his father died. When he was eight, he went to live with his grandfather in Illinois. He stayed there until he was sixteen, when Soulé returned to New York. Soulé married **Lucinda Maria Boyes** (1842–1928) in July 1858, when she was just sixteen. He worked as a farm laborer until 1860 when he and Lucinda headed west to California. Soulé drove a four-horse team with his family and brother Andrew. The Soulés arrived in Little Shasta, Siskiyou County, in September 1861, where they purchased eighty acres. Over time, Stephen and Andrew purchased more land and expanded their holdings. The Soulés had nine children: George; Stella; Damia; Cornelia; Ernest; Annie; Charles; John; and Ray. Stephen, the family patriarch, died in 1917 and was buried in the **Little Shasta Cemetery**, located outside of Montague, Siskiyou County.

Before settling in Little Shasta, in 1855, **Samuel Musgrave** (unknown–1895) struggled to get to America from northern England. The family moved to Cumberland, where Musgrave spent his early childhood working in the mines. When he tried to attend school the first time, the teacher whipped him for knocking down another boy who had stuck him with pins, so he refused to go back to school. Instead, in 1845, Musgrave sailed to America on a steamer, the *Queen of the West*. It was a thirty-day journey and after landing, Musgrave ended up in Pennsylvania until February 1852. Finally, he set sail for California via Panama. The journey across the Isthmus and by ship took twenty-six days to reach San Francisco. Twenty-seven men died crossing the Isthmus.

Before becoming a farmer in Siskiyou County, Musgrave spent time in the mines along the American River and then settled

The Soulé family settled in Little Shasta in September 1861 and became one of the area's well-known ranchers.

permanently in Little Shasta. He and his wife had four children: Mark; MaryAnn; Elizabeth Jane; and George. Ellen preceded her husband in death and was buried at Little Shasta. Samuel Musgrave passed away in 1899 and was also laid to rest at Little Shasta Cemetery. He was eighty-five years old.

Abner Weed (1842–1917) was born in Maine. After serving in the Civil War—where he witnessed Lee's surrender at Appomattox—he married **Rachel Cunningham** (1842–1940) in September 1866. They migrated to California in 1869, settling for a time in Truckee before moving to Siskiyou County. Engaged in lumbering, Abner built a sawmill (in the town that came to be known as Weed) and purchased timberlands to supply his sawmill. He also owned a

22,000-acre ranch in Oregon, where he became quite successful. For a number of years, Abner's mill produced more lumber than any other mill in the nation. Eventually he sold his Weed Lumber Company to Long-Bell Lumber Company. After Abner fell ill, he died in 1917 and was buried in the **Dunsmuir City Cemetery** off of Dunsmuir Avenue, Dunsmuir, Siskiyou County.

Abner and Rachel had four children, but only three lived to adulthood. **Elenore May Weed** (1878–1880) lived two years. **Edward Chandler Weed** (1873–1911) died when he was thirty-seven years old. **Horace Atwood Weed** (1880–1932) lived to fifty-two, while **Abbie Cunningham Weed Albee** (1867–1945)— their oldest child—lived to be seventy-seven. Rachel Weed lived to be ninety-seven years old, and when she passed away, she was buried beside Abner in the Dunsmuir City Cemetery.

A tragic event occurred near Hawkinsville, east of Yreka, Siskiyou County, during the winters of 1852, 1853, and 1854, and again in 1861 and 1862, when the area was hit with smallpox. At least 580 cases had already erupted in San Francisco. In 1854, a rash of smallpox occurred at Deadwood, a mining camp up McAdams Creek, outside of Fort Jones, killing a dozen or more people. The Costa family, who had been given cast off clothing as a donation, all perished after it was discovered that the clothing had been worn by children infected by smallpox. Rather than laid to rest in an established cemetery, the family was buried on a hillside near their home, and trees, as a memorial, were planted alongside their graves. The trees still mark the location.

John Daggett (1833–1919), one of Salmon River's most successful pioneers, came west in 1852. He purchased and worked the famous Black Bear mine off and on from 1862 to 1885. Mule trains hauled the massive equipment in from the coast, while supplies arrived in large burden baskets carried by Indian women from nearby tribes.

The mine yielded 200,000 ounces of gold and consisted of two rich veins, one running north and south and the other east and west. Daggett was not only enterprising, but he was also known to be fair. He hired 300 Cornish miners to work the mine, and later he hired Chinese miners. When one of the Chinese workers was murdered, Daggett hired a gunslinger to protect them. Daggett was also elected to the State Assembly and served as lieutenant governor in 1882. He was appointed the superintendent of the U.S. Mint in San Francisco in 1893, a position he held for four years. When he died in 1919, he was interred in the **Etna Cemetery**, located on

The Costa family from Hawkinsville, near Yreka, perished after the entire family contracted smallpox.

Old Sawyers Bar Road in Etna, just "over the mountain" from his beloved Black Bear Mine.

Born and reared in the mountains surrounding their father's Black Bear Mine, John Daggett's daughters and son were raised to understand and appreciate the Klamath Mountains. **Hallie Morse Daggett** (1878–1964) was an especially competent outdoorswoman, although she and her sister **Leslie D. Daggett Hyde** (1884–1961) had both been schooled at female seminaries in San Francisco and Alameda.

The First Female Fire Lookout

In 1913, thirty-year-old Hallie M. Daggett applied to the U.S. Forest Service for the position of fire lookout. No woman had ever served in this position heretofore, and Ranger McCarthy who reviewed her qualifications hoped she could do the job—especially because the only other applicants were entirely unreliable: one was a drunk and the other had poor eyesight. McCarthy wrote to his superiors, "She [Hallie] knows every trail on the Salmon River watershed, and is thoroughly familiar with every foot of the district."

Hallie Daggett's lookout station was the Eddy Gulch Station, which sat high atop Klamath Peak, accessible only by horse or foot. Her cabin was a twelve-foot by fourteen-foot structure next to which flew the American flag she had to raise and lower each day. Her job was demanding, with only two days off a month, and all day, every day, she stood scanning the forest in every direction for smoke—even at night. In 1912 alone, local forest fires had killed seventy-five people and devastated $25 million in timber loss. Hallie was diligent and, in a sense, in competition with the men who sat atop other fire lookouts, but in her first summer fire season, she reported the most fires—which she reported via an antiquated

Hallie Daggett was the first woman to work as a fire lookout in the United States and opened the door for women to work at such jobs.

phone system. When interviewed about her job as lookout, Hallie replied, "It was quite a swift change in three days, from San Francisco, civilization and sea level, to a solitary cabin on a still more solitary mountain, 6,444 feet elevation and three hours' hard climb from everywhere, but in spite of the fact that almost the very first question asked by everyone was 'Isn't it awfully lonesome up there?' I never felt a moment's longing to retrace the step."

In the end, Hallie Daggett spent thirteen summers working lookout—all alone except for her dog, her horse, and her gun.

By 1918, with World War I, other women were hired to do what Hallie Daggett had been doing. Two women were appointed that first year, but by 1919, there were more women serving atop mountain peaks than men. As her superior, McCarthy, reported to one newspaperman, "No man ever performed the duties more conscientiously or effectively." Hallie died in 1964 and was buried in the Etna Cemetery, near her sister Leslie Daggett Hyde.

Charles Kappler was born in Alsace, France in 1834 and emigrated to Yreka, Siskiyou County, California, in 1860 where he worked as a brewer. He returned to France to marry **Florentine Kriner** in 1865; the couple returned to Yreka in 1867. In 1868, Charles bought a brewery from A. P. Hartstrand located three miles east of Etna. In 1872, Charles moved his family to Etna where he built a brewery. A fire destroyed it in 1875. In rebuilding, he enlarged and modernized the operation. A successful entrepreneur, in 1895, Charles built an enormous three-story home on Main Street. For a time, Catholic services were held there and it also functioned as a school. Workers at the brewery often boarded there. Charles built the first ice plant in Etna and the area and provided the town's first electric lights, in 1898. From a power plant on nearby Johnson Creek, he powered fans to cool the icehouse and brewery, which produced 30,000 gallons of beer each year. Beer was shipped all over Southern Oregon and Northern California. Etna Beer even won a gold medal at the 1915 World's Exposition in San Francisco. Though the brewery closed with Prohibition, a new Etna Brewery was "reopened" in 1990 on the original site and is now a brewery and pub. Members of the Kappler family, including Charles and Florentine, are buried in the Etna Cemetery.

One early Fort Jones, Siskiyou County, rancher was **Israel Smith "Matt" Mathews** (1827–1904), who, along with pioneer John Fairchild, drifted into Fort Jones, located within Scott Valley, in 1852. Mathews homesteaded 160 acres. He married **Ann Elizabeth Coffin** (1844–1903), who had crossed the plains to California with her grandmother, **Orpha McMechen Davidson**, and family. Family lore has it that with each child, Israel received an additional 160 acres; thus, Mathews and his seven sons ended up with a substantial ranch outside of the fort at Fort Jones. They also opened up five butcher shops around the county. Ann and Israel did lose one daughter, **Ann Elizabeth Mathews** (1865–1867), at age two. She was buried in the Fort Jones Cemetery, Siskiyou County. Both Ann and Israel were also interred at the Fort Jones Cemetery.

Sergeant James Bryan (1838–1913), the third of seven sons, was born to James Bryan and Mary Bridget Whelan. He emigrated from Ireland and a year later enlisted in the U.S. Army Company F, Fourth U.S. Calvary. He was eventually stationed at Fort Jones. After mustering out, Bryan became one of the first pioneers to farm in Scott Valley, Siskiyou County. He married **Mary Josephine Fragly** (1846–1918)—also from Ireland—and together they had nine children, although only seven reached adulthood. To this day, the Bryan ranch continues to be run by members of the sixth generation of the Bryan family. James and Mary were both interred in the Fort Jones Cemetery.

Fort Jones

Established on October 16, 1852, Fort Jones was an isolated 640-acre-long U.S. Army post located on the east side of Scott River near today's community of Fort Jones (first known as Wheelock). The post was established by Edward H. Fitzgerald, with Companies A and E, First Dragoons, and named after Colonel Roger

Jones, who died on July 15, 1852. The post was evacuated in 1858, although it was reoccupied in 1864 for a short time. General George Crook, who later gained fame during the Civil War, was stationed at Fort Jones when he first left West Point. In one report, he complained that his stipend of $64 a month was not enough to cover his food bill. However, Crook and the other officers, including the future Confederate general John B. Hood, combined their funds and "as we were fond of hunting and game was plentiful [we were able] to supply our own table with every variety thereof and to send the surplus to market for sale. This financial plan worked admirably."

Another early rancher from Siskiyou County, was **George F. Smith** (1825–1901). Born in England, he immigrated to California in 1852. He married **Cleopatra H. "Cleo" Fairbrother** (1837–1893) and they had six children. One of their daughters, **Minerva "Minnie" E. Loos** (1859–1938), became the mother of **Corinne Anita "Nita" Loos** (1889–1981), renowned Hollywood screenwriter of award-winning early films like *Gentlemen Prefer Blondes* and *Gentlemen Marry Brunettes*. In 1912, Anita Loos became the first female scriptwriter in Hollywood, and between 1912 and 1915, she wrote 105 scripts. She lived to be ninety-two and was buried in the Etna Cemetery, along with her grandparents, parents, and siblings.

Crystal Creek, Siskiyou County, was one of the original settlements in Scott Valley, Siskiyou County. Today all that is left is an historical landmark marking the site along Highway 3 outside of Etna, and—tucked up along a hillside, is the tiny, abandoned and well-hidden **Crystal Creek Cemetery**. Difficult to determine its size, the site is covered in layers of leaves, sticks, and broken stones. Sagging bits of

Native Daughters of the Golden West posted names of those who were once interred in the Crystal Creek Cemetery. Many more have been lost to time.

page wire suggest that the area was once fully enclosed. A large slab monument stands near the center and attached is a faded list of names of those interred here. It's a raw reminder of a time that has been lost to just about anyone who still lives in the area. The weeds, the leaves, and the skeleton trees leave the visitor with a haunting sense of the forlorn.

AUTHOR'S NOTE

This project was all-encompassing, as it required travel; hundreds of photographs, interviews, and phone calls; online research; and library research. Unfortunately, I had to leave as much out of the book as is included in the book! One disappointment came with the COVID-19 shutdown, as I had to immediately suspend all travel around the state. That left me without a significant number of photographs.

However, coupled with the statewide shutdown was the fact that I suffered two accidents even before the shutdown. In August 2019, as I was visiting a cemetery in Lake County, I overlooked a raised curb and—in my excitement—fell to the cement, breaking four ribs and damaging a lung. In spite of the fall, I managed to visit three more cemeteries before driving five hours home, at which point my older son insisted I go to the Emergency Room. I was admitted into the hospital for three days, then sent home with strict instructions to rest. Of course, I still had hundreds of miles to cover! While I had visited dozens of cemeteries already, I had dozens more to see.

As if one fall was not enough, in February 2020, I fell down our 1870s farmhouse staircase—a full fourteen stairs—headfirst.

This time I took an ambulance to the hospital. Thankfully, no broken bones, but I did sustain a concussion and this time, not only was I ordered to rest, but I was also forbidden to read, to watch television, or to work on a screen, that is, NO computer time. Two or three weeks later we entered the shutdown, and while I had plenty of time to write, I still had more sites and cities to visit and research.

Two more accidents befell our family before the entire project was finished, which left me wondering if 2020 was, indeed, a year to sweep under the carpet!

Even with these setbacks, however, the project has been rewarding. Always attracted to cemeteries, and as a genealogy junkie, I was excited and determined to bring to life as many individual stories as I could. My intent was to select large, small, abandoned, or just historic cemeteries or graves and find representative families or individuals whose stories could/would reveal a more honest picture of the life and times in which they lived.

One of the most powerful but disquieting revelations was how the reality of "DEATH" pervaded everyone's life. It seemed to stalk some families with an intensity that most of us rarely have to endure. Today we even seem impervious to it, or at least to its frequency, and many people refrain from "getting too close" to the dead; a quick visit to a funeral home is a stretch for some. Yet these people, regardless of how often they had to bear it, were resolute and courageous, generally preparing their own for burial, including setting aside time for a wake (where family and others "sat" with the body before burial). If it didn't harden some to death, it certainly reveals how close everyone lived to it.

Even as we are now fighting our own pandemic in 2020, studying the losses suffered by so many during the 1918–1920 flu pandemic made the cost of disease all the more real. The anxiety, fear, anticipation, confusion, loss, and grief we are facing today were fully realized by people in the past, and for those of the eighteenth, nineteenth, and twentieth centuries, it was not a once-in-a-lifetime event but was frequently repeated over and over.

Finally, I regret I could not include more cemeteries and more stories! With the thousands that exist up and down the state, I was forced to make selections and to trust my instincts. Sometimes I began with findagrave.com (a cemetery research website that genealogists use frequently) for information or for the names of pioneers, in addition to possible photographers whose last-minute photo contributions were appreciated.

To share just how meaningful an experience tramping around an old cemetery can be, just as I was finishing up my edits on this manuscript, I got a message from the daughter of an old-timer, Sharon Holmes Sanborn. She related how, after 9/11, her cousin came home from Houston, Texas, and while visiting, the two decided to do a little investigation into family history. They went to the cemetery in search of the grave of their great grandfather, Ensign Rufus Smith, also known as "Whiskey Smith." They did not uncover his grave (at that time), but they did stumble over a grave under a big oak tree on the side of the cemetery that read: "Age 19, He walked into the bar and they shooted him dead." Sadly, phones did not have cameras then, and when they returned a year later with a camera, the stone was gone, and it took a few more visits before the pair discovered the lost grave of the long-departed ancestor. As noted by Sharon, "Last year (2019), my cousin met me there and he installed a homemade 'plate' to put on great grandfather's grave." Whiskey Smith, one of Aetna Mills's earliest pioneers, had been found and now his story can be told.

And what a perfect door to history to open—to rediscover family after three or four generations—AND to uncover a mystery. In the final analysis, there is only dirt and bone (or dust) to discover, but truthfully what more can we say than this:

We are all stories in the end, remembered by the adventures we had, the achievements we made and the people we loved. So make sure your story is a good one.

—Nishan Panwar

ACKNOWLEDGMENTS

While there are so many to whom I am indebted, I dedicated this book to my two sisters, Patricia Mae Peterson and Teresa M. Davis, because both provided continual and frequent encouragement and inspiration as well as "first aid." They traveled with me up and/or down the state, wandering through cemeteries, carrying cameras and lists of names as I searched and investigated. I also want to acknowledge my husband and family who weathered my long hours of being locked away and unavailable, apart from the weeks of the COVID shut down! Finally, I want to thank my editor, Erin Turner, for believing in this project and giving me an added dose of encouragement. I would also like to thank (in alphabetical order): Tom Allain, Suzanne Birch, Keely Martin Bosler, Paul Boyle, Angel M. Brant, Stephanie Burton, Todd Burton, California Missions Staff, Margie Campbell, Jacob Castellon, John D. Curtis, Teresa Davis, Tyler Dawn, Jan Dishon, Rick Dolwig, Tamar Dolwig, Chris S. Ervin, Wendy Figueroa, Findagrave.com, Vanessa Ford, Fort Jones Museum, Don Garrett, Paul Bailey-Gates, Lisa Gioia-Acres, Gary Gragnani, Julia Baskin Green, Carolyn Wing Greenlee, Dean Hirst, Vickie Hittson, Kim S. Hurst, Michael Imwalle, Daniel Jansenson, Doug Jenner, Francyne Jenner, GloryAnn Jenner, Chris Jepsen, Eric Jopson, Julian Book House, Sunny Lee, Adam Kipp, Robin Lakin, Everett Laustalot, Patricia Laustalot, Sunny Lee, David Lewis, Jose Leyva, Larry Luna, A. J. Marik, Bob Marlowe, Michael Marsalek, Laine Martens, Cynthia Leal Massey, Susan Mayfield, Casey Mayfield, Don McCombs, Carol McCune, Roni McFadden, Mike McGary, Matteo Mereu, Andres Mora, Haley Myers, Chris Nelson, Chris Peterson, Patricia Peterson, Lesa Pfrommer, Cecelia Reuter, Linda Rhoadarmer, Sharon Holmes Sanborn, Gaia San Martino, Selma Schantz, Kathleen Shurber, Mary Simonelli, Siskiyou County Museum, Nalia Campbell-Skipper, Molly Steele, Anne Shurtleff Stevens, John and Peggy Valpey, Tay Vanderlip, Joe Walker, Whaley House Museum, Annette Wells, David Wells, Carl Wimer, and Dan Worley.

Thanks to those who provided some of the images used in the book: Denise Boose; Dee Cramer; Tom K. Cubes; J. Clark McAbee; Carol McCune; Bret Lama; Fort Jones Museum; Julia Baskin Green; Janice Janek; PJH/Angelbird; and Cecelia Reuter.

Finally, thanks to all those who provided images and stories and ideas, and—not least of all—I dedicate this volume to those individuals whose names and life stories I was not able to include. Life is a story and each of them deserves a place in history.

BIBLIOGRAPHY

Adams, Charles F. *The Magnificent Rogues of San Francisco*. Palo Alto, CA: Pacific Books, Publishers, 1998.

"American Gravestone Evolution—Part 2: Monuments of North America in the 1800s." *Atlas Preservation* (2016). Accessed November 10, 2019. atlaspreservation.com/pages/historical2.

Ammenheuser, Maura. "A Look Back: 19th Century Businessman Dreamed of Town." *The Press Enterprise*, January 11, 2011. pe.com/2011/01/01/a-look-back-19th-century-businessman-dreamed-of-town/.

Armor, Samuel. *History of Orange County California with Biographical Sketches of the Leading Men and Women of the County Who Have Been Identified with Its Growth and Development from the Early Days to the Present*. Los Angeles, CA: Historic Record Company (1921). Accessed December 11, 2019. archive.org/details/cu31924028881965/page/n4/mode/2up.

Bagley, Will, ed. *Across the Plains, Mountains, and Deserts: A Bibliography of the Oregon-California Trail, 1812–1912: For a Historic Resource Study of the Oregon & California National Historic Trails*. N.p.: Prairie Dog Press (2014). Accessed January 15, 2020. nps.gov/cali/historyculture/upload/NPS-HRS-Biblio-Master- February2014 WillBagley.pdf.

Barrows, H.D. "The Lugo Family of California." *Annual Publication of the Historical Society of Southern California* 9, no. 1/2 (1912): 34–40. Accessed April 7, 2020. JSTOR, jstor.org/stable/41168892.

Baugher, Sherene, and Richard F. Veit. *The Archaeology of American Cemeteries and Gravemarkers*. Gainesville: University Press of Florida, 2015.

Bell, Major Horace. *Reminiscences of a Ranger, Or, Early Times in Southern California*. N.p.: Yarnell, Caystile & Mathes, Printer (1881). Accessed January 11, 2020. play. google.com/books/reader?id=sQINAAAAIAAJ&hl=en&pg=GBS.PA3.

"Bernardo Yorba Timeline." *Yorba Linda History*. Accessed March 23, 2020. yorbalindahistory.org/timeline.html

Berner, Noah. "Locals Seek to Locate, Protect Old Hospital Cemetery in San Andreas." *Calaveras Enterprise*, January 22, 2020. calaverasenterprise.com/ news/article_9fb30a20–3d68–11ea-9d30–9f5f02869306.html

"Biography of John Daubenbiss." *Online Biographies*. Last modified 1931. Accessed December 2, 2019. onlinebiographies.info/ca/sf/daubenbill-j.htm.

Bissell, Laurie. "San Diego Cemeteries: A Brief Guide." *The Journal of San Diego History* (1982). Accessed April 2, 2020. sandiegohistory.org/journal/1982/ october/cemeteries/.

Boardman, Patricia M. "Mini Biographies of Pioneers Buried in the Santa Ana Cemetery." *A Walk to Remember* (2009). Accessed December 10, 2019.

Brigandi, Phil. "A Collection of Articles about the History of Orange County, California." *OC Historyland* (2019). Accessed March 8, 2020. ochistoryland. com/index.

Brigandi, Phil. "Orange County's First Rancheros—Manuel Nieto and Juan Pablo Grijalva." *OC Historyland* (2019). Accessed March 8, 2020. ochistoryland.com/ firstrancheros.

Brigandi, Phil. "Questions and Answers about the History of Orange County, California." *OC Historyland* (2019). Accessed March 8, 2020. ochistoryland. com/ask.

Burton, Fred W. "Fred C. Burton, 1909 to Now." *The Siskiyou Pioneer* 3, no. 8 (1965): 4.

Burton, Fred W. "Gertrude Bryan Burton." *The Siskiyou Pioneer* 3, no. 8 (1965): 5.

Caesar, Clarence. "The Historical Demographics of Sacramento's Black Community, 1848–1900." Last modified 2020. Accessed June 1, 2020. Online.ucpress.edu.

"Calaveras County History." *California Genealogy and History Archives* (1891). sites.rootsweb.com/~cagha/history/history-calaveras.htm.

Carpenter, Aurelius O., and Percy H. Millberry. *History of Mendocino and Lake Counties California with Biographical Sketches*. 1914th ed. Vol. 1. Los Angeles, CA: Historic Record Company (1914). Accessed April 5, 2020. 1914_ History_of_Mendocino_and_Lake_Count.pdf.

Cataldo, Nick. "This Longtime San Bernardino Resident Was 'Always More Than a Doctor'". *The Sun*, March 23, 2020. sbsun.com/2020/03/23/this-longtime-san-bernardino-resident-was-always-more-than-a-doctor/.

Chamberlain, Newell D. "Chapter XXXIV: Color around Hornitos." *The Call of Gold* (1936). Accessed May 10, 2020. yosemite.ca.us/library/call_of_gold/ hornitos.html.

"Chung Wah Cemetery." *National Register of Historic Places Registration Form NPS 10–900* (1990). Accessed March 2, 2020. U.S. Department of the Interior National Park Service. https://npgallery.nps.gov/NRHP/GetAsset/ NRHP/95000999_text.

"The City of Benicia Is Born 1847." *Benicia Historical Museum*. Accessed May 19, 2014. beniciahistoricalmuseum.org/the-city-of-benicia-is-born-1847/.

Colman, Patty R. "John Ballard and the African American Community in Los Angeles, 1850–1905." *Southern California Quarterly* 94, no. 2 (2012): 193–229. jstor.org/stable/10.1525/scq.2012.94.2.193.

Conmy, Peter T. *A Parochial and Institutional History of the Diocese of Oakland 1962–1972.* Mission Hills, CA: Saint Francis Historical Society, 2000.

Cook, Roy. "Antonio Garra: Tarnished California Gold." *American Indian Source.* Accessed January 16, 2020. americanindiansource.com/gara/gara.html.

Daly, Walter J. "The Black Cholera Comes to the Central Valley of America in the 19th Century—1832, 1849, and Later." *PMC US National Library of Medicine* (2008). Accessed March 9, 2020. ncbi.nlm.nih.gov/pmc/articles/ PMC2394684/.

Davis, David A. PCC and General William Passmore, eds. *Partial Bibliography of the Civil War and Civil War Veterans' Activities in the Western United States.* Accessed January 8, 2020. http://www.suvpac.org/docs/Western%20CW%20 Bibliography.pdf.

Diamond, Dick. "Local History: Louis Wolf and His Store." *Temecula Valley Historical Society.* Last modified 2010–2020. Accessed March 20, 2020. temeculahistoricalsociety.org/html2/Wolf_Louis.html.

Douglas, Laurelyn. "Health and Hygiene in the Nineteenth Century." *The Victorian Web* (1991). Accessed March 13, 2020. victorianweb.org/science/ health/health10.htm.

Durflinger, Keith. "Whittier's Founders Park Is the Former Site of Two Cemeteries." *Whittier Daily News*, October 21, 2012. whittierdailynews.com/2012/10/21/ whittiers-founders-park-is-the-former-site-of-two-cemeteries/.

Epting, Charles, ed. *Orange County Pioneers: Oral Histories from the Works Progress Association.* Charleston, SC: History Press, 2014.

"The Experiences of the First California Volunteer Infantry." *The Spanish American Centennial Website.* Last modified 1996–2020. Accessed April 13, 2020. spanamwar.com/1stCAinf.htm.

"Exploring Main Street Placerville: A Self-Guided Walking Tour." *El Dorado County Historical Museum* (2010). Accessed June 3, 2020. ExploringMainStreetPlacerville.pdf.

Faison, Glen. "New Chapter Opens in Historical Figure's Civil Rights 'Journey'." *The Porterville Recorder*, September 11, 2008. recorderonline.com/new-chapter-opens-in-historical-figures-civil-rights-journey/article_0b6c24cd-5c0e-59d9-ad01–112345eb9e91.html.

Fardon, G. R. *San Francisco Album. Photographs of the Most Beautiful Views and Public Buildings of San Francisco (1919).* San Francisco, CA: Dover Publications, 1977.

Felson, Gregg. *Tombstones: Seventy-Five Famous People and Their Final Resting Places.* Berkeley, CA: Ten Speed Press, 1996.

Findagrave.com. Accessed 2019–2020. findagrave.com

Geissner, Jo. "A Tuttle Gulch Cemetery History." *Shasta County Cemetery Records, Access Genealogy* (2013). Accessed April 6, 2020. accessgenealogy.com/cemetery/shasta-county-california-cemetery-records.htm.

Glass, Dean. *The History & Mystery of the Whaley House: Old Town San Diego.* San Diego, CA: Our Heritage Press, 2016.

Gorelick, Ellen. "The Wright Family." *Tulare Historical Museum.* Last modified 2014. Accessed June 3, 2020. tularehistoricalmuseum.org/wright.html.

Green, David B. "This Day in Jewish History 1913: A Jewish Civil War Hero Dies." *Haaretz Israel News,* July 17, 2014. haaretz.com/jewish/1913-civil-war-hero-governor-dies-1.5255885.

Greene, Meg. *A History of American Cemeteries*. Minneapolis, MN: Twenty-First Century Books, 2008.

Greer, James K. *Colonel Jack Hays: Texas Frontier Leader and California Builder*. College Station: Texas A&M University Press, 1987.

Greve, Eric. "James Herman Banning (1899–1933)." *BlackPast*, March 26, 2012. Accessed April 2, 2020. blackpast.org/African American-history/banning-james-herman-1899–1933/.

Gubert, Betty Kaplan, et al. *Distinguished African Americans in Aviation and Space Science*. N.p.: Greenwood Publishing Group (2002). Accessed March 18, 2020. https://books.google.com.jm/books?id=QAXWwVrc9TsC&printsec=frontcover#v=onepage&q=Banning&f=false.

Gutglueck, Mark. "Don Antonio Maria Lugo." *San Bernardino County Sentinel*, August 3, 2017. sbcsentinel.com/2017/09/don-antonio-maria-lugo-2/.

Hagaman, Wallace R. *A Short History of the Chinese Cemetery at Nevada City, California and Chinese Burial Customs during the Gold Rush*. Nevada City, CA: Cowboy Press, 2001.

"Hallie M. Daggett." *USD.A. Forest Service*. Accessed December 4, 2019. fs.usda.gov/detail/r2/learning/history-culture/?cid=stelprdb5360607

Hayden, Dolores. "Grandma Biddy: Biddy Mason's Place, a Midwife's Homestead." *Los Angeles, California: Power of Place* (1988). Accessed March 1, 2020. imgzoom.cdlib.org/Fullscreen.ics?ark=ark:/13030/hb0g50073p/z1&&brand=oac4.

Historic American Buildings Survey. "Mission San Rafael Arcangel, San Rafael." *Library of Congress*. Last modified 1933. Accessed April 21, 2020. loc.gov.

"History." *Temecula: The Heart of Southern California Wine Country*. Accessed April 8, 2020. temeculaca.gov, 2020, temeculaca.gov/159/The-Wolf-Family.

"History and Facts." *Pechanga Band of Luiseno Indians* (2020). Accessed April 4, 2020. pechanga-nsn.gov/index.php/history.

"History and Facts." *Whittier Museum, Whittier Historical Society* (2019). Accessed March 12, 2020. whittiermuseum.org/research/cemeteries/.

"A History of Chinese Americans in California: Historic Sites." *Five Views: An Ethnic Historic Site Survey for California.* Last modified November 17, 2004. cr.nps.gov/history/online_books/5views/5views3h.htm.

History of Humboldt County, California, with Illustrations. San Francisco, CA: Wallace W. Elliott & Co, Publishers, 1881.

Interment.Net: Cemetery Records Online, edited by Steve P. Johnson, Clear Digital Media, December 19, 1999. interment.net/data/us/ca/sandiego/julian/julian_pioneer.htm.

"Jewish Cemetery, Ocean House Road, Mission Dolores." *Library of Congress.* Last modified 1866. Accessed April 6, 2020. loc.gov.

Jewish Museum of the American West: Kusel Family: Pioneer Jews of the Northern California Gold County (2018). Accessed March 1, 2020. jmaw.org/kusel-jewish-california/.

Jewish Museum of the American West: Professor Albert Abraham Michelson: Nobel Prize Winning Jewish Physicist from Calaveras County, California (2015). Accessed March 1, 2020. jmaw.org/michelson-jewish-california/.

"John Bidwell Facts." *Your Dictionary.* Last modified 2010. Accessed January 24, 2020. biography.yourdictionary.com/john-bidwell.

Jones, J. Roy. *Saddle Bags in Siskiyou.* 2nd ed. Happy Camp, CA: Naturegraph Publishers, Inc., 1953/1980.

Jopson, Eric. "The Value of Life: The Struggles of Civil War Veteran Lucien Hoyt with the Pension System, 1836–1892." CSU Chico: History 492, Archival Research, 2019.

Keister, Douglas. *Going Out in Style: The Architecture of Eternity*. New York: Facts on File, Inc., 1997.

"Kern Turns 150: Thomas Baker, Our City's Namesake." *Bakersfield Californian* (May 2016). Accessed April 7, 2020. bakersfield.com/archives/kern-turns-thomas-baker-our-city-s-namesake/article_81c7c3ca-62a1–5b9b-ac3f-e4d0f92fe3a9.html.

Kindell, Alexandra. *Iowa State University Digital Repository: Settling the Sunset Land: California and Its Family Farmers 1850–1890s*. Iowa State University Capstones, Theses and Dissertations, 2006. Accessed January 6, 2020. lib. dr.iastate.edu/rtd.

Kiniry, Laura. "Famous Graves and Cemeteries in San Francisco." *trip savvy*, December 21, 2019. Accessed April 1, 2020. tripsavvy.com/famous-bay-area-grave-sites-2939371.

Klauber, Laurence M. *One Hundred Years Ago: Two Days in San Francisco-1906*. *The Journal of San Diego History* (1958). Accessed June 5, 2020. Two_Days_in_San_Francisco.pdf.

Kot, Elizabeth, and Shirley P. Thomson. *California Cemetery Inscription Sources: Print & Microfilm*. Vallejo, CA: Indices Publishing, 1994.

Lamm, Maurice. "The Interment in Judaism." *Chabad.org*. Last modified 2020. Accessed June 2, 2020. chabad.org/library/article_cdo/aid/281565/jewish/The-Interment-in-Judaism.htm.

Lamm, Maurice. "A Jewish Burial and Procession: Death & Mourning." *Chabad. org*. Last modified 2020. Accessed May 7, 2020. chabad.org/library/article_cdo/aid/281569/jewish/A-Jewish-Burial-and-Procession.htm.

Landis, Mark. "Bartons Were Active in Early Development of SB." *Redlands Daily Facts*, February 3, 2009. redlandsdailyfacts.com/2009/02/03/bartons-were-active-in-early-development-of-sb-valley.

"L.A. Philanthropist Chloe Canfield Murdered in Cold Blood." *The Dead Bell*, May 26, 2017. Accessed February 10, 2020. deadbell.com/2017/05/26/l-a-philanthropist-chloe-canfield-murdered-in-cold-blood/?blogsub=flooded#subscribe-blog.

Lewis, David. *Last Known Address: The History of the Julian Cemetery*. 2nd ed. Julian, CA: Headstone Publishing, 2008/2015.

Lloyd, Annie. "The 7 Most Iconic Cemeteries in Los Angeles." *N.p.: LAist*. Accessed February 10, 2020. laist.com/2017/09/21/iconic_cemeteries_la.php.

Lloyd, Paula. "Abandoned Cemetery South of Selma Dates from 1870s." *Fresno Bee*, August 27, 2016, special ed. Accessed March 4, 2020. fresnobee.com/news/local/news-columns-blogs/ask-me/article97866927.html.

Lopez, Jose A. "Lopez: María Amparo Ruiz de Burton (Wonder Woman of the West)." *Rio Grande Guardian*, September 23, 2019. riograndeguardian.com/lopez-maria-amparo-ruiz-de-burton-wonder-woman-of-the-west/.

Lovret, Juanita. "Remember When: Rancher, Developer, Businessman, Civic Leader." *Orange County Register*, February 3, 2009. tustin.k12.ca.us/utt/about-our-school/charles-edward-utt.

Mansfield, George C. *History of Butte County California with Biographical Sketches of the Leading Men and Women of the County Who Have Been Identified with Its Growth and Development from the Early Days to the Present*. N.p.: Historic Record Company (1918). Accessed January 10, 2020. books.google.com/books?id=VTREAQAAMAAJ&printsec=frontcover&source=gbs_ge_summary_r&cad=0#v=onepage&q=Bidwell&f=false.

"Marcus Schiller: San Diego's Jewish Horatio Alger." *Jewish Museum of the American West*, edited by Linda Kern, 2013. Accessed April 4, 2020. jmaw.org/marcus-schiller-san-diegos-jewish/.

Martin, Edward. *History of Butte County California with Biographical Sketches of the Leading Men and Women of the County Who Have Been Identified with Its Growth and Development from the Early Days to the Present*. N.p.: Historic Record Company (1911). Accessed April 4, 2020. archive.org/details/historyofsantacr00mart.

Martinez Historical Society, edited by Gregg Burtop. N.p.: Martinez Historical Society. Accessed June 13, 2020. martinezhistory.org/index.html.

Mauldin, Henry. *Mountains & Pioneers of Lake County*. 2nd ed. Kelseyville, CA: Earthen Vessel Production, Carolyn Wing Greenlee, 1995.

"Meanwhile Out West: Colonizing California, 1769–1821." *California Historical Society*. Last modified 2017–2018. Accessed December 11, 2019. californiahistoricalsociety.org/exhibitions/meanwhile-out-west-colonizing-california-1769-1821/.

Meschery, Joanne. *Truckee: An Illustrated History of the Town and Its Surroundings*. Truckee, CA: Rocking Stone Press, 1978.

Meyer, Richard E., ed. *Ethnicity and the American Cemetery*. Bowling Green, OH: Bowling Green state University Popular Press, 1993.

"The Mizners: A Very Interesting Family." *Benicia Historical Museum*. Last modified May 19, 2014. Accessed May 18, 2020. beniciahistoricalmuseum.org/the-mizners-a-very-interesting-family/.

"Mokelumne Hill, California." *Western Mining History*. Last modified 2020. Accessed December 6, 2020. westernmininghistory.com/towns/california/mokelumne-hill/.

Moore, Shirley Ann. *Sweet Freedom's Plains: African Americans on the Overland Trails 1841–1869.* Salt Lake City, UT and Santa Fe, NM: National Park Service, 2012. Accessed January 9, 2020. https://www.nps.gov/oreg/learn/historyculture/upload/Sweet-Freedom-s-Plains-508.pdf.

Munro-Fraser, J. P. *History of Santa Clara County, California: Including Its Geography, Geology, Topography, Climatography and Description. Together with a Record of the Mexican Grants; Its Mines and Natural Springs; the Early History and Settlements, Compiled from the Most Authentic Sources; the Names of Original Spanish and American Pioneers; Full Legislative History of the County; Separate Histories of Each Township, Showing the Advance in Population and Agriculture. Also Incidents of Public Life; the Mexican War; and Biographical Sketches of Early and Prominent Settlers and Representative Men; and of Its Cities, Towns, Colleges, Secret Societies, Etc.* San Francisco, California: Alley, Bowen & Co., 1881. Accessed January 24, 2020. Digital copy at archive.org/details/historysantacla00munrgoog.

"Mt. Whitney, Lone Pine, Inyo County, California." *Stone Quarries and Beyond.* Last modified, 2020. Accessed May 13, 2020. quarriesandbeyond.org/states/ca/structures/ca-lone_pine_whitney_cem_1.html.

Neighbors, Joy. *The Family Tree Cemetery Field Guide.* Cincinnati, OH: Family Tree Books, n.d.

"Newmark," *Jewish Virtual Library: A Project of AICE.* American-Israeli Cooperative Enterprise (2020). Accessed January 10, 2020. www.jewishvirtuallibrary.org/newmark.

Nunis, Doyce B. Jr., ed. *The Bidwell-Bartleson Party, 1841 California Emigrant Adventure: Documents and Memoirs of the Overland Pioneers.* Santa Cruz, CA: Western Tanager Press, 1991.

"OC Parks: Historic Yorba Cemetery." *OCgov.com.* Accessed January 19, 2020. ocparks.com/historic/cemetery/.

Oliver, Myrna. "William Mason: California Historian, Author." *Los Angeles Times*, November 2000. latimes.com/archives/la-xpm-2000-nov-25-me-57012-story. html.

"Perez Nieto, Jose Manuel." *Schwald Family Genealogy* (2020). Accessed March 4, 2020. schwaldfamily.org/getperson.php?personID=I10775&tree=RodSchwald.

Perry, Patricia. "Sonora's Old City Cemetery." *City of Sonora: Queen of the Southern Mines*. Last modified August, 2012. Accessed January 6, 2020. sonoraca.com/visit-sonora/sonora-california-history/cemeteries/.

Piatt, Michael H. "The Death of Madame Moustache: Bodie's Most Celebrated Inhabitant." *Bodie History*. Last modified March, 2009. Accessed June 19, 2020. bodiehistory.com/madame.htm.

Raphael, Ray, and Freeman House. *Two Peoples, One Place*. Vol. 1. Eureka, CA: Humboldt County Historical Society, 2007/2011.

Reader, Phil. "Uncle Dave's Story: The Life of Ex-Slave Dave Boffman." *Santa Cruz Public Libraries Local History*. Last modified 1991. Accessed June 3, 2020. history.santacruzpl.org/omeka/items/show/134485#?c=0&m=0&s=0&cv=0.

Rechcigi, Mila. "Czech California Pioneers." (DOC) Accessed March 1, 2020. academia.edu/26734847/Czech_California_Pioneers?email_work_card=title

Rouse, Wendy L. "Chinese-American Death Ritual in 19th Century California." *What We Didn't Understand*. Accessed February 2, 2020. http://npshistory. com/publications/nhl/theme-studies/finding-path-forward.pdf.

Rubio, J'aime. *More Stories of the Forgotten*. Vol. 2. San Bernardino, CA: J'aime Rubio. 2019.

Rubio, J'aime. "Remembering Nat Cecil." *Dreaming Casually (Investigative Blog): A Step Back in Time to Explore Stories and Mysteries of the Past*, edited by Steve

P. Johnson, Clear Digital Media (October 17, 2017). dreamingcasuallypoetry. blogspot.com/2017/10/remembering-nat-cecil.html.

Ruffell, Marcia. "Gasquet Ranger District History." *Smith River National Recreation Area.* Last modified 1995. Accessed June 3, 2020. Gas_Ran_Dis_His_Prt1.pdf.

Ruiz, Russell A. "The Santa Barbara Presidio." *Noticias: Quarterly Bulletin of the Santa Barbara Historical Society* XIII, no. 1 (1967): 1–6.

Sacramento Pioneer Association. *Gone to Rest: Biographies of Sacramento Pioneers Buried in or Nearby Pioneer Grove of the Old Sacramento City Cemetery.* N.p.: Sacramento Pioneer Association, 2001.

"San Juan Capistrano Mission." *Digital Public Library of America.* Last modified 1922. Accessed May 14, 2020. dp.la/item/ df35219a4a83be36dedbad82bb9a0420.

Santos, Robert LeRoy. "The Gold Rush of California: A Bibliography of Periodical Articles." *University Llibrary California State University, Stanislaus.* Last modified 2002. Accessed December 27, 2019. library.csustan.edu/sites/ default/files/Bob_Santos-The_Gold_Rush_of_California-A_Bibliography_of_ Periodical_Articles.pdf.

Santos, Robert L. "An Anthology of Personal Life Sketches." *Stories of California Azorean Immigrants.* Denair: Alley-Cass Publications, 1998. Accessed January 21, 2020. library.csustan.edu/bsantos/sketches.html[6/10/2014 10:26:53 AM].

Santos, Robert LeRoy. "The Gold Rush of California: A Bibliography of Periodical Articles." *University Library California State University, Stanislaus.* Last modified 2002. Accessed December 27, 2019. library.csustan.edu/sites/ default/files/Bob_Santos-The_Gold_Rush_of_California-A_Bibliography_of_ Periodical_Articles.pdf.

Schafer, Joseph, ed. *California Letters of Lucius Fairchild*. XXXI ed., Madison, State Historical Society of Wisconsin, 1931, cdn.loc.gov//service/gdc/calbk/004.pdf. Accessed February 3, 2020.

Schiller, Gerald A. *True Stories of Old California*. Fairfax Station, VA: InterContinental Publishing, 2001.

Seiser-Alexander, Kathy, ed., N.p.: Legends of America 2020. Accessed November 4, 2019. legendsofamerica.com/ah-lynching/8.

"Small Cemeteries of Shasta County." *Shasta Genealogical Society*. Last modified 2019. Accessed December 17, 2020. shastagen.org/cemeteryRecords.php?cid=3.

Smith, Jeff. "Ah Quin: Unofficial Mayor of San Diego's Chinatown." *San Diego Reader* (July 30, 1998). sandiegoreader.com/news/1998/jul/30/unofficial-mayor-chinatown/.

Speer, Robert. "Close to Annie." *Local Stories*. Last modified November 11, 2004. newsreview.com/chico/close-to-annie/content?oid=32592.

Steele, James. *Old Californian Days*. Chicago, IL: Belford-Clarke Company, 1889. Accessed December 16, 2019. loc.gov/resource/calbk.

Stuart, David R. "The Native Peoples of San Joaquin County: Indian Pioneers, Immigrants, Innovators, Freedom Fighters, and Survivors." *The San Joaquin Historian*. Last modified 2016. Accessed March 2, 2020. sanjoaquinhistory.org/documents/HistorianSummer2016.pdf.

Swift, Carolyn. "A Sequel History Tale." *CityofCapitola.org*. Accessed February 7, 2020. cityofcapitola.org/capitola-museum/page/soquel-history-tale.

Terkelsen, Lee. "Not-so-Living History: Tales from the Tomb Recounts Visalia's Past." *Visalia Times Delta*, October 16, 2019. visaliatimesdelta.

com/story/entertainment/2019/10/16/tales-tomb-recounts-visalias-history/3989920002/.

"Today in Earthquake History: Owens Valley 1872." *Berkeley Seismology Lab*, UC Berkeley, March 26, 2019. Accessed April 10, 2020. seismo.berkeley.edu/blog/2019/03/26/today-in-earthquake-history-owens-valley-1872.html.

Toler, Jr., David L. *Blood of the Band: An Ipai Family Story*. San Diego, CA: Sunbelt Publications, Inc., 2015.

UCSC Special Collections Archives. "Rowland Card Collection Database." MS51, UCSC. Accessed February 16, 2020.

"The Valley of Heart's Delight." *Dr. John Townsend—California Pioneer Biography*. Santa Clara County Biography Project. Accessed June 1, 2020. santaclararesearch.net.

Vandor, Paul E. *History of Fresno County California with Biographical Sketches of the Leading Men and Women*. Vol. 1, Los Angeles, CA: Historic Record Company, 1919, 2 vols. books.googleusercontent.com/books/content?req=AKW5QadYJ95dYtxRDmwOyf_adATcFsIav0qi4tGjlPiXs9_5IibymmN4Lx WNj0MPvIvQKCKHAIS7EtyvSUqiFiZ8DbeV95B3WKTmZRdY1rz_B5Y4nBo-Bdy0FPPFkfOyDSZepWqDrzDb4EnkR0.

Varney, Philip. *Ghost Towns of California*. Minneapolis, MN: Voyageur Press, 2012.

Wang, Claire. "A Chinese Fishing Village Regains Its Rightful Place in California History." *Atlas Obscura* (March 31, 2020). www.atlasobscura.com/articles/how-chinese-fishermen-helped-build-california?utm_source=California+Historical+Society&utm_campaign=ed672a7e72-Society+Happenings_COPY_01&utm_medium=email&utm_ter.

"The Wives and Children of John Brown." *National Park Service*. Accessed June 3, 2020. nps.gov/articles/wives-and-children-of-john-brown.htm.

INDEX

Italicized page numbers indicate illustrations.

INDEX

INDEX

INDEX

ABOUT THE AUTHOR

Gail L. Jenner is a former secondary history and English teacher and is married to a fourth-generation cattle rancher in the mountains of Northern California. She and her husband live on the Jenner Cattle Company's 150-year-old, original homestead. She has spent fifty years working with her husband, maintaining a large garden, teaching, raising children and chickens, and cooking for family and hired help, and now, writing full-time. She is the author of *Ankle High and Knee Deep, Sourdough Biscuits and Pioneer Pies, One Room: Schools and Schoolteachers in the Pioneer West*, and other titles for Globe Pequot and TwoDot.